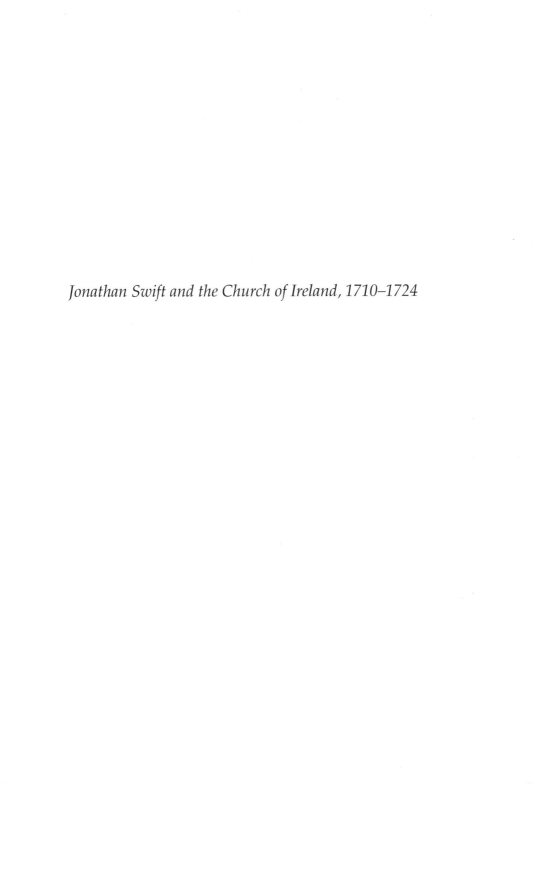

Jonathan Swift and the Church of Ireland, 1710–1724

Jonathan Swift
and the
Church of Ireland
1710–1724

CHRISTOPHER J. FAUSKE

IRISH ACADEMIC PRESS
DUBLIN • PORTLAND, OR

First published in 2002 by
IRISH ACADEMIC PRESS
44, Northumberland Road, Dublin 4, Ireland
and in the United States of America by
IRISH ACADEMIC PRESS
c/o ISBS, 5824 NE Hassalo Street,
Portland, OR 97213-3644.

website: www.iap.ie

British Library Cataloguing in Publication Data
Fauske, Christopher
  Jonathan Swift and the Church of Ireland, 1710–1724: an accidental patriot
  1. Swift, Jonathan, 1667–1745 2. Ireland – Foreign relations – Great Britain
  3. Great Britain – Foreign relations – Ireland 4. Ireland – Politics and
  government – 18th century 5. Great Britain – Politics and government –
  1714–1727
  I. Title
  941.5' 07

  ISBN 0-7165-2728-6

Library of Congress Cataloging-in-Publication Data
Fauske, Christopher J., 1963–
  Jonathan Swift and the Church of Ireland, 1710–24 / Christopher J. Fauske.
    p. cm.
  Includes bibliographical references (p.) and index.
  ISBN 0–7165–2728–6 (hardback)
    1. Swift Jonathan, 1667–1745 – Religion. 2. Authors, Irish – 18th century –
  Biography. 3. Ireland – Church history – 18th century. 4. Church of Ireland –
  Clergy – Biography. 5. Clergy – Ireland – Biography. I. Title.

  PR3728.R4 F38 2001
  828'.509—dc21
  [B]   2001039127

Typeset in 10.5 pt on 12.5 pt Palatino by
Carrigboy Typesetting Services, County Cork
Printed by MPG Books Ltd., Bodmin, Cornwall

No Prospect of making my Fortune, shall ever prevail on me to go against what becomes a Man of Conscience and Truth, and an entire Friend to the established Church.

Jonathan Swift to William King,
Archbishop of Dublin, 9 November 1708

for we have rights drawn from the soil and sky;
the use, the pace, the patient years of labour,
the rain against the lips, the changing light,
the heavy clay-sucked stride, have altered us;
we would be strangers in the Capitol;
this is our country also, no-where else;
and we shall not be outcast on the world.

John Hewitt, 'The Colony'

Contents

'The teasing particularity of Swift's ironies': reflections on the Dean

> We can scarcely not say something about [Swift], even though everything has been said already.
>
> D.J. Enright[1]

Jonathan Swift is a man about whom much has been said and to whom almost every conceivable motive has been attributed. Swift has been read as just about all things to all people for so long that he has become public property. In general, his readers divide into two camps – those attracted to (or repelled by) the misanthrope, and those drawn to the question of Swift's Irish patriotism. Can a great patriot really be a great misanthrope? Probably not, but if you are not interested in combining the two, either can make sense on its own. You can have your misanthrope or you can have your patriot. Unless, that is, you are willing to compromise on both counts. But readers like their writers to make sense, both on the page and in 'real' life. Swift, notoriously, doesn't make 'sense', at least not easily.

And yet writers about Swift often insist on focusing on his works as discrete entities, determined to make sense of Swift *the writer*. He remains the possession of both literary theorists and popular historians, as Victoria Glendenning's recent biography reminds us, precisely because tracts inconvenient to broad arguments can easily be dismissed as the result of 'ambition' or some other human trait. Each camp has an interest in finding and identifying its 'Swift', a writer who wrote so much on such diverse topics it is not difficult to argue that some of the work is of lesser interest than the rest and can therefore safely be ignored.

As with all generalities, the above remarks risk coming undone as soon as one sits down to think about them. Most immediately, one can

1

think of Irvin Ehrenpreis' monumental three-part biography, *Swift: The Man, His Works, and the Age*. It is a model biography and a model biography of a writer (which is not necessarily the same thing). In its broad view it is careful to balance arguments, to reflect upon what is to be found in writing. Rightly sceptical of wild conjecture, Ehrenpreis is cautious of making even considered speculations, but as Aileen Douglas, Patrick Kelly and Ian Campbell Ross remind us: 'Ehrenpreis's view of Swift had been largely formed by the time he began writing in the late 1950s [and so] . . . took only limited account of contemporary shifts in British and, more significantly, Irish historiography.'[2]

Other studies have avoided the didactic by refusing to dismiss as nothing more than irony those works of Swift that potentially raise problems. These are the works of writers who are as interested in Swift's sense of his times as they are in Swift himself, with the occasional exception of David Nokes' wonderful and historically grounded *Jonathan Swift, a Hypocrite Reversed* which at times simply revels in all the contradictions to be found in Swift's work. Ian Higgins' *Swift's Politics: A Study in Disaffection*, for example, draws its strength from the recognition that 'critical disagreement about Swift's political character derives in part from disagreement about the nature of party politics and ideology when Swift is writing'.[3] Indeed, too many modern critics are willing to assume that 'Tory' and 'Whig' in Swift's time meant roughly what we think they mean today, and to assume that everyone involved in the debate at the time agreed on the meaning of these terms. To do this, as Higgins points out, makes it easy to see in Swift (and others) a shift in loyalty from one grouping to another when, in fact, there may well have been little, if any, shift. While discussion of 'party' politics after 1714 is only partially useful, use of the term to describe the events prior to that date is essentially anachronistic. 'Faction' may be an appropriate word, 'party' seldom is.

Other recent studies have concentrated on the broader contexts, most noticeably and informatively Carole Fabricant's breathtaking *Swift's Landscape*. Swift perhaps more than most writers benefits from these studies. Thus, in 'Swift as Irish Historian', Fabricant argues that:

> although Swift never wrote a history of Ireland *per se*, he produced a large number of tracts pertaining to Irish affairs. In proposing that we consider these as historical writings, as continuing expressions of his early resolve to be the historian for a nation and an age . . . I want to consider these tracts as historical writings in the sense that they actively engaged in the historiographic controversies of the time, not only addressing the central

issues highlighted by contemporary histories of Ireland, but also functioning as calculated interventions in the combined historical and historiographic enterprise as it had come to be defined by the English and their representatives in Ireland.[4]

This is an approach that certainly helps get around the issue of how to find a single Swift in the miasma of his writings but, as Fabricant is careful to acknowledge, we must be wary of the apparent powers of hindsight. What we think was happening at a certain point in history is not necessarily what contemporaries thought was going on around them.

As Christopher Hill reminds us, 'it is easy to note the recurrence of certain ideas [in a particular period] and to assume that they recur because everyone accepted them'. However, he points out that 'it is equally possible that they were repeated . . . because they were under attack'.[5] However, it is possible to understand what a writer thought he was up against in his own time, not necessarily based upon what is said but also upon what is left unsaid, or what is said in an opportune, occasional manner. Higgins' book opens with a consideration of 'Swift's political character'. It offers a fine demonstration that Swift can be just about all things to all people, not because that was what he wanted to be, but because it was what the times demanded of him. It is a commonplace to imagine Swift as some sort of lonely hero defying his contemporaries to do their worst, but the fates of Alexander Pope, John Arbuthnot and other 'Tory' literary figures suggest we exaggerate if we assume that Swift's life was at stake in the aftermath of the Hanoverian succession. It is probably a stretch even to argue that his liberty would have been at risk for any extended period of time, whatever Swift might have wished to think, or to have had others think. After the failed revolt of 1715 demonstrated how secure Ireland was in the Protestant cause, Swift's political fears lessened but he still needed an audience and so his works come with a context – a context determined not just by particular events but by popular conceptions and misconceptions of what ideas were shaping contemporary discourse.

A reading of Swift's work during his least public period in Ireland, and an examination of the contemporary secular political conditions which he sought to influence and to respond to, provide an almost coherent view of the stresses and concerns of the man who ended his career as dean of St Patrick's, Dublin. This is not to suggest that Swift is any less complex a character and writer for that emerging coherence.

If only melancholy, misanthropy or malice – the stereotypes of Swift biographical criticism[6] – primarily motivated Swift's activities between 1714 (when he returned to Ireland after the death of Queen Anne) and

1724, when *The Drapier's Letters* began to appear, then those years of disillusionment and frustration should have been some of the most productive of his life. They were not. However, to attribute Swift's silence only to fear of possible retribution is to distort and confuse the issues, for Swift had before demonstrated a willingness to be outspoken, even to the point of facing censure. Swift's almost total lack of involvement in the debates of 1714–24, and his idiosyncratic defences of the Tories, make perfect sense when viewed as a consequence of his own sense of frustration about the relevance of the debate itself. Despite the personal risks involved, Swift might, as some of his surviving sermons suggest,[7] have been willing to engage in a partisan attack upon the Whigs immediately after George I's accession had he thought doing so could have served a practical purpose. The nature of Swift's silence also explains the tenor of his writings of that period, both published, as in his 1720 *Proposal for the Universal Use of Irish Manufacture*, or unpublished.

The three major studies of Swift's relationship with Ireland, Oliver Ferguson's *Jonathan Swift and Ireland*, Louis Landa's *Swift and the Church of Ireland* and Fabricant's *Swift's Landscape*, while all excellent and essential reading, nonetheless explain Swift's years in Ireland as in some manner illuminating his experiences in England. They all see Swift's time in Ireland as important and interesting in its own right, but all hint that his interest in Ireland was a way of diverting himself while he was not in England. However, although Swift undoubtedly enjoyed himself more in England, his loyalties were theoretical rather than geographic, idealistic rather than physical, and his response to events in Ireland was in keeping with those theoretical loyalties. In short, Swift's activities in Ireland between his return in August 1714 and the publication of *The Drapier's Letters* are an integral part of his almost life-long engagement with questions of church–state polity and are not simply a useful means of illuminating more dramatic events in Swift's life. They tell us as least as much about what he thought was going on around him as they do about the man himself.

The primary motivation of his life's work was his conservative loyalty to old ideas of the church–state relationship. Swift was a much shrewder political tactician than is often recognised – though not, ultimately, a particularly successful one. His political manoeuvering was predicated upon an interest beyond mere political principle. He was a man firmly committed to what he saw as the best interests of his church, which he understood to have little to do with God and everything to do with a socio-political compact. Swift's own ideals looked back to an imagined Golden Age when the temporal and the spiritual had been organically related, to a time when political and religious institutions were uncorrupted and existed in harmony. What prevented Swift's near nostalgia from becoming static was his determination to engage the moment in defence of this ideal, whatever the strain inevitable in such engagements.

Theology and political philosophy Swift left to others. His own inclinations and polemical skills led him to join the political debate not for what he might accomplish but for what he could prevent. His efforts were effectively a sustained rearguard action conducted against a backdrop of ever-changing alliances and political expediency. Swift was engaged in an extended guerrilla-like defence of an idealistic and profoundly radical conservative concept. He took his allies where he could, changed allegiances when need dictated and sought to engage the enemy only when he had the twin advantages of surprise and momentum on his side. His main goal was to preserve what little power and privilege he thought the Church of Ireland still enjoyed, and he believed that struggle honourable and vital to society's well-being. Swift had as a working principle the conviction that the interests of his church were so paramount that just about any alliance that could serve those interests was worth pursuing, irrespective of its costs to him and without regard to his own reputation.

This character made him an almost perfect foil for the man who would come to occupy much of Swift's time, namely his neighbour but not, technically, his immediate superior, Archbishop King. King was a descendant of a Scots Presbyterian family who, through hard work and careful support of church doctrine accompanied by polemics exposing the short-comings of Presbyterian theology, had made his way in the church with little obvious patronage to help him. King's political instincts were perhaps less shrewd than Swift's, but he had political power where the dean did not. King, therefore, could seek to use a system that Swift identified as part of the problem.[8] These two men's actions helped identify the various fault lines that were to grow increasingly defined as the Stuart era was replaced by an entirely new political system during the early Hanoverian years.

The 1714 accession of George I coincided with an ongoing strengthening of secular, rationalist discourse in British, and hence in Irish, political life. In many ways, this presented the Church of Ireland with an opportunity it would not otherwise have had because it was suddenly in a position to define its role in society in something other than purely religious terms. Swift was a churchman comfortable, whatever his personal faith, with making the case for his church along other than traditional doctrinal lines. In this willingness to engage in the arguments, Swift was helped by Anglicanism's profoundly undoctrinaire roots. It is a commonplace that the Church of England was born of political and genealogical needs, but Henry VIII never abandoned the title 'defender of the faith' which the pope had granted him in recognition of his intellectual opposition to the continental Protestants. Indeed, it would take more than fifty years for the first significant Anglican theological apologies to appear – Richard Hooker's *The Laws of Ecclesiastical Polity* (beginning 1594) and Lancelot Andrewes' *Tortura Torti* (1609) and *Responsio ad Apologiam Cardinalis Bellarmini* (1610).

The two standard histories of the Church of Ireland, both in need of updating, reflect the complexity of the Church of Ireland's relationship with the Church of England. The first full-length history of the Church of Ireland was Richard Mant's *History of the Church of Ireland from the Reformation to the Revolution*. The subtitle, *with A Preliminary Survey, from the Papal Usurpation, in the Twelfth Century, to its Legal Abolition in the Sixteenth*, also reflects the difficulty of deciding the historical, episcopal relationship with the church founded by St Peter in Rome. Mant's opening remarks refer to the Church of Ireland's place in the 'British empire in general', to the 'history of that National Church, of which the Irish Church forms an integral member, the United Church of England and Ireland', and to the 'history of the Reformed Church of Ireland'.[9] He is uncertain from the outset about the status of the body whose history he presumes to write. The *History of the Church of Ireland from the Earliest Times to the Present Day*, edited by Walter Phillips, grew out of a General Synod resolution of 1929 calling for 'a standard history of the Church of Ireland . . . with special reference to the origins and the continuity of Faith and Order in the Church of Ireland'.[10] The history of the church is flexible enough that it can fit into almost any scheme of events.[11]

As a spokesman (albeit sometimes self-appointed) for an institution with so confused an identity, it is hardly surprising that Swift's writings do not always appear coherent in relation to other work of his. This is not because they were inherently contradictory but because Swift's 'writing', in Warren Montag's lucid analysis, 'is not so much determined by a set of guiding ideas as by the institution in relation to which he defined himself . . . and this institution was from its origins confused, radically disarticulated and riven with contradictions'.[12]

Swift's stubborn temperament was perfectly matched to the temper of his time. He engaged willingly in secular debates in an attempt to strengthen the position of his allies in his own church, even as many of his allies looked with scepticism upon his apparent lack of faith. As Michael DePorte observes in 'The Road to St Patrick's: Swift and the Problem of Belief', what 'comes across most strongly in Swift's references to God is a sense of God as remote and unknowable'.[13] This is, of course, hardly a radical posture for a cleric and it owes at least something to the fideism of such early Christian thinkers as Tertullian and Augustine. However, much consequent consideration of Swift has since been taken up with the question of the nature of the dean's faith. It is a fascinating question but, as DePorte recognises, there is a profoundly political aspect to Swift's statements about the church and God, their relationship to each other and the place of humanity in relation to both. Swift grasped that following the Glorious Revolution of 1688 the church was on a different footing politically to its pre-Revolution status. His sense of the place of the church was increasingly apparent and, in DePorte's words:

> the importance of preserving established religion is so persistent in Swift's later writings that even a change to a new religion 'that is more pure and perfect, may be an Occasion of endangering the publick Peace'.[14]

This was a view Swift had come to over many years, but it was after his return to Dublin that the truth of it became so apparent that he could discover no choice but to re-enter the political arena when the moment was right. We should remember this as we read Swift, 'accept[ing]' in Edward Said's words, 'the discontinuities [Swift] experienced in the way he experienced them: as either actual or imminent losses of tradition, heritage, position, history'.[15]

At the time Swift was reaching his conclusions, some clerics within the Church of Ireland had begun to consider the ramifications of being a state-sponsored church in an Enlightenment-era polity. The need to engage civic society as something other than an agent of that society would have significant consequences for the Church of Ireland. Swift was centrally located and so was fully aware of the debates being conducted publicly and privately. He was lucky enough to be unencumbered by an office that prevented him from applying his own analyses to the situation – analyses that provide us with important clues as to the forces which would shape the new, Hanoverian Church of Ireland.

Along with his position at St Patrick's, Swift was also able to take advantage of his own lack of public interest in the nature of God. This freed him to respond to specific concerns with particular comments, and because those concerns were not constrained by pre-existing doctrinal statements of his own, Swift was able, as Montag demonstrates, to develop an 'imaginary solution: a vision of Church and State, an ideal'.[16] Montag argues that this idea, incapable of expression in 'expository form', found its voice 'negatively in literary satire'.[17] However, Swift on several occasions evoked his ideal 'vision of Church and State' in his public considerations of the political issue of the day. In every case, he suggested that the cause of the immediate problem at hand was a falling away from the ideal and hinted at a resolution to be found in some re-establishment of that ideal. For Montag, Swift's satire was a consequence of the fact that ideologically:

> it was less and less possible to state the Anglican philosophy; instead one had to learn how to be an Anglican *in* philosophy, to occupy positions that, no matter how foreign to traditional Anglican thought, objectively favored the interests of the Church.[18]

This was not simply Swift's literary position. It was also his political inclination.

Swift had an agenda. It was simple yet complex – simple in that it centred around the preservation of the established church, complex in that he recognised the limits of the traditional audience to whom such an agenda would appeal. And so Swift co-opted whatever political discourse of the moment suited his agenda. At times he sounds positively 'Old Whig', at others, distinctly 'Tory'. For many of his contemporaries these terms were practically synonyms for 'Jacobite', but that does not mean Swift himself held Jacobite opinions.[19] At other times, Swift would shape his appeals to reach a broader public audience, but that, too, does not mean his intentions were populist. This is the stuff out of which myths are made and reputations unfairly earned, but as Nokes reminds us, while we should be wary of the myths, we ignore them at our peril. There is an:

> ever-lengthening bibliography of Swift studies . . . [Where] specialist works often produce partial or lop-sided views of his writings . . . while the broad sweeps of the generalising critic run the risk of missing the teasing particularity of Swift's ironies.[20]

There is a middle way. Swift's commitment to the church provides a core which establishes his body of work as one of those rare collections that can be argued to have grown organically from first to last. It was Fabricant who first extensively argued for the 'gains' Swift experienced from those challenges confronting him.[21] Fabricant's study definitively demonstrates the influences, positive and negative, that helped make Swift the man and writer he was. Landscape alone, however, even in Fabricant's generous interpretation of the term, was only a part of what provided Swift with a fixed point in his psychological and moral temperament against which all his work can in some manner be assessed.

The Dean of St Patrick's was fortunate in that he could leave obtuse theoretical considerations to King, who had a penetrating intellect, a faith in reason and argument and a powerful position from which to engage in theoretical discourse. Swift was of a different ilk altogether, but he did possess one talent King did not – the ability to join the political moment with the immediate concerns of his church. It is important, therefore, to better understand the political and economic pressures upon the Church of Ireland, in addition to the broader implications of those strains on Irish society as a whole, to understand how Swift came to be taken as a patriotic defender of a country for which he never expressed much sympathy. Swift was able to draw upon the still potent political position of men such as King and the Irish-born Anglican Irish aristocracy to promote church causes, albeit in his own distinct manner. It was his luck to be effectively exiled to a society where political discourse was still defining its parameters. In understanding how those parameters evolved we gain an invaluable insight into the complex dance which made up the Church of Ireland's relations with its secular sponsors. The language of Swift was informed by the moment and so of the moment, but that does not mean it lacked consistency.

Modern readers of Swift are wiser than was Swift's contemporary Colley Cibber. We do not, and should not, 'improve' the work of earlier writers to provide some greater currency for our time. Yet we often overlook the currents of the time in which they wrote, forgetting that writers and their contexts were often more intertwined than literature alone allows us to understand.

Swift's accomplishments were not the result of some well disguised affection for Ireland but the inevitable result of a series of historical, political and cultural stimuli and a commitment to the well-being of the established church in which he served. Because of this commitment, Jonathan Swift became an Irish patriot by accident, but his patriotism was no less sincere for that.

* * *

Jonathan Swift and the Church of Ireland, 1710–1724 is designed as preliminary and exploratory. It will perhaps raise more questions than it answers, but it is my hope that this examination of the period in

Swift's life between 1710, when the Tories came to power, and 1724 will help to demonstrate the essential integrity of Swift's political views that would resurface in his so-called 'Irish' writings, an integrity intimately connected with the struggle for identity of the Church of Ireland.

Of Swift's major works, I deal in detail with only one, *A Proposal for the Universal Use of Irish Manufacture*, and I end just as Swift is about to embark on his seminal 'Irish' work, *The Drapier's Letters*. Those already familiar with Swift's writings will find themselves reminded of passages in those works when reading these pages. I have decided to leave these connections by and large unremarked, confident that readers will themselves make those connections they consider pertinent, and I do not wish to draw attention to some connections while seeming to ignore others I have, no doubt, overlooked. In any case, I am loathe to prejudice the use others might care to make of this work by seeming to seek to guide readers to certain ancillary texts.

As this study is intended as introductory and for an audience perhaps unfamiliar with church affairs, I have tried to explain terms that might cause some confusion. However, I have not annotated certain clerical terms as they seem to me to be perfectly clear within the text itself. I have used the technical term where possible, so that, for example, bishops are 'translated' to their new 'living', rather than being posted to a new job. I have done my best to annotate appropriately any terms relating to the structure of the Churches of England and Ireland in the years under study, but to the modern reader the role played by those churches in society at that time, and their own internal operations, are perhaps cause as much for confusion as for anything else. If I have overdone the occasional political or economic note, that is because I felt it better to err on the side of the generous. The busy or otherwise engaged reader should be able to complete the body of the text without needing to refer to the notes at all as they are intended either to explain terms or to suggest possible ideas for development at a later stage.

This might be the best place to quickly mention the two women most significant in Swift's life – Stella and Vanessa, as he called them in his correspondence. Stella was Esther Johnson and Vanessa, Esther Vanhomrigh. Much has been made of Swift's relationships with these two women, none of it pertinent to this work. I mention them here only so that readers unfamiliar with the women may at least recognise the real names behind 'Stella' and 'Vanessa' when they appear in the pages that follow. Should you wish to know more, you must look elsewhere.

This study grew over many years. It was at the University of Delaware that I finally limited what seemed like various disparate interests and questions into a single one that led somewhere. There, the encouragement and enthusiasm of Donald C. Mell, Jr made this work possible. His understanding and support were both greater than I deserved, and I hope I have rewarded his patience and his generosity. I have also been extremely lucky to have had the encouragement of Michael DePorte at the University of New Hampshire. He introduced me to Swift while I was an undergraduate and persuaded me to return to Durham for my first graduate degree. Both these teachers gave far more of their time and interest over the years than I would have dared asked for.

James Dean read a very early version of the first chapter and helped me understand the commitment and responsibilities demanded of those who would presume to do this work. At least as importantly, his course on William Langland demonstrated the virtues of reconsidering assumptions, in his case about Geoffrey Chaucer, and offered me the confidence to undertake a study that is only in part literary. Also at the University of Delaware, Jerry Beasley was kind enough to offer advice when I asked. His skills as an editor and reader were invaluable.

Without the encouragement and support of Carl Dawson I would never have believed myself capable of this work, and to him much thanks is due. Jill Jones and Michael Pugh both read drafts and helped me master material which informs much of my thinking. Bernard J. McKenna helped me with research at the University of Delaware library. He was always cheerful in the process, and exactly the same can be said of Jon Worley in Belfast, who looked things up when I could not find them in the United States and who, with his wife Elizabeth, was always a gracious host when I was over in Ulster. I am grateful to have had the opportunity to share my ideas with all these people.

Shayne Annett helped with the computer work and kept me informed of England's progress (or lack thereof) in the 1993, 1994–95, 1997 and 1998–99 Ashes series – this latter obligation he has happily offered to continue to undertake every two years.

I would like, too, to keep a promise made to Stefan Kanfer and mention his wonderful novel, T*he International Garage Sale,* which introduced me to the maxims and essays of the Marquis of Halifax.

Although this is ostensibly a book about Jonathan Swift and the Church of Ireland, Swift's neighbour, William King, Archbishop of Dublin, plays an important role. King is a greatly underappreciated presence in Irish history of the period from 1688 until the mid-1720s. He was a devout Anglican, motivated by a sincere devotion to God, Christ and his church's doctrine. Few in King's circle were as intellectually honest, as charitably inclined or as genuinely courageous as he. King is a man deserving of much greater recognition and, unlike Swift, also of emulation. The relations and misunderstandings of Swift and King, for so many years intertwined in political and ecclesiastical affairs, shed much light on the two men's strengths and weaknesses. For much of my understanding of King I have relied on the work of Andrew Carpenter, who almost alone has recognised the complexity and attraction of King's character, as well as his central role in Ireland at that time. Additionally, he was kind to a young graduate student who wrote to him for advice and help and has been supportive of my efforts ever since. I trust he will find some reward in these pages. One other scholar in Ireland who showed much patience and offered help and encouragement was Kenneth Milne. I am grateful to him as well.

At Newbury College I have been honoured to be allowed to learn from my colleagues Debbie Mael, Peter Galeno, Gary Bonetti and David Daniel. Jane Gentry read the final draft of this work and many of the resulting felicities of language are hers. It was to the staff of the Newbury College library that help with the last minute checking and double-checking of information and documentation fell. I would especially like to thank Nellie Lyubomirsky and Janet Hayashi for their always cheerful assistance despite the numerous difficulties besetting the library at that time.

Finally, but of course not least, I have to thank my father, Tore Fauske, and my mother, Susan Rogerson. At the risk of sounding like Gwyneth Paltrow on Oscar night, I shall simply say that without them . . .

CHAPTER ONE

'Putting the world in order': when Jonathan Swift met his destiny

I

> When we see a natural style, we are quite surprised and delighted, for we expected to see an author and we find a man.
> Blaise Pascal, *Pensées*[1]

Jonathan Swift was a man fiercely committed to the protection of the privileges of the state-supported Anglican church. For him, although he longed for a position within the Church of England, this meant the church of his native country, the Church of Ireland.[2] The Anglican church was established in both England and Ireland and protected by the laws of those countries. In Ireland, legal protection was reinforced by the historical memory of the governing class. The senior clerics of both churches sat in their respective parliamentary House of Lords, and the expenses of running the church were at least in part met by state appropriations. Additionally, in England at the beginning of the eighteenth century, and in Ireland almost until the end of the same century, a variety of laws effectively reserved government and public service appointments for members of the Anglican church.[3]

One inherent strain facing any established church, despite the obvious and significant benefits, is the inevitable involvement of the church in political debate. What parliaments and monarchs have granted, they can revoke. It was Swift's destiny to serve his church at a time of enormous upheaval in relations between the church and parliament. Many of the apparent 'discontinuities' of Swift's writings grew out of his commitment to the church, combined with a stubborn pride and determination to appear no man's servant.

Swift had a sincerely conservative notion of what should be the church's position in society, but he combined that with an adeptness at political manoeuvring that often obscured his intentions. At odds with the secular trends of his time, but determined to try to influence those trends, Swift should not have been surprised by the charges of inconstancy and opportunism that dogged him throughout much of his career. However, Alexander Pope understood well that Swift's various guises were all part of a coherent whole. He dedicated *The Dunciad* of 1728 to Swift, celebrating his friend's achievements:

> O Thou! whatever titles please thine ear,
> Dean, Drapier, Bickerstaff, or Gulliver!
> Whether thou chuse Cervantes' serious air,
> Or laugh and shake in Rab'lais' easy chair,
> Or praise the Court, or magnify Mankind,
> Or thy griev'd Country's copper chains unbind . . .[4]

The changes in Swift's expectations following the death of Queen Anne have rightly been seen as pivotal to an understanding of his writings. His later re-emergence as champion of a country he professed to find a 'land of slaves, / Where all are fools, and all are knaves'[5] has been explained most readily as a way for a disappointed man to castigate both his neighbours and a government he despised. But to say that what explains Swift's increasing stridency is a personal vendetta is to do him a significant injustice. As far as Swift was concerned, what the death of Queen Anne changed most profoundly was the balance of power between the church and the law-makers. In Ireland, Swift did his best to restore the balance he believed vital. He saw in the troubles of his native country evidence of what happens when the church–state compact is undermined. His anger, though sharpened by personal disappointment, was that of a displaced public servant who saw everything he believed vital for the common good being systematically undermined.

Swift was installed as Dean of St Patrick's, Dublin, on 13 June 1713. He stayed in that city barely two weeks before retiring to his country living at Laracor, County Meath. From there he wrote to Vanessa (Esther Vanhomrigh) that:

> if they have no further service for me, I will never see England again: At my first coming I thought I should have dyed with Discontent, and was horribly melancholy while they were installing me, but it begins to wear off, and change to Dullness.[6]

Despite his anxieties, Swift did return to England as part of an unsuccessful attempt to save the Tory ministry. Less than a year later, he was back in Ireland and he soon composed one of his most bitter poems, 'In Sickness':[7]

> But, why obscurely here alone?
> Where I am neither loved nor known.
> My state of health none care to learn;
> My life is here no soul's concern.
> And, those with whom I now converse,
> Without a tear will tend my hearse.[8]

Swift returned to Ireland embittered and frustrated, but in the confusion surrounding an evolving Anglican Irish identity,[9] and in his own fight on behalf of a church embattled, he would find a new outlet for his own particular brand of radical conservatism.

Ireland, like England, would fail the dean. 'Whose fault is it if poor Ireland still continues poor?' asked George Berkeley, Bishop of Cloyne, ending the 1750 edition of *The Querist* with the sort of resignation that typifies so many reformers' conclusions.[10] It was a question Berkeley's friend Swift had often asked, taking care always to absolve himself. In his late poem *The Legion Club*, Swift paints a graphic picture of some of the people behind 'poor Ireland's' fate, people whom he had once thought to influence for the better. 'The language suggests', says Irvin Ehrenpreis, 'Christian associations of devils and damned souls, along with bestiality and lunacy'.[11] In such 'Christian associations' is to be found Swift's ideal of the social fabric – the interests of the state were identical with those of the established Anglican church. Challenges to establishment threatened more than the church itself; they jeopardised the very foundation of the state. Indeed, *The Legion Club* was inspired by one of the many arguments over tithes between the lay politicians in Ireland and their clerical counterparts. In 1736, the Irish House of Commons denied the Church of Ireland's right to collect 'agistment' (a tithe on certain types of pasturage) and Swift responded with his last lengthy polemic.

Toward the end of his life, Swift saw that his struggle for the integrity of the Church of Ireland, and so, as he thought, for the welfare of Ireland, had failed. He blamed neither himself nor, particularly, the Whigs whom he despised. His anger he chose to vent on his fellow Anglican Irishmen who had put personal profit ahead of the good of the state. J.A. Downie takes exception to critics who 'bestow high praise on Swift's tirade', noting that 'there is surely little that is original in calling one's adversary fool and knave, madman or devil . . . Swift's libel is remarkable more for its testimony to the depth of his feeling'.[12] Setting aside the question of who is right on the literary merits of the poem, the point is precisely that aged 69 Swift was still moved to anger not by any of the various culpable or foolish acts of the Irish House of Commons, but by a specific attack upon an institution he loved dearly but about which the majority of his countrymen could not care less, the Church of Ireland.

If Swift's tenure as dean began with 'melancholy' and finished in something approximating despair, it also witnessed genuine achievement which assured him lasting fame. Ironically, it was a fame which flourished in English radical circles long before his eventual literary rehabilitation. After his period of deepest distress, Swift published tracts, essays and poems anonymously for a public that seldom had much doubt who was the author. He wrote to defend his old friends and to explain the failure of the Tory ministry. Swift wrote from Ireland to remedy the troubles of England, and when that failed he wrote to castigate England for Irish troubles and to suggest domestic Irish solutions, just as he had suggested domestic English solutions when writing in that country. So certain was Swift of the validity of his analysis, he was at least as hurt that it was *his* plans that were rejected as he was that nothing got done.

Swift worked with a deliberateness of which it can be easy to lose sight. Much in *The Drapier's Letters* seems as intemperate to today's first-time reader as it did when it appeared on the streets of Dublin. Swift argued not simply for revolt but for a political order that had to be re-established. It was a political order that would justify the dreams and expectations of a middle-age spent in the company of Viscount Bolingbroke and the Earl of Oxford. Although the words and ideas of M.B. Drapier would seal Swift's reputation as an 'Irish patriot', Ireland was incidental to the most important aspect of that work. Unconcerned by geography, circumstance forced Swift to use Ireland. His mind, however, was primarily focused upon ideas and only partially upon that unhappy country.

Swift was not unused to being categorised by his opponents and supporters in terms he did not necessarily appreciate or understand. The most damaging of those characterisations was based upon his actions in 1710 when he had, so his opponents claimed, crossed party lines from Whig to Tory with unbecoming ease. That reputation was to haunt him throughout the remainder of his life, and beyond, but charges of opportunism cannot explain why Swift gave every appearance of remaining loyal to the more reactionary Tory faction after 1714. Many Tories, chief among them the minister Lord Harcourt, successfully mended fences with the Whigs. Swift did not.

In September 1714, Swift's friend Constantine Phipps was removed as Lord Chancellor of Ireland, leaving him without an ally within the administration at Dublin Castle. Phipps himself was one of the most strident and partisan of politicians and had been a member of the defense team at the trial of Dr Henry Sacheverell, Bursar of Magdalen College, Oxford, a trial which had helped catapult the Tories into power in 1710. Phipps was 'pugnacious, hot-tempered and contemptuous of opposition', writes David Hayton in 'The Crisis in Ireland and the Disintegration of Queen Anne's Last Ministry'.[14] He had 'plunged into the party battle in Ireland' and had managed to make the situation in Ireland in the concluding period of Queen Anne's life actually represent the kind of partisan government Robert Walpole was determined to find in Britain to justify his own theories of politics.[15] 'The goings-on in Ireland excited great interest in England', Hayton records, and Swift's old paper, *The Examiner*, and Richard Steele's *The Englishman* 'debated in print the rights and wrongs' of attacks on Phipps.[16] Swift knew full well that Phipps' days in Dublin were numbered once Anne had died, and while he might have sympathised with the out-going Lord Chancellor's politics, and while he liked him personally, he knew better than to stand up for him in public.

At the same time, Walpole's 'Committee of Secrecy' was established in London to provide proof of Tory treason.[17] Swift, who knew enough to stay silent while the committee worked, quickly found himself one of the few remaining Tories of significance in Ireland. Ehrenpreis places him in a peculiarly lonely isolation:

> Letters kept coming from his sweet-tempered, high-church friend, Dr Arbuthnot, who was still prosperous but no longer a royal physician and no longer welcome at court. Letters came from the magnificent but malleable Duke of Ormonde, grandest of Irish peers, but now vilified . . . As tidings and salutations arrived from these and other friends he left behind, Swift was bitterly reminded of his distance from society he admired . . . [H]e seemed isolated, old, dependent on enemies.[18]

Swift missed England enormously. He missed even more the friendships that allowed him indulgence in literary talk and escape from politics. Restless, authoritarian and meddlesome, Swift was obliged to restrain his natural impulses but at first could find little else with which to divert himself and chafed under the constraints he felt imposed upon him.

The Committee of Secrecy reported in July 1715 that there were grounds on which to impeach Bolingbroke, Ormonde, Oxford and the Earl of Strafford. In mid-July, Oxford was escorted to the Tower of London. Bolingbroke fled to France and joined the Old Pretender's camp (a palpable act of treason) and Swift was stunned when, on 20 July, Ormonde went too. In the summer of 1715, revolts supporting the Old Pretender broke out in Scotland and England. Aware of the seriousness of the situation, Swift had ceased corresponding with his erstwhile political colleagues. The implication was that he wished to be left well enough alone. Such prudence helped him survive a potential danger when Ormonde sent him a package of papers that was confiscated by a customs officer and sent to the Lords Justice in Dublin. William King, Archbishop of Dublin and one of the three Lords Justice, exonerated Swift, pointing out that the letters 'seemed to acquit the dean by complaining of his not writing, which [Ormonde] interpreted as forbidding [him] to write'.[19]

Whatever the true extent of the danger, Swift survived the period in style, helped perhaps by finding an outlet for his political instincts in a demarcation dispute with Archbishop King over the prerogatives of the deanery. He wrote sundry texts, pamphlets and defences of the last Tory administration but made no attempt to publish them. Refusing to be completely silenced by Walpole's cronies, Swift did undertake one splendid act of defiance, writing and preaching what is now preserved as the sermon 'On False Witness'. George I had decreed on 11 December 1714 that sermons should not 'intermeddle in any affairs of state' and Swift decided to do just that. There existed at that time a healthy trade in selling information about Jacobite supporters to the Whig government. Swift chose for one of his sermons a warning to those who would bear false witness. It would be hard to castigate a dean for preaching on one of the Ten Commandment.[20]

Swift makes clear at the outset the true topic of this particular sermon:

> In those great Changes that are made in a Country, by the prevailing of one Party over another, it is very convenient, that the Prince, and those who are in Authority under him, should use all just and proper Methods for preventing any Mischief to the Publick from seditious Men . . . [W]hoever knoweth any Thing, the

telling of which would prevent some great Evil to his Prince, his Country, or his Neighbour, is bound in Conscience to reveal it.[21]

But, Swift cautions, 'Holy *David* numbers this among the chief of his Sufferings; *False Witnesses are risen up against me, and such as breath out Cruelty*'.[22] Swift warns his congregation against this particular sin, which is 'so horrible and dangerous in itself', before going on to give advice to his political sympathisers:

> Innocence is the best Protection in the World; yet that is not always sufficient without some Degree of Prudence. Our Saviour himself intimateth [this] to us, by instructing his Disciples *to be wise as Serpents*, *as well as innocent as Doves* . . . Neither is Virtue itself a sufficient Security in such Times, because it is not allowed to be Virtue, otherwise than as it hath a Mixture of Party.[23]

This is a vision of society not dissimilar to the account of the Kingdom of Tribnia (a not-all-that subtle anagram of Britain) in *Gulliver's Travels*, where:

> the Bulk of the People consisted wholly of Discoverers, Witnesses, Informers, Accusers, Prosecutors, Evidences, Swearers; together with their several subservient and subaltern Instruments; all under the Colours, the Conduct, and pay of Ministers and their Deputies. The Plots in that Kingdom are usually the Workmanship of those Persons who desire to raise their own Characters of profound Politicians; to restore new Vigour to a crazy Administration . . . as . . . shall best answer their private Advantage.[24]

Downie uses this passage as one of the cornerstones of his review of Swift's relationship with Walpole, to which he devotes one chapter of his study.[25] However, while Swift blamed Walpole for much of what happened in the years after the death of Queen Anne, Swift's animosity was not particularly personal. Rather, he saw Walpole as the personification of the consequence of the collapse of the church-state compact, not as the primary cause of it. Walpole's greed, corruption and continued exercise of power were only possible because of what had failed in British polity; they were not the cause of that failure. It is not at all clear that Swift's antipathy toward Walpole was any more personal than his numerous other political opinions.

Apart from demonstrating the skill and courage with which Swift consistently invested his appeals for the restoration of the civic values, the sermon 'On False Witness' is typical of Swift's analysis of what happened to political discourse in Britain immediately after the accession of George I. Swift had first been introduced to British politics in the household of Sir William Temple at Moor Park immediately after the Glorious Revolution of 1688. The significance of 1688 was that, Ireland aside, it in many ways concluded the struggles that had come to a head with the civil war between parliament and Charles I, the father of the deposed James II. The largely peaceful transition from James to the one-of-a-kind co-monarchy of William of Orange (son of Charles I's daughter) and his wife Mary (elder daughter of James II) was accompanied by a series of agreements between parliament and monarch. The cornerstone of these agreements was the Bill of Rights which finally demarcated the respective rights and privileges of monarch and parliament.

From 1688 until 1714, English political life enjoyed one of its most stable periods as parliamentary factions began to emerge in their modern form even as their members remained careful not to jeopardise the nature of parliamentary authority. Debate was significant and often intense, but it remained constrained by memories of civil war. Temple himself was so confident of the new arrangement, and so fed up with the old squabbles, that he retired to Moor Park, refused various commissions from the new monarchs and enjoyed his peace. It was to this house that Swift came from Ireland to make his way in the world, a time A.C. Elias details so thoroughly.[26]

Perhaps because of his earlier exposure to Temple's apparent contentment, Swift was at first almost alone among his peers in Ireland in realising the shift in atmosphere heralded by the rise to power of the militant Whigs. Aware of the new king's reliance on his ministers, the Whig ministers dispensed with the old assumptions and expelled Tory supporters from even the most trivial of county positions. The extensive machinery of government patronage was used to ensure that even the most minor officials of the new government relied upon the Whigs for job security. The new ministry exaggerated fears of the Old Pretender and Roman Catholic ambitions for reclaiming England to purge posts that since the Restoration of 1660 had passed from office holder to office holder without regard for party (and often without regard for ability). All these moves polarised political discourse and reduced debate to a matter of 'party'.

That 'Virtue itself . . . is not allowed to be Virtue, otherwise than it hath a Mixture of Party' was an insight that profoundly affected Swift's work in Ireland.[27] An exponent of expedient alliances, Swift understood the fundamental change in the political discourse and decried the manifestations of 'party', even as he appreciated the opportunities presented by the creation of so much disaffection with the new system. Swift was to use for his own ends the ravages of 'party' he so despised.

The boost to his morale from the successful preaching of his sermon 'On False Witness' aside, Swift was at the nadir of his political career. The exclusionary nature of the Whig agenda after Anne's death surprised him, but even before that he had struggled with the increasingly obvious: Oxford and Bolingbroke were barely on speaking terms and each acted decisively only where he saw an opportunity to scotch the plans of the other. In any case, it is hard not to suspect that, even had Queen Anne lived, Swift would have fallen out with precisely those people who should have been his political allies. Jonathan Swift was no John Robinson and political success seems never to have been in his stars.[28] The already apparent failure of the Tory ministry could only have fostered what was, as F.P. Lock argues, an overarching psychological trait. Swifts 'Cato Complex', writes Lock:

> was a temperamental affinity with, and admiration for, a partic-
> ular type of hero: the man of complete integrity who is defeated
> in terms of this world but vindicated by his spiritual triumph.[29]

In Ireland after 1714, this 'complex' would find fertile soil and would be strengthened by Swift's 'Old Whig' sympathies, sympathies which, as Lawrence Klein demonstrates, placed Swift firmly in the mainstream of a genteel, increasingly irrelevant tradition with out-dated notions of the meaning of the word 'liberty'. As the republican and sometime-commander of English forces in Ireland, Algernon Sidney, wrote in *Discourses Concerning Government*, 'the Strength, Vertue, Glory, Wealth, Power and Happiness of *Rome* proceeding from Liberty, did rise, grow and perish with it'.[30]

Swift thought that 'few States are ruined by any Defect in their Institution, but generally by the Corruption of Manners'.[31] Furthermore, in ancient Greece and Rome when:

> Arbitrary Government of single Persons [was commonplace]
> *Arts* and *Sciences* took their rise, and flourished only in those few
> small Territories where the People were free, . . . *Slavery*, the first
> natural Step from *Anarchy* or the *Savage Life*, [was] the greatest
> Clog and Obstacle to *Speculation*.[32]

Swift would refer to Ireland as in a state of 'slavery' on several occasions, but as his *Sentiments of a Church-of-England Man* had stated, the solution lay as much in the institutions as in 'society' in its more modern meaning. In the *Sentiments* (published in 1711 but probably written in 1708), Swift had admitted that in a corrupt society 'the best Institution is no longer security', but in Ireland, with its greater political potential for the Church of Ireland, he saw upon his return a society not yet beyond redemption.[33] By protecting the legacy and heritage of the Church of Ireland, as he thought it should be expressed, Swift envisaged the possibility that, for once, society as it might have been could be at least touched upon. It was not Ireland that interested him; it was the institutions he found there.

While such a temperament gave Swift the mettle with which to act so coolly in the period immediately after Anne's death, it could not prevent him struggling to reconcile retrospectively the competing factions of the late-Tory ministry in works such as *Some Free Thoughts upon the Present State of Affairs* and *An Enquiry into the Behaviour of the Queen's Last Ministry*. What Swift found drove him to despair, but he continued his own exertions precisely because his commitment to his church was greater than the inclination to retire to the willows he had planted at Laracor. Out of that struggle would grow Swift's reputation as an 'Irish' patriot, but his patriotism, though it relied upon circumstances specific to Ireland, was a loyalty to the ideal of the church established and was only incidentally Irish.

II

[Query:] Whether the whole and sole duty of an Irish patriot be not to nourish opposition, to guard against influence, and always to suspect the worst?

George Berkeley[34]

In *Before Novels: The Cultural Contexts of Eighteenth-Century English Fiction*, J. Paul Hunter reminds us that works of literature are inseparable from their contexts:

No book comes into the world altogether naked, new, or alone. Every text has a past and a history of its own . . . Some of what clothes a text or comes along as baggage is authorially chosen, but some is not.[35]

This is perhaps hardly a novel insight, but it is one which in Swift's case presents a particular set of challenges. Swift's 'authorially chosen baggage', introduced with a variety of excuses and with a diverse set of immediate aims, stated and unstated, is of an order quite distinct from that of those other eighteenth-century English writers with whom we are most familiar today. Swift's primary concern in his prose was nearly always political, and in none of his fictions was he ever occupied by the theoretical demands of the novel, not even in his quasi-novelistic *Gulliver's Travels*. His work was consistently inspired by an immediate need, but, like any good polemicist, Swift understood that his writing had a function that existed beyond the demands of genre. His own idiosyncratic outrages and ironies combined with stylistic skills to distinguish his work from the hundreds of other tracts and pamphlets appearing on the themes he chose to address. This felicity with language has led to his work often being considered for its literary achievements without reference to its more mundane ambitions. Although Swift's work has enormous merit on a purely literary basis, overlooking its immediate political objectives naturally produces conclusions similar to, if usually less extreme than, F.R. Leavis's assertion that Swift's writings show 'probably the most remarkable expression of negative feelings and attitudes that literature can offer'.[36]

Leavis believed Swift to be 'distinguished by the intensity of his feelings, not by insight into them'.[37] This is certainly one implication of Swift's 'literature' when considered in isolation from his letters and less famous political pamphlets. Leavis's interpretation echoes that of many of Swift's contemporaries, but Swift's 'insight' into what he was about in his writing was this: that he had an overtly political purpose, one served not by dispassionate analysis, but by an immediate appeal to his readers' own sentiments. Swift was writing in the midst of a savage political debate. Swift believed everything he stood for and held most important was being destroyed in the England the Whigs were seeking to create. What Leavis thought were his 'negative feelings and attitudes' were the weapons of an embattled Anglican conservative waging an often lonely fight.

In his own study of the emergence of various Protestant sects, Donald Davie reminds us of Ferdinand Brunetiere's observation that John Calvin's *Institutes* represented the first *classique* work in French, 'classique' meaning that the whole was greater than the sum of the parts.[38] Davie uses this remark to question whether it can be said of *The Dunciad* that its whole is greater than its parts. He thinks not. Whatever it may do to Pope's reputation, Brunetiere's definition of 'classique' helps identify the integrity of much of Swift's prose.

It was not just the periodic political realignments that helped obscure the thematic consistency of much of Swift's work; his own explosive irony added a further layer of complication. At times, Swift rejoiced in the confusion his writings could cause, as he demonstrated in his long autobiographical poem 'Verses on the Death of Dr Swift, D.S.P.D.':

> Arbuthnot is no more my friend,
> Who dares to irony pretend;
> Which I was born to introduce,
> Refined it first, and showed its use.[39]

Readers have, of course, long wondered at the nature of that irony. A precise description of Swift's position can be found in Søren Kierkegaard's at times exasperating dissertation, *The Concept of Irony, with Continual Reference to Socrates*. Kierkegaard touches directly on the nature of Swift's irony when examining 'The Validity of Irony'. The subject of an ironist's attention, writes Kierkegaard:

> has become for him an imperfect form that is a hindrance everywhere. But on the other hand, he does not possess the new. He knows only that the present does not match the idea. He is the one who must pass judgment . . . [T]he ironist . . . has stepped out of line with his age, has turned around and faced it.[40]

This was precisely the position in which Swift found himself, and he understood only too well the warning of a man whose politics he must have despised – the seventeenth-century embodiment of compromise and discretion, George Savile, Marquis of Halifax. 'In a corrupted Age', the marquis wrote, 'the putting of the World in order would breed Confusion'.[41] Swift knew the truth of Halifax's maxim; unlike Halifax, however, he was willing to risk confusion, and his own reputation, to preserve at least what order did remain. Swift found some of his motivation in an apparently far simpler idea: that, in Edward Rosenheim's words, 'there remain . . . relative degrees of truth; the course of political action or of religious belief which flies in the face of common interest is plainly a greater folly than the systematic pursuit of that interest'.[42] In practice, however, those 'relative degrees of truth', each measured against the best interests of the established church at a particular moment, required of their proponent a significant degree of political skill and rhetorical accomplishment. Where most of those who could not adjust to the new politics engaged in what Isaac

Kramnick calls 'the politics of nostalgia',[43] Swift adapted his approach to take account of the demands of his age. This ever-present sense of urgency, combined with an increasing certainty of failure, in the end makes it hard to distinguish the tone of Swift's satires from that of the 'straight' political manifestos, for, as Rosenheim demonstrates, Swift's 'satire moves toward rhetoric as the fictional quality becomes subordinate to literal polemic'.[44] In Swift's case, however, the 'literal polemic' is very often not so 'literal', and we would do well to remember the perplexity of Christopher Bayliss in Alan Wall's novel *The Lightning Cage* when he ponders the question, 'Whoever taught us to assume that the hearts of books should be easier to come by than our own? What is a book but someone's heart and soul?'.[45]

Swift's tactics in Ireland were similar to those he had employed in England, but he did have to pick his fights more carefully. In England, he had worked within existing circles of public debate centered in the coffee houses of London and the court at Windsor. In Ireland, he had the far harder task of trying to align with his notion of the church's interest an otherwise nervous and disjointed opposition with no apparent focal point. Unpublishable defences of his friends gave way to intricately argued explications of a displaced but no less articulate high church faith in just government and a well ordered society. Inexorably, Swift moved further and further from the ranks of the befuddled but increasingly compliant Tory opposition in England. As time and circumstance changed, Swift abandoned the Tories as he had once abandoned the Whigs, compelled to continue his defence of the Church of Ireland in a different political arena.

The basic principle from which Swift always worked was his conviction that the role of the church in society was not simply one issue among several. It was a matter so integral that even when he considered the fate of his Tory friends, or Ireland's economic woes, religion was never far from the surface. When there were policy disputes that he honestly could not imagine affecting the church, Swift, uninterested in partisan disputes, was willing to amuse himself with personal vendettas or harmless banter. More often than not, however, Swift's prose addressed the polity of England and Ireland from the position that he believed best represented the established church's interests at that particular time.

Swift's living was within the Church of Ireland, and he had been its emissary for six years. While he had hoped for translation to the English church, that had not happened, and in 1714 he returned to Ireland aware that it was probably to be his home for the rest of his life. However uncertain Swift was of Ireland's exact constitutional status, he viewed Ireland as akin to a foreign country.[46] For the Irish Anglicans, their church was the established national church. The English, in contrast, generally treated that church as an adjunct to the Church of England, more as the Church of England in Ireland, rather than as its own agency. With English government policy so inherently damaging to the established church's position, Swift quickly grasped the potential in distinguishing the Church of Ireland as an integral, and independent, part of Ireland's Anglican political structure. Consequently, on his re-emergence upon the Irish political scene in 1720, Swift seized upon economic issues to drive home the advantage he believed would accrue to the Church of Ireland by separating Irish Anglican interests from their English counterparts. This is a crucial pointer to understanding Swift's later defence of Irish economic and political liberty. Though the country had changed, neither Swift's motives nor his tactics had undergone any significant transition. The later Irish patriot was to all intents and purposes the same man who had made his name defending first a Whig and then a Tory ministry in England.

For six years, from 1708 to 1714, Swift tenaciously worked in England on behalf of the church of a country he repeatedly claimed to despise. He hoped for personal advantage, but whenever a choice had to be made Swift unhesitatingly put aside personal gain for the sake of his church. Confident of his talents, though unsure of the respect they commanded, Swift could not hide his indignation when events conspired against him. He was wont to combine conviction and pique when he wrote, as he so often did, to correct injustices done both to him and to society. And yet, the scheming politician of the London years and the ill-tempered gadfly of Irish exile were one and the same person, motivated by, and responding to, the need to protect the interests of the established church. Whig or Tory, English or Irish, Swift's writings struggled to neutralise fundamental political challenges to the church within a secular politics inimicable to its interest.

CHAPTER TWO

'We were in danger to be over-run': the church's plea

I

Look down, *St Patrick*, look, we pray,
On thine own *Church and Steeple*;
Convert thy *Dean*, on this *Great Day*;
Or else God help the People!
Jonathan Smedley[1]

In England after his return in 1707 Jonathan Swift combined his lobbying for remission of the First Fruits and Twentieth Parts with his own passion for secular politics.[2] So complete was this merger of the public and private that Swift's appointment in 1713 as Dean of St Patrick's, Dublin, was greeted as a victory for politics over ecclesiastical common sense. The prayer asking St Patrick to convert his dean, supposedly pinned to the cathedral door on the day of Swift's inauguration, was far from unique in its assessment of the new dean's merits.

Abel Boyer, capable and vitriolic spokesman for the Whigs, saw in Swift one of the Tories' *'prostituted tools* and a *clergy-man*, who was hardly suspected of being a Christian'.[3] Archbishop King greeted the news of Swift's promotion with pointed relief, comforted that 'a dean could do less mischief than a bishop'.[4] Swift was known as a political propagandist and as the author of sundry apologies for a Christianity the church did not dare recognise. He had written little in the way of theological discourse and had often been removed from Ireland. Though his work in London was sanctioned by the Church of Ireland, Swift's own proclivities for political involvement and his obvious preference for life in London made it easy to mistake Swift for that stereotypical Irish cleric – the absentee priest.

Absentee clerics had long been a major concern within the Church of Ireland. When Anthony Dopping, Bishop of Meath, wrote in 1690 to Henry Compton, Bishop of London, asking for help in putting the Church of Ireland's case in England, Compton replied coolly: 'I am told that the Clergy of Ireland lived in great luxury . . . We have heard likewise great complaints of non-residence & Dispensations for holding Benefices at extravagant distances'.[5] Foreshadowing later criticism of Swift, Compton also remarked that '[i]t has been talked as if some who formerly recommended to Church preferments, had too great a regard to their secular friends & relations'.[6] Swift was absent from Ireland almost continuously from 1707 until 1714. Throughout that time he was the parish priest for the combined benefices of Laracor, Agher and Rathbeggan. Swift's work for remission of the Queen's Bounty required him to conduct his business in the corridors of power. His temperamental liking for political intrigue and the literary opportunity available in London supplied Swift with additional impetuses which made it relatively easy to see him as a cleric who seemed increasingly to fit Compton's profile of a man who preferred to throw in his lot with 'secular friends and relations'.[7]

This was especially true after Swift's return to London in 1710 to again pursue the Queen's Bounty. His account of what happened during the next year demonstrates the remarkable degree to which Swift himself was responsible for the reputation that was to dog him throughout the remainder of his career. Within a week and a half of his return to England, Swift was writing to Stella about a meeting with the Earl of Godolphin, whose ministry was then disintegrating. He writes angrily of having been 'received . . . with a great deal of coldness, which has enraged me so, I am almost vowing revenge.'[8] In similar vein, he wrote seventeen days later to John Stearne, then Dean of St Patrick's, Dublin, concluding with the now famous remark: 'I am weary of the caresses of great men out of place'.[9] Landa sees in this 'a letter which in retrospect shows that [Swift] was ready for his great change in allegiance from Whig to Tory'.[10] But Swift's actions were not really a change of allegiance; they were, rather, a necessary realignment in his lobbying for the Queen's Bounty. It would have been foolish to continue to petition the out-going ministry for a favour only the new one could now grant. Private protestations of personal insult aside, Swift knew Godolphin's star was on the wane and he could claim personal satisfaction simply by playing the hand most likely to benefit the Church of Ireland.[11]

More tellingly, Swift demonstrated an unwillingness to overstep the frustratingly vague terms of his appointment to London. He had been sent to London to work with, and report to, Bishops Ossory and Killaloe. However, by the time Swift arrived in England the bishops had left the capital and his letter of commission addressed to them was now useless. Rather than take matters into his own hands, Swift wrote to King. He asked King to tell him what, if anything, Ossory and Killaloe had achieved and reported that, Godolphin's greetings aside:

> Upon my arrival here, I found myself equally caressed by both parties, by one as a sort of bough for drowning men to lay hold of; and by the other as one discontented with the late men in power . . . and therefore ready to approve present things.[12]

While trying to insinuate himself into a position of greater authority, Swift nonetheless promised not to act further until he had heard from King. He was as good as his word and did nothing until he received from King various memoranda relating to the petition.

The matter of the First Fruits and Twentieth Parts progressed well and, on 4 November 1710, Swift wrote to King that 'I have only now to tell you, that Mr. Harley has given me leave to acquaint my Lord Primate [Narcissus Marsh] and your Grace, that the Queen has granted the first fruits and twentieth parts'.[13] Unfortunately for Swift, there had been considerable unease in Ireland at the idea of a man who had been so closely identified with the previous Whig administration lobbying Harley, and on 2 November, King had written to Swift stating plainly that 'I am not to conceal from you, that some expressed a little jealousy that you would not be acceptable to the present courtiers'.[14] The letters crossed somewhere between Dublin and London. Swift had proved himself 'acceptable to the present courtiers', but that success served only to underline the misjudgment of his superiors.

Swift could hardly restrain himself and regularly pleaded with King for help in getting the credit he thought he deserved. On 15 August 1711, he commented that:

> the grudging, ungrateful Manner of some People, which upon several Occasions I could not but give Hints of for my Justification, hath not been prudent. I am sure that it hath hindered me from any Thoughts of pursuing another Affair of yet greater Consequence . . . What can be the Matter with those People? Do I ask either Money or Thanks of them?[15]

Of course, it was thanks he was asking of them, and Swift certainly expected some sort of ecclesiastical promotion when the opportunity presented itself.[16]

The 'affair of yet greater consequence' Swift had in mind, remission of the Crown Rents, would have been a singular coup. This was a matter entirely in the hands of the queen, and Swift hoped to use what he saw as his closeness with the Earl of Oxford to get Anne's ear on the matter.[17] It was an audacious idea, particularly in that such a request had been sanctioned neither by the Irish bishops nor by a convocation of the Church of Ireland. But it is important in understanding Swift to realise that remission of Crown Rents was not an idea new to him in 1711. Indeed, on New Year's Eve 1704, acting as a sort of self-appointed spokesman for the lower clergy, Swift had written from Trim to Archbishop King, not for the first time mistakenly assuming the Queen's Bounty to have been granted. He told King:

> what I would mind your Grace of is, that the Crown Rents should be added, which is a great Load upon many poor Livings, and would be a considerable Help to others.[18]

Seven years later, Swift hinted at his willingness to take on a project he had earlier urged on his archbishop.

It is not surprising that writing to the Archbishop of Dublin, the Rector of Laracor and Prebendary of Dunlavin suggested an ecclesiastical role for himself. What is most telling, however, is the nature of Swift's offer to King. Swift was willing to undertake the arduous task of getting remission of the Crown Rents – a remission not then granted even to the Church of England – but he would do so only if assured some suitable recognition from within the Church of Ireland. For a man without independent patronage it was an entirely reasonable position. When he wrote to King, Swift was increasingly engaged in political writing on behalf of Oxford, editing *The Examiner* and defending the Peace of Utrecht. In addition, he had proposed an academy to preserve the English language, and his own poems and bagatelles were increasingly admired within certain circles. Just as his secular career was taking off, Swift was seeking a further commission from the church, hardly the actions of a man oblivious to the calling of his cloth. Typical of Swift, however, was the fact that he presented his suggestion to King not as an essential next step for the Church of Ireland, though he certainly saw it as such, but as a project only possible as a result of his own relationship with Oxford and, furthermore, as one he would undertake only if credit for his earlier activities was forthcoming.

In suggesting for the Church of Ireland a course of action even its English counterpart had yet to secure, Swift argued that he alone could undertake such a task, and all as a result of his secular political accomplishments. But whatever his protestations might have led others to believe, Swift's commitment to the Church of Ireland did not deserve to be so sceptically received. Most instructive should have been his politically risky behavior in 1708 when, in the midst of preparing the First Fruits/Twentieth Parts argument, he published his *Letter From a Member of the House of Commons in Ireland to a Member of the House of Commons in England, Concerning the Sacramental Test.*[19] Part of the deal the Whigs were offering the Church of Ireland in 1708 would have required church support for repeal of the Test Act in return for the Queen's Bounty. Repeal of the Test Act would have been a major concession to Dissenters and it would have further separated Irish political life from its British counterpart. The Act of Toleration, one of William III's first legislative initiatives in England, had not excused Dissenters from the Test Act requiring occasional attendance at the Church of England, merely from the penal laws. The repeal of the Test Act would have removed almost all bars to Dissenters taking a full role in civil society. If the Test Act were repealed in England, Irish Dissenters would have had yet more cause to resent the protected position of the Church of Ireland in Irish life. The very provenance of the Act of Toleration, however, served as a reminder to opponents of repeal of the Test Act that the Anglican communion's legal position was increasingly threatened from the Protestant side more than from the threat of Catholicism. For, explains Gordon Schochet, the chief sponsor of the 1689 'Act for Exempting Their Majesties' Protestant Subjects Dissenting from the Church of England from the Penalties of Certain Laws', legislation better known as the 'Act of Toleration', was the Earl of Nottingham, and his intention had been:

> the reunification of Anglicans and moderate Dissenters. . . . But in the end, it was indulgence (toleration) that carried the day. The Toleration Act at least left Protestant Dissenters somewhat better off than it had found them. . . . It had the further consequence, with the failure of comprehension, of forcing into their number the Presbyterians, who had to surrender their hope of reuniting with the Church of England.[20]

While King might have been quite happy to have seen a clear separation develop between the Presbyterian and Anglican communions, Swift's attitude would have been more complicated, concerned as he was with the idea of a state church and a public which conformed regardless of personal faith. They both recognised the threat to establishment in the consequences of the Act of Toleration, whatever its intentions, and saw the need for opposing any further dilution of protections for the established church.

Swift and King's correspondence of this period is almost as concerned with the status of the various dissenting sects as it is with Swift's mission in England, remission of the First Fruits and Twentieth Parts. As would often later be the case, Swift appears to have been eager to undertake the role of propagandist for his side's case in the argument, offering to publish public appeals for support while King undertook the less overt but more politically useful mustering of votes among those actually involved in the decision. Many of Swift's letters of this period went in packets addressed to the Dean of St Patrick's at that time, John Stearne, who would become Bishop of Clogher, with the request that they be forwarded to the archbishop. Swift sent his letters in this manner to avoid having them read by unwanted parties. This suggests that, whatever King thought, Swift believed the two of them engaged upon some joint exercise of political action. The tone of the two men's relationship on affairs outside the day-to-day running of the church, upon which they would disagree with varying degrees of ferocity once Swift was appointed dean, is clear by the time Swift writes, under cover to Stearne, on 15 April 1708, stating that 'unless y^r Grace would send me your Absolute Commands to the Contrary, wch I should be sorry to receive, I should hardly forbear publishing some Paper in opposition' to the proposed repeal of the Test Act should the measure be reintroduced in the next session of parliament.[21] King did not forbid it and the *Letter Concerning the Sacramental Test* appeared later that year.

Swift firmly believed that in Ireland especially, but also in England, repeal of the Test Act would have had an irreversible and profoundly negative effect upon both the church and society as a whole. The grist of Swift's contention in the *Letter* would determine everything he would later have to say about Ireland and religion:

> It is grown a mighty Conceit, among some Men, to melt down the Phrase of a *Church established by Law*, into that of *the Religion of the Magistrate*; of which Apellation it is easier to find the Reason than the Sense: If, by the *Magistrate*, they mean the *Prince*, the Expression includes a Falshood; for when King James was *Prince*, the Established Church was the same it is now: If, by the same Word they mean the Legislature, we desire no more.[22]

For Swift, the established church was ultimately a secular and not a divine creation, but that did not absolve the secular state of the need to protect that establishment. Ironically, too, it required the church to be willing to engage the state to preserve its powers if necessary. The ultimate irony was that because the possibility of parliamentary alteration to the status of the church existed, Swift could claim that its establishment was a validation of the liberties enjoyed by British and Irish citizens, albeit that only those who adhered to the church's creed were permitted to engage in the very parliamentary activities that theoretically allowed the nature of the church's relationship with the state to be reviewed periodically.

Despite some considerable support for repeal from within the Churches of England and Ireland, and despite the political realities which he knew would at best severely hamper his quest for remission, Swift unhesitatingly put what he saw as the greater good of the church above the financial needs of some very hard pressed clerics. He also risked political connections which his own ambitions would have benefited from preserving.

On the face of it, his *Letter Concerning the Sacramental Test* was a clumsy move for a supposed Whig lobbying the ministry for a favour. The theme of the *Letter* is that, regardless of either party political interests or other secular concerns, the Church of Ireland must be protected from the Dissenters. While the Whigs were busy manoeuvring to retain the already slipping power of their governing Junto, Swift launched an attack on the very piece of legislation with which they were trying to woo support.[23] It was, says Landa, 'a shining personal moment, one must say, in an illiberal cause'.[24] Offered the opportunity to win passage of the very law he had been sent to England to secure, Swift had not hesitated to put the interests of his church ahead of his own short-term political objectives. When the *Letter Concerning the Sacramental Test* appeared, King was moved to ask Swift 'by what artifice did you contrive to pass for a Whig?'. It is a question redolent with both irony and wonder, for, King adds, 'As I am an honest man I courted the greatest Whigs I knew, and could not gain the reputation of being counted one'.[25] King's surprise that Swift ever passed as a Whig was more perceptive than would be attempts by later critics and biographers to determine when, and why, Swift became a Tory.

Indeed, Swift's sympathy for conservative Anglican interests had been known to some observers long before his open break with the Whig faction. Most indicative of Swift's already formed loyalties is perhaps his relatively early poem, 'Ode to Dr William Sancroft, Late Lord Archbishop of Canterbury'. The poem was written at the request of Francis Turner, sometime Bishop of Ely. Sancroft and Turner were among the leading Non-jurors, Anglican clerics who refused to acknowledge William III's right to the throne. In addition to nine senior clerics, the Non-jurors numbered some four hundred lower ordains, and with the Archbishop of Canterbury in their ranks they had symbolic influence far beyond their actual number. The Non-jurors, although allowed to remain within the Anglican communion, were deprived of privilege and livings. In retrospect, their stance seems strangely quixotic, especially as Sancroft himself had led a long fight against James II's treatment of their church. They had courage where their compatriots relapsed into casuistic cowardice, swearing allegiance to William as *de facto* king while recognising James II as *de jure* monarch.[26] Swift's sympathies in the 'Ode' are clear:

> Ill may I live, if the good SANCROFT in his holy rest,
>> In the divinity of retreat,
> Be not the brightest pattern earth can show
>> Of heaven-born truth below:
> But foolish man still judges what is best
> In his own balance, false and light,
>> Following opinion, dark, and blind,
>> That vagrant leader of the mind,
> Till Honesty and Conscience are clear out of sight.

Swift was no less reticent in prose than he was in verse and wrote on 3 May 1692 to his cousin Thomas Swift about 'Dr Sancroft, a gentleman I admire at a degree more than I can express'.[27]

When the Tories were in power, Swift defended them in a variety of ways, but his retrospective defence of their conduct in opposition prior to 1710 concentrated on their implicit compact with high church interests, rather than on matters of economy or other secular policies. For example, his closely argued 1712 attempt to provide *Some Reasons to Prove that no Person is Obliged by his Principles, as a Whig, to Oppose Her Majesty or her Present Ministry, in a Letter to a Whig-Lord*, written when the Peace of Utrecht was the most pressing of Tory goals, looks back to that party's consistent support of the Church:

> If your Lordship will please to consider the Behaviour of the *Tories* during the long Period of this Reign, while their Adversaries were in Power, you will find it very different from that of your Party at present . . . We opposed Repealing the *Test*, which would level

the Church Established, with every sniveling Sect in the Nation. We opposed the Bill of General Naturalization, by which we were in danger to be over-run by Schismaticks and Beggars . . . [S]everal others of the same Stamp, were strenuously opposed, as manifestly tending to the Ruin of the Church. [28]

The Tory ministry was busy grappling with matters of foreign affairs and trying to end the War of Spanish Succession.[29] Their supposed lead propagandist was meanwhile occupied with a pamphlet suggesting that the ministry should be supported because of its past record on church policy. But more than that: if the *Letter to a Whig Lord* is to be believed, just about every action of the Tory party was to be explained by a consideration of the established church's interests.

Swift was writing in a highly politicised time when few on either side were interested in reading past the immediate political objectives of a particular pamphlet. Back in Dublin, however, William King was the one man willing to search beyond Swift's rhetoric of political debate, but he was seeking something Swift would never produce: a fully fledged theological treatise. And so, even as his star rose, Swift began to lose the support of an uncompromisingly honest and committed cleric who disdained but nonetheless engaged in the political machinations Swift believed so necessary to their church. In Dublin, Archbishop King, one of the few Irish bishops prepared to acknowledge Swift's role in gaining the Queen's Bounty, began to sense that he had lost another cleric to the delights of London.

Swift and King's relationship throughout the remainder of Queen Anne's reign was to be fundamentally weakened by the two men's mutual misunderstanding of the other's position. Years of dealing with politicians had reinforced Swift's sense that cynicism and personality were surer prompts to move them in the right direction than were appeals to their integrity or their honesty. Unfortunately for him, he did not feel the need to shape his own appeals for help to King in a different light. King read what he received and responded to that, overlooking the record and diligence of his church's representative in London. The restoration of relations between the two men was to take many years and to suffer through several further disappointments.

II

> We are blinded with Prejudice, and thereby render'd very
> *partial Judges* of the Goodness or Badness of other Men. He that
> is our Acquaintance and befriends us is a good Man, he that
> favours our Enemies is a very bad one.
>
> William King[30]

Swift's first mission to London for the Church of Ireland had brought
him into King's immediate sphere of influence, and after that he was
never again to be free of having to explain himself to the archbishop.
Yet King and Swift consistently misunderstood each other in ways
that would significantly affect the way they worked together and the
tone in which each reported on the other's activities. King was a
complex character, fiercely loyal to his church, and more successful in
it than his initial sources of patronage would have suggested. Irish-
born, King displayed remarkable courage when his church most
required it and stubborn regard for its needs when discretion would
have argued for a different course of action. King was one of those
churchmen who, despite occasional successes in political endeavours,
seem genuinely confounded by the world of secular politics, even
though he understood its importance to him and his church. Never
less than his uncompromising self, he was unsuited to the intrigues
which his position demanded. He and Swift in some respects represented two sides of the same coin – the archbishop, who, to protect his
church's integrity, would not compromise himself; and his dean, who
was willing to risk his reputation to protect his church's position.

King had been fearless in promoting the Church of Ireland's
welfare, even remaining in Dublin when his archbishop had fled
during the upheavals of 1688–89. He was twice imprisoned before
William III finally secured Ireland. Such courage aside, King's
determined support of the claims of Irish-born clergy and his concern
for the welfare of his tenants, whether Catholic or Protestant, often left
him isolated within his own church. In the autumn of 1697, Andrew
Carpenter records, King had written to an old friend, Nathaniel Foy,
Bishop of Waterford: 'I speak it with sorrow, I have not one friend near
me that I can with reliance & necessary freedom consult'.[31] When
Archbishop of Dublin, King continued to exemplify those ideals he
believed necessary to a cleric. Reporting a conversation with one of
those improving landlords then busy replacing tenants with cattle,
King says he questioned:

whether it cou'd be agreeable to equity or reason that 490 persons sho'd be turn'd out of their Livlihood without any manner of provision merely that the landlord might get more rent.[32]

But what distinguished King from most eighteenth-century church-men was his intellectual integrity as a defender of Anglican doctrine. King's intellect is typified by his lengthy treatise *De Origine Mali*, which remains one of the most graceful and compassionate of Anglican theodicies. King and Swift, however, disagreed profoundly on the efficacy of theological justifications of church doctrine, even as they agreed on the social implications of such doctrine. King believed the truth of the church's doctrine to be sufficient cause for its privileged position, and so he concentrated as much upon justification of doctrine as upon political manoeuvring. Swift was more impressed by the safeguards of political power than he was by doctrinal disputation. More significant still in determining their relationship was that the two men were to remain at odds over what King owed Swift for the latter's work in England. King, writes Carpenter, 'was in the habit of tendering advice freely . . . [A]nd one of the main causes of friction between them during the years 1707–1710 was that King never offered Swift anything more tangible than advice'.[33] King advised Swift how to make his way in the world while Swift believed he had demon-strated a commitment to the church that should have resulted in specific acts of patronage from the archbishop.

Ironically, it was a shared interest in the church's position in society that fostered King's and Swift's misunderstanding of each other. King felt as strongly as Swift about the idea of toleration. He consistently used not only his seat in the Irish House of Lords, but also his access to the pulpit to oppose any concessions with respect to the Test Act. On 15 May 1709, for example, King used a sermon preached before the Lord Lieutenant of Ireland, the Earl of Wharton, as an opportunity to engage in a doctrinal debate that had grave implications for the whole issue of the toleration of the Protestants in Ireland. A careful doctrinal defence of the Anglican concept of predestination, King's sermon, *Divine Predestination and Fore-Knowledge Consistent with the Freedom of Man's Will*, is also an unmistakable attack upon toleration. In his opening remarks, King admits that:

> learned Men have engaged with the greatest Zeal and Fierceness in this Controversy, and the Disputes have proved so intricate . . . that considering Men of all Parties seem at last, as it were by

> Consent, to have laid it aside . . . except some very young and imprudent Preachers.[34]

Nonetheless, King thought the issue important enough to venture to set out for his congregation 'that which I take to be the edifying Part of the Doctrine of *Predestination*', and for the greater part of its length the sermon is essentially a doctrinal dissertation. But as he reached his conclusion, King suddenly asked the seemingly mundane, and distinctly social rather than doctrinal, question, 'how we are to behave our selves in a Church', a church of which Wharton, as Lord Lieutenant of Ireland, was the supposed political champion. 'And here', King suggested to his audience:

> I think the resolution is easy. We ought to be quiet, and not unseasonably to disturb the Peace of the Church, much less should we endeavour to expose what she Professes . . . On the contrary, we are obliged . . . to discourage all who make them, as Enemies of peace, and False Accusers of their Brethren.[35]

King's distinctly secular purpose in his sermon is characteristically predicated on a careful and elaborate theological defense of Article 17 of Anglican doctrine, which holds that:

> *Predestination to Life is the everlasting purpose of God, whereby . . . he hath constantly Decreed by his Counsel, secret to us, . . . whom he hath chosen in Christ out of Mankind.*[36]

Given King's analysis, this becomes an unexpectedly optimistic item of dogma, for 'we can have no Expectation of obtaining the Benefit of [Predestination], but by fulfilling the Conditions', a conclusion that appears to put the onus as much upon the individual person to conduct himself as one likely to be predestined to salvation as upon God's decision as to each person's fate.[37]

Rigorous though King's argument in the *Sermon on Predestination* was, there is an underlying aspect to it that Swift would have understood immediately. As David Berman writes in his introduction to the sermon, there was a crucial difference between 'Locke, Tillotson, and Berkeley (among others) [for whom] a certain religious practice is called for because one holds a certain theoretical belief in God', and William King, who 'seems to construct his particular conception of God from an attachment to a certain religious practice'.[38] King chose to conclude an intellectually and theologically rigorous sermon with the thought that it is unwise 'unseasonably to disturb the peace of the church', because that was, after all, the lynch pin upon which his church would stand or fall. Swift, who had little time for such theoretical niceties in the face of immediate political challenges, recognised in King's conclusion an apposite starting point for his own ecclesiastical activities, as his 1720 *Letter to a Young Gentleman Lately Entered into Holy Orders* makes abundantly clear. Swift writes:

> I do not see how it can be agreeable to *Piety, Orthodoxy*, or good *Sense*, to go about [explaining religious mysteries]. For . . . if you explain them, they are Mysteries no longer; if you fail, you have laboured to no Purpose.[39]

While King and Swift agreed on the social ramifications of Anglican doctrine, the essential difference in their justifications of that position can be seen in the Swift sermon which most explicitly attacks toleration, *On The Testimony of Conscience*. The backbone of Swift's sermon is a discussion of what 'Liberty of Conscience' means, not within the framework of church doctrine, but as a social consideration. 'Properly speaking', Swift argued, liberty of conscience is:

> no more than a Liberty of knowing our own Thoughts . . . But those Words have obtained quite different Meanings. Liberty of Conscience is now-a-days not only understood to be the Liberty of believing what Men please, but also of endeavouring to propagate the Belief as much as they can and to overthrow the Faith which the Laws have already established.[40]

Once such toleration is allowed, great social danger must surely follow, because:

> those very Persons who under a Pretence of a public Spirit and Tenderness towards their Christian Brethren are so jealous for such a Liberty . . . are of all others the least tender to those who differ from them in the smallest Point relating to Government.[41]

There is an obvious parallel here to King's reflection that 'we are obliged . . . to discourage all [Dissenters] as Enemies of peace, and False Accusers of their Brethren'. However, where King based his critique upon an analysis of church doctrine, an analysis which then justified state-sanctioned protections for the Anglican church, Swift thought the church's social function justification enough for its privileges. Doctrine, for Swift, was of secondary importance to the church's social role; for King, the church's civic function was the consequence of its doctrine.

King's intellectual proclivities led him to see in Swift a potential companion in theological discourse. He wrote to the younger man offering advice, advice which Swift saw only as an insincere attempt to avoid offering material help. It was an example of the kind of mutual misunderstanding that was always to plague their relationship. Where King appears genuinely to have been willing to have befriended Swift, Swift desperately wanted something else – a hand in gaining promotion and recognition for his services in England. So when King suggested that Swift make his reputation engaging in some new area of doctrinal discourse, the reply was as dismissive as convention and discretion permitted. 'God has given you parts and learning, and a happy turn of mind', King wrote to Swift on 1 September 1711. 'You are answerable for those talents to God', he added:

> and therefore I advise you, and believe it to be your duty, to set yourself to some serious and useful subject in your profession . . . Say not, that most subjects in divinity are exhausted; for . . . the most curious and difficult are in a manner untouched, and a good genius will not fail to produce something new and surprising on the most trite, much more on those that others have avoided.[42]

One wonders if King had paid any attention at all to Swift's nonclerical work for, as Nokes remarks, there is here 'an almost comical' lack of understanding about Swift's views of the 'new and surprising' when developed on the 'most trite' of themes.[43] Swift replied testily:

> I have often thought of some Subjects, wherein I believe I might succeed: But, my Lord, to ask a Man floating at Sea what he designed to do when he goes on shore, is too hasty a Question: Let him get there first, and rest and dry himself, and then look about him.[44]

What Swift wanted was public recognition; what he got was an archbishop who read his letters literally.

Earlier in his letter to Swift, King directly addressed an issue raised by Swift when he had written of his distress at having received no credit for his part in the matter of the Queen's Bounty. Replying from his residence at Swords, King remarks without a trace of irony that:

> I can't but admire, that you should be at a loss to find what is the matter with those, that would neither allow you, nor any one else, to get any thing for the service of the Church . . . It is, with submission, the silliest query I ever found made by Dr Swift.[45]

King wearily reminds Swift that 'there are some, that would assume themselves to be the only churchmen and managers, and can't endure that any thing should be done but by themselves'.[46] This was a lesson King had learned many years earlier, and which Swift was forever to bridle against. In his letter to Foy quoted above, King had complained about the inevitable political complications attendant on being the established church: 'If we vote with the court . . . we are flatterers; if against it, ungrateful. In short we are used as our master was, & I can find no other comfort besides that consideration'.[47] It was a comfort a man of Swift's temperament was not likely to suffer gladly.

If even Swift's most sympathetic superior was consistently unable to understand the dean's motives, it is hardly surprising that less friendly observers consistently found opportunity to comment upon Swift's apparent personal ambition as proof of a lack of commitment to the church. Swift's opponents had no trouble chastising him for cynical political activities, while his supporters within the church had a difficult time making sense of often apparently contradictory statements. It was Swift's ill-luck to understand the consequences of another of the Marquis of Halifax's maxims, a maxim of which Swift's natural allies within the church had an understandable distrust. Confident of their rights by virtue of doctrine, men such as King would have blanched at the ramifications of Halifax's 1688 observation that 'our Church is a *Trimmer* between the frenzie of Phanatick Visions, and the Lethargick Ignorance of Popish dreams'.[48] Swift instinctively understood the practical applications of this observation even as he, too, opposed any watering down of Anglican doctrine. Indeed, almost thirty years after Halifax's remarks, Swift would use his pulpit to revisit the Marquis's tenets.

The sermon 'On Brotherly Love', preached on 1 December 1717, took for its text the innocuous plea in Hebrews 13.1 to 'let Brotherly Love continue'. Swift delivered a sermon that was by his own confession 'more suited to the present Times, than to the Nature of the Subject in general'.[49] He argued that:

> A man truly Moderate is steady in the Doctrine and Discipline of the Church, but with a due Christian Charity to all who dissent from it out of a Principle of Conscience; the Freedom of which, he

thinketh, ought to be fully allowed, as long as it is not abused, but never trusted with Power. He is ready to defend, with his Life and Fortune, the Protestant Succession, and the Protestant established Faith . . . He is for giveing the Crown its just Prerogative, and the People their just Liberties. He hateth no Man for differing from him in Political opinions; nor doth he think it a Maxim infallible, that Virtue should always be attended upon Favour, and Vice upon Disgrace.[50]

Christian concepts of love and charity were for Swift little more than guidelines for proper conduct in society. Once again, he chose to leave their doctrinal justification to others.

Or, put another way, as he would in his later sermon 'On the Martyrdom of King Charles I':

Between . . . two extremes, it is easy, from what hath been said, to chuse a middle; to be good and loyal subjects, yet, according to your power, faithful assertors of your religion and liberties.[51]

However, sympathetic though Swift might have been to the political instincts of the trimmers, he recognized that there were limits to moderation and toleration, for, the above passage concludes, it is proper,

to avoid all broaches and preachers of new-fangled doctrines in the church; to be strict observers of the laws, which cannot be justly taken from you without your own consent. In short, *to obey God and the King, and meddle not with those who are given to change.*[52]

This is close to a recusant position, deeply sympathetic to the Non-juror movement and politically explosive in any environment where people are fighting over their 'rights', an argument Swift specifically thought appropriate for Ireland and its established church.

Swift might have helped himself by adhering to Halifax's desire that 'those who are in possession of the Pulpit would quote at least as often the authority of the Scriptures as they do that of the state'.[53] But then, Swift liked to keep his sermons simple, recognising with King the danger of those who:

being either puff'd up with the Vanity of appearing wise above the Vulgar, or impos'd upon by their own Subtilty, often frame Monsters of their own, and deny things that are the most manifest: while they are striving to pursue Truth thro' Coverts impervious and inaccessible to human Wit, they leave her behind their Backs, and are blind in full Light.[54]

Swift's belief that conduct was a sufficient guide to character, as most clearly and famously outlined in his 1708 *Argument to Prove that the Abolishing of Christianity in England May . . . Be Attended with Some Inconveniences*, does gain a considerable measure of intellectual integrity when reviewed in the light of its author's conception of Christian doctrine as being at least as much a social code of ethics as a matter of faith. Indeed, many of Swift's attitudes can be sympathetically reassessed if we bear in mind the social nature of his interpretation of biblical commands. Swift's charity, for example, was perhaps more accurately described by the notoriously hostile Samuel Johnson than by more sympathetic commentators. Swift's 'beneficence', says Johnson, 'was not graced with tenderness or civility; he relieved without pity, and assisted without kindness, so that those who were fed by him could hardly love him'.[55] Swift's apparently distinctly unconventional concept of the church's mission only helped to obscure the motivations of a man Smedley suggested 'might a bishop be in time / Did he believe in God'.[56] It was left to Johnson to untangle the political from the religious. Swift was, Johnson thought:

> By his political education . . . associated with the Whigs, but he deserted them when they deserted their principles . . . ; he continued throughout his life to retain the disposition which he assigns to the 'Church-of-England Man', of thinking commonly with the Whigs of the State, and with the Tories of the Church.
>
> He was a churchman rationally zealous; he desired the prosperity and maintained the honour of the Clergy.[57]

Prior to 1714, Swift's distinctly secular concept of the church's proper place was encouraged by a sense that the 'Constitution in Church and State' was still a defensible foundation upon which political discourse was to be built. After 1714, Swift could no longer convince himself of the structural integrity of that particular church-state compact. Unlike King, Swift had no faith in the efficacy of doctrine and so was compelled to make increasingly political defences of his church. Such defences foreshadowed those of Episcopalians in the American colonies who faced the dual challenge of non-Establishment and low membership, exactly the fate Swift and others feared for the Church of Ireland. For Swift, as later for the New Jersey cleric Thomas Bradbury Chandler, the ultimate justification of the Anglican church was political and not theological:

Episcopacy and Monarchy are, in their Frame and Constitution best suited to each other. Episcopacy can never thrive in a Republican Government, nor Republican Principles in an Episcopal Church. For the same Reasons, in a mixed Monarchy, no Form of Ecclesiastical Government can so exactly harmonize with the State, as that of a qualified Episcopacy.[58]

Threatened by the superior numbers of non-Anglicans and by the spiritual descendants of those who had executed Charles I, both Swift and Chandler tried to protect their vision of the social compact by irreducibly linking the established church to the welfare of the entire body politic. Such an analysis obscured any religious sensibilities that might have otherwise been cited as evidence of genuine spiritual commitment to the church.

This vital link between church and state, where the interests of the latter were necessarily those of the former, had already been seriously weakened in England by the time Swift arrived at Moor Park, the home of Sir William Temple. That Swift appreciated this is amply demonstrated by *A Tale of A Tub*, whose distinctive defence of Anglican moderation in the face of Presbyterian and Catholic extremism derides the Freethinkers and Deists as much as the more traditional enemies of the Anglicans. Swift would later make the same claims far more clearly in his sermon 'On the Martyrdom of King Charles I,' when, commenting upon William III's overthrow of James II, he reflected that:

> a house thrown down by a storm is seldom rebuilt, without some change in the foundation, so it hath happened, that, since the late Revolution, men have sate much looser in the true fundamentals both of religion and government, and factions have been more violent, treacherous, and malicious than ever, men running naturally from one extreme into another; and, for private ends, taking up those very opinions professed by the leaders in that rebellion, which carried the blssed Martyr to the scaffold.[59]

Swift was not alone in making this analysis, for as W.A. Speck notes in *Stability and Strife*:

> In the early eighteenth century the Church of England turned from defending itself against puritan dissenters and catholics to taking up the challenge from the deists and freethinkers. Dissent and catholicism no longer appeared to be formidable opponents.[60]

In Ireland, however, the Catholics and especially, as Swift saw it, the Dissenters, continued to offer the greatest threat to the Church of Ireland. The nature of the respective challenges to the Churches of England and Ireland was increasingly to become the crucial difference between the two churches. In Ireland, Swift could continue his religious polemics at least for a while without regard to changing realities in London. Later, when it was the very government itself that sought to change the status of the church, Swift would alter his arguments, responding with an appropriate counter-thrust, one which this time sought to offer the church as the defender of the people's ancient liberties.

Unhampered by a need to refer to doctrine for justification, Swift was consistently able to engage himself in political causes on behalf of his church whenever it seemed opportune to do so, even if his work could not readily be identified with the church's welfare. Thus, in England after 1710 Swift was delighted to defend such issues as the Peace of Utrecht, but only for so long as those secular goals served to preserve a political alliance that included the high church interest – the one faction of the Church of England committed to preserving the church-state compact in all its glory. Swift's support of the high church faction was fundamentally reactionary and conservative, but only coincidentally Tory. That Swift's politics were those of expediency in defence of a cause helps explain the apparent contradictions within his various appeals from London to Dublin. Those politics also provide a basis for understanding the apparently idiosyncratic nature of Swift's defences of the Tories after 1712.

III

> The Dunkirk beach is silent now,
> The seething ranks are gone.
> But still across the broken chairs
> He smiles as if he'd won.
>
> Will Healey[61]

Swift often wrote to his friends hinting at retirement from politics. In a lengthy letter from London written while Harley's ministry was still taking shape, Swift was uncharacteristically sanguine: 'We shall have a strange Winter here between the struggles of a cunning provoked discarded party, and the triumphs of one in power', he told Stella and Rebecca Dingley back in Ireland. He added, 'I shall be an indifferent spectator, and return very peaceably to Ireland, when I have done my part in the affair I am entrusted with'.[62] Disingenuous though this letter was, it does indicate a side of Swift always disdainful of purely secular politics.

From the beginning of his first mission to London, Swift had been peculiarly ambivalent about his own expectations. Despite occasionally grandiose dreams of bishoprics and prestigious English deaneries, Swift's cynicism meant he also retained a realistic understanding of his more likely reward. On 9 November 1708 Swift had written a convoluted letter to King requesting a variety of help as the Junto emerged in its final form. The letter is marked by both veiled threats and a desperate searching for signs of favour. '[A]lthough I care not to mingle publick Affairs with the Interest of so private a Person as myself', Swift told the archbishop:

> Yet, upon such a Revolution, not knowing how far my Friends may endeavour to engage me in the Service of a new Government, I would beg your Grace to have favourable Thoughts to me on such an Occasion; and to assure you, that no Prospect of making my fortune, shall ever prevail on me to go against what becometh a Man of Conscience and Truth, and entire Friend to the established Church.[63]

Swift was temperamentally unable to ask for help directly, and he was quick to hint that King need not overly concern himself with the other's fate – a hint King was altogether incapable of overlooking. '[M]y own Thoughts are turned another Way', Swift added, suggesting a possible appointment to the entourage that would travel to Vienna should Lord Berkeley re-engage himself in diplomacy:

> by which I shall be out of the Way of Parties until it shall please God I have some Place to retire to, a little above Contempt; or, if all fail, until your Grace and the Dean of St *Patrick's* shall think fit to dispose of that poor Town Living [St Nicholas Without] in my Favour'.[64]

A letter of the same day to Archdeacon Thomas Walls indicates Swift's willingness to retire from London. Having just asked King for help in procuring preferment to St Nicholas Without, albeit in a manner guaranteed to ensure disappointment, Swift looked to Walls to help secure the archbishop's 'favourable thoughts' concerning another possible appointment, this one at Swords, just north of

Dublin, should the then-incumbent, Thomas King, pass away. Swift already held the living at Laracor but he did not consider it sufficient to meet his needs. He was willing to return to Ireland as a cleric, but only if he could reside in, or close to, the centre of activities in Dublin. Swift asked Walls to remind King that 'I like [Swords], and he told me I should have the first good [benefice] that fell', but, he added, doubtful as ever about the promises of others, 'you know, great men's Promises never fail'.[65] Swift's lobbying for both St Nicholas Without and Swords on the same day grew directly out of his reservations about remaining in London. '[I]t is thought', he told Walls, 'that most of those I have credit with will come into play', with the change in ministers, 'but yet, if they carry things too far, I shall go to Vienna, or even to Laracor, rather than fall in with them'.[66] About to enter upon his two most successful years of alignment with the Whigs, Swift was already expressing doubts about their anti-establishment levelling tendencies: 'The Whigs carry all before them', he wrote to Robert Hunter on 12 January 1709, worried that 'how far they will pursue their Victoryes, we moderate Whigs can hardly tell'.[67] Swift's loyalty to his church and to the ideals expressed in work such as the *Letter Concerning the Sacramental Test* and the 'Ode to Sancroft' coloured his dealings with the Junto. A similar pattern is increasingly apparent during the years Swift worked with Oxford. While the Treaty of Utrecht was being negotiated, Oxford needed to consolidate his position and he asked Swift to help calm the reactionary Tory October Club. This request led in 1712 to *Some Advice Humbly Offer'd to the Members of the October Club, in a Letter from a Person of Honour*. After dwelling on the troubles that had beset the ministry from abroad, Swift looked to domestic issues. He immediately saw an:

> Adverse Party [which] consists of an Union so monstrous and unnatural, that in a little time it must of necessity fall to Pieces. The *Dissenters* with Reason think themselves betray'd and sold by their *Brethren*. What they have been told, that the present *Bill* against *Occasional Conformity*, was to prevent a greater Evil, is an Excuse too gross to pass.[68]

Most contemporary observers believed the principal division between Tory and Whig to be an economic one of landed interests versus an emerging merchant class. Swift was aware of the economic division, but he sought always to make the church the focus of debate. He was so successful that when the anonymous author of *Torism and Trade Can Never Agree*, which was written around 1713, paused to consider *The Examiner*, he could not avoid the links with the church:

> The *Examiner*, who was possess'd more than any Man with the
> *Daemon* of *Torism*, was always launching out in his Panegyricks
> on the *Landed Interest* and *Church Interest*.[69]

Just as the author of *Torism and Trade* understood the ecclesiastic
implications of Swift's work, so Swift sought to whip into line the
October Club by warning its members that opposition to the Treaty of
Utrecht would only hurt the established church. Swift argued that:

> It is enough to arm Ourselves against [the Whigs], when we
> consider that the greatest Misfortunes which can befall the Nation,
> are what would answer their *Interest* and their *Wishes*; a perpetual
> War encreases their Mony, breaks and beggars their *Landed Enemies*.
> The Ruin of the Church would please the Dissenters, Deists, and
> Socinians, whereof the Body of their Party consists.[70]

While Swift's convergence of landed and church interests co-opted
contemporary issues, it followed a time-honoured tradition that had
been employed just twenty years earlier by the then Dean of St Patrick's,
William King. In 1691 King had published the immediately popular
tract, *The State of the Protestants of Ireland under the Late King James's
Government*, his account of the 1688–91 administration of Richard
Talbot, Earl of Tyrconnell.[71] King's analysis of life in Ireland at that
time argues that James was seeking to promote 'that constitution of
slavery under which he designed to bring the kingdoms'.[72] It was a
slavery predicated upon depriving Protestants 'of their estates and
improvements and send[ing] them to die or beg'.[73] So persuasive
did he consider this argument, Swift would revisit it writing as
M.B. Drapier some thirty years after King's tract:

> The *farmers* must *rob* or *beg*, or leave their *country*. The *shopkeepers* in
> this and every other town, must *break* and *starve*; for it is the *landed
> man* that maintains the *merchant*, and *shopkeeper*, and *handicraftsman*.
> (*A Letter to the Shop-keepers, Tradesmen, Farmers, and Common-People
> in General, of the Kingdom of Ireland*.)[74]

It was appropriate for landowners and farmers, therefore, to support a
regime that would respect their interests – interests both King and
Swift believed coincided with those of the established church.

Swift always understood the power of self-interest as a motivating
agency. He also understood that in politics cynicism is not necessarily
an impediment to action; he was willing to be frank in appealing to
self-interest where he thought it would help. His 1712 *Letter to a*

Whig-Lord is an excellent example of this cynicism openly deployed to defend a worthy cause:

> Whatever good Opinion I may have of the Present Ministry, I do not pretend, by any thing I have said, to make your Lordship believe that they are Persons of sublime abstracted *Roman* Virtue: But, where two Parties divide a Nation, it so usually happens, that although the Virtues and Vices may be pretty equal on both sides, yet the publick Good of the Country may suit better with the private Interest of one Side than of the other.[75]

Swift believed in the efficacy of such appeals, but here an apparently lukewarm defence serves the additional purpose of undermining the charges of fanaticism which Whig managers were consistently levelling against the Tories. It was this perpetual convergence of Swift's innate cynicism, his careful political manoeuvring, and his easily over-looked attachment to the church that earned him his reputation for opportunism. Similarly, the long and determined defence of Oxford's administration, *Some Free Thoughts Upon the Present State of Affairs* (begun as the government collapsed and subsequently revised throughout the years in Ireland), clearly reveals Swift's thinking about the nature of Oxford's ministry: 'Interest made it necessary for [the cabinet] (although their Inclinations had been otherwise) to act upon those Maxims which were most agreeable to the Constitution in Church and State'.[76]

Sustaining alliances built on the shifting sands of secular politics strained even Swift's talents, and the increasing despair with which he watched the activities of the Oxford and Bolingbroke camps is evident in his correspondence. Swift wrote to Walls on 1 October 1713 in connection with plans to elect Swift as prolocutor of the much-anticipated Irish Convocation. Swift must have recognised the singular advantage such an appointment would have given him, but his frustration got the better of him and he left Walls with the clear impression that what he most wanted was an escape from political machinations of any sort. He was, he reported, 'heartily weary of Courts and Ministers, and politics, for several reasons impossible to tell you'.[77]

By the last day of 1713, Swift was even more depressed and he sounded an uncharacteristically weary note when closing a letter to Archbishop King. 'As to myself', he wrote:

> I take *Ireland* to be the worst Place to be in while the Parliament sits, probably I may think the same of *England* in a Month or two. I have few Obligations (further than personal Friendship and

> Civilities) to any Party: I have nothing to ask for but a little Money
> to pay my Debts, which I doubt they never will give me . . .[78]

Nonetheless Swift concluded this letter with exactly the type of comment that left King exasperated and uncomprehending of his dean's motives: '[W]anting the Wisdom to judge better, I follow those who, I think, are most for preserving the Constitution in Church and State, without examining whether they do so from a principle of Virtue or of Interest'.[79] Reading these lines, it could not have been hard to imagine Swift preparing another shift in allegiance, either to a more flexible Tory grouping or to a moderate Whig alliance. Such political fickleness could only have infuriated less cynical observers. As it turned out, events beyond his control would ensure that Swift would be identified as a Tory for the rest of his life. Late in 1713, however, he was still willing to reconsider his secular political allegiances.

This ever increasing certainty that the collapse of Oxford's ministry was inevitable freed Swift to turn his attention directly to personal animosities that had been festering for some considerable time. That there was little he could do to reconcile Oxford and Bolingbroke helps to explain one of the most elusive of all Swift's political tracts, *The Importance of The Guardian Considered*. Swift had returned from his inauguration as dean to find the squabble over the failure of the French to destroy the fortifications at Dunkirk, as required by the Treaty of Utrecht, threatening to hasten the collapse of the ministry. As editor of *The Guardian*, Richard Steele had been trying for some time to drive home the Whig attacks over Dunkirk's still intact fortifications. He finally hit a nerve in *The Guardian* of 7 August 1713 when he adopted Cato's rallying cry, 'Delenda est Carthago', and implied Dunkirk had the potential to become England's Carthage.

The Tories were quick to reply, and, recognising their vulnerability, Steele went on to produce an extended consideration of his theme, *The Importance of Dunkirk Considered*. Steele's lengthy essay is an example of political argument neatly coinciding with personal anger. Had Swift been anything other than an irreconcilable foe he would have appreciated both the motivation of the essay and Steele's considerable courage in quoting verbatim large parts of Defoe's defence of the Tories. Defoe's blisteringly rude *The Honour and Prerogative of the Queen's Majesty Vindicated* lambastes Steele for his treatment of the Queen's person, suggesting that Steele's experience as a West Indies plantation owner had affected for the worse his ability to communicate with anyone other than slaves. Indeed, Defoe's defence is remarkable in that its personal animosity toward Steele stands out in a time when personal antagonism was a staple of most such literature.

When Swift finally joined the debate in October he also opted for an *ad hominem* attack. *The Importance of the Guardian Considered* struck out in a direction entirely unrelated to party politics. It did, however, borrow heavily from Defoe in continuing to question the tone of Steele's remarks to the Queen. Nokes is impressed that 'Swift prudently waited until the demolition of the Dunkirk fortifications had begun before replying'.[80] Ehrenpreis, meanwhile, is 'surprised' that 'the contempt . . . becomes not that of a professional writer for an incompetent craftsman but a civilized gentleman for a mercenary hack'.[81] The nature of his attack is exactly the reason Swift had to wait until either the demolition had begun or the controversy had subsided: He was not so much interested in the fortifications as he was in completing a personal vendetta against Steele.[82] Swift 'prudently waited' because whether Dunkirk were razed or not was of little import to the church. Swift knew that Oxford's ministry was disintegrating. All the debate over Dunkirk could do was hasten that process. Winning the debate, even if that were possible, would not significantly strengthen Oxford's hold on power.

The internal tensions of *The Importance of the Guardian Considered* have often been remarked upon. F.P. Lock argues that party was the driving force behind Swift's work and is unhappy because *The Importance of the Guardian* is so unpolitical.[83] Indeed, as Ehrenpreis notes:

> Swift may have it all over Steele as a rhetorician or a moralist, but when he does interrupt his witty performance to examine political principles, his case collapses.[84]

Had he promptly joined the debate over Dunkirk, Swift would have embroiled himself in a purely political debate that had little, if anything, to do with the well-being of the church. Restless, bored and uninterested in doing more than revenging himself on Steele, 'resolv'd, as I am told, / Some strange arcana to unfold'.[85] Swift simply could not bring himself to join the publisher of his *Miscellanies in Prose and Verse*, John Morphew, Daniel Defoe and others in defending the Party.[86]

From the outset it is apparent that Swift's pamphlet is more interested in personality than policy. '[Y]ou will observe', the author tells John Snow, Bailiff of Stockbridge, to whom the whole is addressed, 'that the Letter called, *The Importance of Dunkirk*, is chiefly taken up in shewing you the *Importance* of Mr *Steele*'.[87] The sharpness of the claim that in giving a character of Steele the author will do so 'without running into his early History, because I owe him no Malice'[88] shows Swift at his most acerbic: This tract has nothing to do with Dunkirk and everything to do with Richard Steele. Swift does make a token attempt to link the Whigs with certain Jacobite tendencies but the effort is abrupt and half-hearted, polemical without being analytical. 'There is a wonderful resemblance between [the French king] and the Party of Whigs among us', Swift observes:

> Is he for arbitrary Government? So are they: Hath he persecuted Protestants? So have the Whigs: Did he attempt to restore King *James* and his pretended Son? They did the same. Would he have *Dunkirk* surrendered to him? This is what they desire. Does he call himself the *Most Christian*? The Whigs assume the same title, though their Leaders deny Christianity: Does he break his Promises? Did they ever keep theirs?[89]

An attempt to link the Whigs with the French when it was the Tories suing for peace could hardly have been expected to be taken seriously and is developed no further.

More indicative of Swift's intent in this diatribe are the frontal assaults on Steele's intellect and integrity. Swift harps on Steele's cumbersome turns of phrase, turning the subject into a literary grudge match rather than a political debate:

> [H]e tells you, *he cannot offer against the* Examiner *and his other Adversary, Reason and Argument without appearing void of both.* What a singular Situation of the Mind is this! How glad I should be to hear a Man *offer Reasons and Argument, and yet at the same time appear void of both!*[90]

The whole work moves steadily toward damning Steele for having weathered the sea-changes, questioning whether Steele's past history and his now professed change of heart are compatible, for, says Swift:

> I think Popish Writers tell us, that the greatest Sinners make the greatest Saints; but so very quick a Sanctification, and carried to so prodigious a Height, will be apt to rouze the Suspicion of Infidels, especially when they consider that this Pretence of his to so Romantick a Virtue, is only advanced by way of Solution to that difficult Problem, *Why has he given up his Employments?*[91]

When at last faced with the complicated issue of actually defending the Tories, Swift is remarkably casual for a man who had so often demonstrated an impressive ability to plausibly interpret almost any set of facts to his own advantage. In a concluding paragraph he simply suggests that 'there may be some few Reasons of state, which have not been yet communicated to Mr *Steele*' as to why things were progressing as they were.[92] Oxford and his ministers could apparently see no reason to communicate those 'Reasons of state' to their chief propagandist either. If they did, he chose not to weaken a perfectly good attack on Steele by explaining what those reasons might be. Swift ignored his erstwhile sponsors' needs in favour of a personal vendetta. While the wreckage gathered around him, Swift ignored the consequences of Dunkirk and declared victory in his war with Steele. But the private impulse behind *The Importance of the Guardian Considered* was only indulged when Swift was sure of the impossibility of 'reconcil[ing] My Lord Treasurer, and My Lord Bolingbroke: from the quarrel between which two great men all our misfortunes proceeded'.[93]

The mass of material on which Swift worked around the time of the final collapse of Tory aspirations all points to his increasing disappointment and frustration with Oxford and Bolingbroke. Further support of their cause was pointless. What Swift realised very quickly was that the next change in administration would not come with the opportunities for the church that the previous switch from Godolphin to Harley had offered. The impending death of Queen Anne, and with it the almost certain emergence of a very different Whig administration, would seriously weaken the church's influence. Swift understood this and he began to write obituaries for an administration that was not quite dead.

The rearguard action had begun in earnest sometime before 12 June 1714 when Swift wrote to Charles Ford, telling him 'I am going on with the "Discourse [Concerning the Fears from the Pretender"]'[94] which would become *Some Free Thoughts Upon the Present State of Affairs*. It was completed and sent to Ford on 1 July, new title and all. As Ehrenpreis notes, Swift's change of title meant the tract 'would not sound so much like a party attack, or a defence of the ministers',[95] even if that was exactly what it was. Swift largely abandoned the Tories before their collapse because he could see no future for his church with them. He hurried to Ireland after the death of Anne because there was no further service he could perform in England. For Tories such as Oxford and Bolingbroke, who at least appeared to retain some sympathy for the high church faction, Swift did retain some sympathy and he would occasionally encourage them to try again. Ultimately, however, unable to sustain his English political career without abandoning his principles, Swift chose to remain loyal to the church rather than join the ranks of the Tories who quickly began to rediscover their Whig sympathies.

CHAPTER THREE

'I had no ill-designs': the Dean and his church

I

> Whoever observed and disliked the causes, has some title to quarrel with the effects.
>   Jonathan Swift to Viscount Bolingbroke, 7 August 1714

Jonathan Swift returned to Ireland after the death of Queen Anne fully aware that his situation had now changed irreversibly. But the self-pity and brave comments to friends were softened by an awareness of the futility of further endeavour in English politics. Swift could take some comfort from the fact that, given the political climate, he would have found little joy in remaining in England. If Swift had complained of being melancholy when he returned to Dublin for his installation as dean, by the late summer of 1714 he was positively dejected. 'I cannot think nor write in this Country: My time passes in doing nothing', he wrote to his old friend Charles Ford immediately after his arrival in Ireland. But, he added, 'I care not to fight against Sea and Wind so late in my Life; and having been beaten with all Advantages on our side, makes me a greater Coward than ever'.[1]

Ireland was a country for which Swift claimed not to care and in which, his earlier suggestions to King and Walls notwithstanding, he saw little prospect for his own advancement. When Knightley Chetwode first made Swift's acquaintance, the dean was flattered enough, and self-importantly nostalgic enough, to let his new friend know that:

> The Person who brought me your letter delivered it in such a Manner that I thought I was at Court again, and that the Bearer wanted a place; . . . and then I recollected I was in Ireland, that

the Queen was dead, the Ministry changed, and I was only the poor Dean of St Patrick's.[2]

But in truth, Swift had adjusted to being 'the poor Dean' better than he would have had others believe, and, despite what he told Ford, he was not busy doing nothing. He quickly became embroiled in a battle with King over appointments within the cathedral's gift, and he worked on finding an appointment for his friend the archdeacon Thomas Walls.[3] Also, Swift was still trying to resolve a dispute with his vicars choral which had begun almost immediately after his appointment as dean.[4] The vicars choral had accepted the Earl of Abercorn's proposal for a long lease for some land under their control in return for a hefty one-time payment and low annual rents. It was exactly the type of deal Swift would later publicly condemn and when news had first reached him in London about the plans he had been furious. In an angry letter to their chief, the Dean's Vicar John Worrall, he had made it clear that he interpreted the proposed lease as an affront to the good of the church, accusing its supporters of seeking to line their own pockets at the expense of their successors. Swift was determined, he warned Worrall, to 'deprive every man of them who consents to any Lease without the approbation aforesaid, and shall think the Church well ridd of such men who to gratify their unreasonable Averice would starve their Successors'.[5] It was a letter which clearly warned the dean's colleagues of his commitment to the long-term welfare of the church and its servants.

Deprived of any opportunity to defend his church in the political arena, Swift began to employ his position as dean to bolster the internal defences of the ecclesiastical establishment. He was, however, not yet ready to give up all hope in his former Tory allies. He took with him to Ireland the completed manuscript of *The History of the Four Last Years of the Queen*. It was a manuscript Swift had hoped would earn him the post of Historiographer Royal, a position for which he was temperamentally unsuited. Whatever his degree of sophistication and skill at political manoeuvring, Swift remained in one crucial sense naïve. As Speck notes:

> the real problem with Swift's *History* is that he had a simplistic view of politics. He believed that they were at bottom perfectly simple and easy to comprehend, being reducible to the ruling passions of politicians.[6]

This naïveté allowed Swift to return to Dublin in a healthier state of mind than might have seemed appropriate. However great his disappointment and frustration, he himself was absolved of responsibility: it was the 'ruling passions' of the Tory ministers that had failed the church and thus the state. Things had all gone wrong, Swift stresses in his bitter and unforgiving preface to *The History*, because of:

> the numberless prejudices of weak and deceived people, as well as the malice of those who, to serve their own interest or ambition, have cast off all religion, morality, justice, and common decency.[7]

Swift's insistence upon the link between character and policies left him unable to excuse many of the compromises necessitated by secular politics. As the Tory coalition was collapsing Swift had sought to rally the party to the church with an appeal in marked contrast to Francis Atterbury's far more sophisticated activities. On 7 August 1714 Swift had written to Bolingbroke, reminding him that 'To be at the head of the Church-interest is no mean station'.[8] With hindsight, it is difficult to imagine the deist Bolingbroke as a convincing leader of a church party,[9] but Swift's letter is revealing precisely because of his appeal to the political advantages of defending the rights of the church.

The advice Swift offered Bolingbroke was a reply to the latter's rather frantic letter of 3 August in which Swift had been offered, in a postscript, the job of gazetteer to Bolingbroke's schemes: 'The Whigs are a pack of Jacobites. That shall be the cry in a month, if you please'.[10] Whatever Bolingbroke's intent, Swift was determined to draw him away from any policy other than advocacy of the church. Frustrated by what had happened, and angry that the church had been so quickly abandoned, Swift's reply was remarkably vitriolic, chastising the Tory ministry and its supporters for 'keep[ing] your bread and butter till it was too stale for anybody to care for it'.[11] He went on:

> Thus your machine of four years modelling is dashed to pieces in a moment: And, as well by the choice of the Regents, as by their proceedings, I do not find there is any intention of managing you in the least . . . But this is too much for what is past; and yet, whoever observed and disliked the causes, has some title to quarrel with the effects.[12]

Unable to find much hope for the church with the Tories, and certain of the Whigs' hostility, Swift left England to concentrate on his duties as dean. He also began to rewrite his history of the Tory ministry as a summons to the church's colours.

The trouble with *The History of the Four Last Years* is two-fold. First, it is more about the first sixteen months of the Tory ministry. Second, and more important, it is as partisan as anything Swift ever wrote. *The History* is an excellent guide to what Swift considered important precisely because any history of the ministry to be found in its pages is, at best, incidental to Swift's main political concern: who was, and who was not, a true friend of the church. Additionally, in writing *The History* Swift took the opportunity to address his own reputation as a turn-coat and political opportunist, a reputation that stood in direct contrast to his oft-repeated refrain that:

> The friendship I had with the late Ministry . . . [was] chiefly applied to do all the service to the Church that I was able. I had no ill designs . . . I was the continual advocate for all men of merit without regard of party.[13]

Swift must have realised the historical shortcomings of the essay, for he was back at work on another history of the change in ministry within three months of his return to Ireland. *Memoirs Relating to that Change which happened in the Queen's Ministry* is a far more personal and, ironically, honest explanation of what Swift thought was happening. It is also noticeably more modest in its claims for the dean's influence, admitting that its writer had not enjoyed 'so much power as was believed, or at least given out'.[14] The contrast with *The History* is further developed in the differing preambles. The preface to *The History* reminds the reader that:

> The materials for this History, besides what I have already mentioned, I mean the confidence reposed in me for those four years, by the chief persons in power, were extracted out of many hundred letters written by our ambassadors abroad, and from the answers as well as instructions sent to them . . . Further, I was a constant witness and observer of all that passed, and entered every particular of any consequence upon paper.[15]

Such a preamble is a bid for authenticity required of a perceived partisan who claims to be writing history rather than a political apology. In October 1714, writing a memoir he knew was unlikely to be published for some time, and in which he could allow himself some greater degree of forthrightness, Swift admitted that 'I was too negligent . . . in taking hints or journals of every thing material as it passed, whereof I omitted many that I cannot now recollect . . . '[16]

Swift made no claims for himself other than that he was 'supposed, whether truly or no, to have part in the secret of affairs'.[17] Indeed, Swift returned to Ireland with a realistic understanding of what his role in affairs of state had been: 'I was either trusted or employed', he wrote of his time in London[18] – never both at the same time, it would seem. Such a statement does not so much belie Swift's opinion of himself as a 'Man of Conscience and Honour'[19] as it does reinforce his argument that he had put the cause of his church ahead of personal gain. Swift's *Memoirs* were the most forceful assertion to date of his primary commitment. In one of the shortest and most clear-cut paragraphs in all his work, Swift reflected on the performance of Godolphin ministry:

> Upon the admission of these men into employments, the court soon ran into extremity of Low-church measures; and although, in the House of Commons, Mr Harley, Sir Simon Harcourt, Mr St John, and some others, made great and bold stands in defence of the constitution, yet they were always borne down by a majority.[20]

Here again, Swift's single-mindedness is apparent. He specifically identifies the three men who led the 1710 Tory ministry in the House of Commons as the champions of the church in opposition to the Whigs. Whatever else their claims to government might have been, Swift draws attention only to their conduct in relation to the church's interests. Harcourt had already bolted from the Tory camp by October 1714, as uninterested in the church as he was determined to further his own career. However that was of no concern to Swift's account of 1710.[21] As far as Swift was concerned, Harley's St John's and Harcourt's defence of the church in the face of Godolphin's attacks sufficiently established their credentials as fit governors of the country.

In *The History*, written less for his own consolation than as a piece of public edification, Swift examined nearly everything in terms of the church, defining even Harley's rise by citing the attitudes of the lower ordains in England, who:

> were altogether in the Interests and the Measures of the present Ministry [i.e. Oxford's], which h[ad] appeared so boldly in their Def[ence] during a Prosecution against One [of] their Members, where the [whole] sacred Order was understood to be con-cerned . . . And they were farther highly gratified by Her Majesty's chusing One of their Body to be a great Officer of State.[22]

It was true that some residual political strength remained with the lower clergy, but the Tory success in the wake of the Sacheverell trial had been masterminded by other interests entirely. Swift's analysis in *The History* was, however, a corollary of the advice he had offered Bolingbroke: that being at the head of the church party was a perfect place from which to plot a political recovery.

Similarly, in *The History* Swift found fault with his former intended patron, Lord Somers. He accused him of agreeing with those who, after William III's accession, argued that because:

> we had accepted a new King from a Calvinistic Commonwealth, we must likewise admitt new Maxims in Religion and Government: But, since the Nobility and Gentry would probably adhere to the Established Church, and to the Rights of Monarchy as delivered down from their Ancestors; it was the Practice of these Politicians to introduce such Men, as were perfectly indifferent to any or no Religion . . . [23]

Swift's analysis of such matters placed him firmly on the side of the lower orders and against the general trend of thinking among the bishops. This division within the church was remarked upon by Swift's longtime antagonist, Gilbert Burnet, Bishop of Salisbury, after one of his visits during the Oxford ministry:

> tho as I went round I kept an open table to all the Clergy, yet nothing could mollify their aversion to a man that was for tolleration and for treating the Dissenters with gentleness.[24]

Swift claimed in his introduction to *The History* that he intended to 'represent so much of the [leading men's] Characters, as may be supposed to have influenced their Politicks'.[25] Instead, the vast bulk of *The History*, which Ehrenpreis recognises to be 'a trackless waste',[26] seeks once again to justify the Peace of Utrecht. It is, in other words, a rehash of earlier, and better, works such as *The Conduct of the Allies* and *Some Remarks on the Barrier Treaty*. In believing his own ideas about the relationship between character, politicians and their commitment to the church, Swift quickly found himself with no consistent rhetoric by which to advance his arguments. He had defended the Peace of Utrecht both because of the financial cost of the war and because he believed that once the war was settled the ministry would support a domestic agenda to the advantage of his church. Unfortunately for him, the Peace of Utrecht turned out to be the bedrock upon which all judgements about the government would be constructed. With the treaty concluded, the ministry collapsed as various personal vendettas were played out. When the time came to write *The History*, events had already disproved Swift's contentions about the role of the church in shaping the government. The contradictions between what should have transpired and what actually did occur denied *The History* any coherent framework.

Throughout *The History* there are sudden and deliberate attacks upon various people and deeds that Swift believed quite inimical to the welfare of his church. It is these passages, with their tone quite distinct from the rest of the work, that provide what little cohesion of expression there is. Quotation from other sources – an all too tedious device elsewhere – is nonexistent. Details are sketchy, rather than being over-elaborated, and the commentary dwells upon the lack of religious scruple among opponents of the ministry, implying that a government composed of such people could only imperil the fabric of society. For example, Swift's consideration of the 'Act passed to prevent the Disturbing [of] those of the Episcopal Communion in *Scotland*' arrives out of the blue, almost as an appendix to unrelated matters. The invective is well-honed, evidence of an author at last able to discuss matters he considers genuinely important:

> The only specious Objection against this Bill was, That it set the Religion by Law in both Parts of the island upon a different Foot, directly contrary to the Union . . . It is manifest, that the Promoters of this Clause, were not moved by any Regard for *Scotland*; which is by no means the Favourite at present; only they hoped, that if it were made part of a Law, it might occasion such a Choice of Representatives in both Houses from *Scotland* as would be a considerable Strength to their Faction here.[27]

Soon thereafter, Swift turns his attention to the Quakers, praising the House of Commons for refusing to extend certain privileges it had already granted them. For, after all, 'it is not easie to conceive upon what Motives the Legislature of so great a Kingdom could descend so low as to be ministerial and subservient to the Caprices of the most absurd Heresy that ever appeared in the World'.[28] Both these outbursts address issues which are never again considered in The *History*, and both follow discussions of progress in negotiating the Peace of Utrecht. It is hard to tell whether Swift believes the peace was justified because of the war's cost to the country, or whether the ministry's support for the church justified its peace treaty.

Swift's analysis of events in the light of their participants' loyalty to the church is so tendentious that when explaining the Earl of Nottingham's refusal to support the peace while supporting the church against occasional conformity, he is reduced to arguing that:

> This he hoped would not only save his Credit with the Church-Party, but bring them over to his Politicks; since they must needs be convinced that instead of changing his own Principles, he had prevailed on the greatest Enemies of the Established Religion.[29]

Similarly, in December 1719 Swift would find himself compelled to describe Archbishop King as 'half a Tory', when trying to explain to Ford the archbishop's support of many measures Swift considered vital to the church but anathema to a supposed Whig archbishop.[30] Looking back on the Tory ministry, Swift defended its secular achievements by lifting large tracts of dry material from the government archives and hoping that such an impressive array of documentation might win the day. It was only when discussing the intertwined issues of personality and religion that the accomplished propagandist of the Tory ministry found his voice.

One of the most important undercurrents in *The History of the Four Last Years* is Swift's doomed attempt to suggest that Oxford had tried to act upon his advice in the May 1714 article, *Some Free Thoughts upon the Present State of Affairs*. This had taken as its premise the idea that:

> There are two Points of the highest Importance, wherein a very great Majority of the Kingdom appear perfectly hearty and unanimous. First, that the Church of England should be preserved entire in all Her Rights, Powers and Priviledges.[31]

It was in *Some Free Thoughts* that Swift had most clearly sought to link the high church with the Hanoverian cause. High churchmen, Swift argued, were:

> instructed in the Doctrines of passive Obedience, Non-Resistance and Hereditary Right, and find[ing] them all necessary for preserving the present Establishment in Church and State . . . must in their own Opinion renounce all those Doctrines by setting up any other Title to the Crown.[32]

This put the Protestant succession via Hanover 'upon a much firmer Foundation, than all the indigested Scheams of those who profess to act upon what they call Revolution-Principles'.[33] By the time *The History* was written, such appeals were still useful only insofar as they demonstrated the means by which the Tories could have served themselves, the new king and the church. By abandoning the latter, they had sacrificed even their own ambitions.

The passion associated with the best of Swift's prose surfaces in *The History* only when the religious principles of the main actors are under consideration. For details of the peace negotiations, Swift relied, word for word, page after page, on cabinet documents. The vitriol and bias evident in *The History* certainly merited Oxford's objection to seeing it in print, but the tedium of much of *The History* demonstrates once again the role of the church in Swift's attachment to the Tory ministry. Unable to connect the subject of his treatise and the criterion by which he believed politicians and governments should be judged, Swift's *History* instead records dreary details, alleviated, as in *The Importance of the Guardian*, only when personal vendettas can be interpolated. Swift hoped to convince by documentation where he could not justify by conviction.

II

> There is love for none except him whom fortune favours; . . .
> Behold me! once supported by many friends . . . I am aban-
> doned on a shattered bark in the midst of the water.
>
> Ovid[34]

Swift responded to his continuing sense of isolation as the Whig administration in Dublin consolidated its power by once again looking back. The summer of 1715 found him putting the finishing touches to another defence of his old allies, *An Enquiry into the Behaviour of the Queen's Last Ministry*. Swift's attempt to emulate Temple by asserting that 'I have not found the Transition very difficult into a private Life, for which I am better qualified both by Nature and Education'[35] is hardly convincing. However, his apparent obsession with what had happened turns out to be not an apology but a further rearguard action, this time designed to protect the high church from charges of Jacobitism. It was a defence necessitated by the Old Pretender's determined, if inept, struggle to regain his throne, and by the flight to his court of a coterie of leading Tories.

Swift's loyalty to friends extended to the most notable Irish peer to side with the Pretender, the Duke of Ormonde. Swift said that his flight to Lorraine:

looks like a Dream, to those who will consider the Nobleness of his Birth, the great Merits of his Ancestors and his own, his long unspotted Loyalty; his Affability, Generosity, and Sweetness of nature. I knew him long and well . . . I have not conversed with a more faultless Person; of great Justice and Charity, a true sense of Religion without Ostentation . . . although under some Disadvantage by an invincible Modesty, which however could not but render him yet more amiable to those who had the Honour and Happiness of being Throwly acquainted with Him.[36]

There is little new in the *Enquiry*, but what is telling is Swift's inability to reconcile his old friend's act of treason with Ormonde's 'true sense of Religion'.

The reiteration of his beliefs and his defence of Ormonde were made easier for Swift by his knowledge that the *Enquiry* could not be published for some time. Fully aware of the political straits in which he would find himself if he offered his ideas to an audience, Swift reported to Ford in a curiously melancholy yet playful letter of 6 January 1719, that:

I chuse all the sillyest Things in the world to amuse my self, in an evil age, and a late time of life . . . Little trifling Businesses take up so much of my time, that I have little left for speculation . . . I do every thing to make me forget my self and the World.[37]

Swift's thoughts must indeed have been turning to more personal matters, for, replying in December 1718 to a letter now lost, Arbuthnot had commented on his old friend's desire to 'find . . . both me & your self to be old & rich'.[38]

The first document to reacquaint the public with Swift appeared early in 1720 with a title that was to undergo a minor, but telling, revision before its appearance in London the next year as *A Letter to a Young Gentleman Lately Enter'd into Holy Orders*. The Irish title of the 1720 edition advertised the work as *A Letter from a Lay-Patron to a Gentleman Designing for Holy Orders*.[39] The 1721 London edition came with a claim on the title page that 'It is certainly known, that the following treatise was writ in Ireland by the Rev Dr Swift, Dean of St Patrick's, in that Kingdom', an assertion Swift did not trouble to deny, making this tract one of the very few prose works he was willing to publicly acknowledge before Faulkner's edition began to take shape.

The original title is indicative of the persona Swift sought to adopt in writing the tract. However, he struggled with the voice required by his choice of author and the change in title prior to the London edition took account of the facts: Swift's clerical years had taken their toll and the advice was that of one vicar to another. The advice Swift had to offer the young cleric might seem at first both harmless and self-evident, but there runs through the whole a radical conservative's alarm at the increasing strength of the Dissenting churches. The success of the Dissenters was especially alarming to Irish Anglicans. The legal protection afforded the Scottish Kirk under the Act of Union encouraged protests over the legal disqualifications imposed on Irish Presbyterians, almost all of whom were of recent Scottish descent. Political moves toward toleration aside, Swift identified one other substantial failing of the church – its inability to foster popular support even among its nominal adherents. 'To the lower classes, and especially the poor', John Wilkes reminds us in his overview of 'The Transformation of Dissent':

> the established church provided little. They could not understand the academic sermons, when a sermon was given at all. They were expected to pay to support the church. They received little personal comfort or advice from the local vicar much less from their bishop. The Anglican Church of the early eighteenth century, in most cases, failed to provide warmth and solace to the unfortunates.[40]

Swift emphasised the importance of encouraging clerics to recognise the needs of their congregants. Much of the advice he offered the would-be cleric was essentially a reiteration of an earlier complaint made while he was in England. In *The Tatler*, issue 230 (26 September 1710), he had complained of 'the continual Corruption of our *English* Tongue',[41] addressing part of his appeal to 'several young readers in our churches, who coming up from University, full fraught with admiration of our Town politeness, will needs correct the style of their Prayer Books'.[42] Swift understood the designs of such men: 'to show us, that they know the Town . . . and have not been poring upon old unfashionable books in the University'.[43] He also understood better than they the consequences of such actions. In *The Tatler* he had even found himself praising 'The Writings of . . . *Parsons* the Jesuit . . . [which] are in a Style that, with very few Allowances, would not offend any present Reader'![44] In that 1710 article, Swift had not designed to offer 'Remedies . . . to be applied to these Evils',[45] but ten years later he undertook to do exactly that.

Swift's opposition to cant, and his recognition that the established church in Ireland could now rely on no-one but her own adherents, led him instinctively to understand the dangers to a church that alienated its communicants by failing to address them in any meaningful manner. Swift's sympathies for Sancroft and other men of principle meant that he looked not to the easy compromises of Bishop Burnet and his colleagues, but back to the Non-jurors. Contemporary Non-juror opinion is to be found throughout Swift's own expressions of proper church conduct. His view on explaining the Christian mysteries, expressed so clearly in the *Letter to a Young Gentleman*, was based on a certainty put most eloquently by the second generation Non-juror William Law in his consideration of *The Case of Reason or Natural Religion Stated*:[46]

> That which is *plain and certain* . . . plainly shews our obligations to every instance of *duty, homage, adoration, love and gratitude*. And that which is *mysterious*, and *inconceivable* in them, is a just and solid foundation of that *profound humility, awful reverence, internal piety* and *tremendous sense* of the Divine Majesty.[47]

Swift's entire religious outlook was dependent upon this interpretation – an interpretation shared by most of those clerics worried by the Dissenters' justification of personal faith. In *De Origine Mali*, a work notable for its intellectual rigour, Archbishop King typically defends apparently random acts of divine intervention with the simple remark that 'there may be a Reason for them, but such as is beyond the mere natural Sagacity of Man to discover'.[48] Like Law, King held that reason was useful for confirming the consequences of particular causes, but the nature of those causes was beyond reason, which could only confirm that the 'Established Doctrine is agreeable to Scripture'.[49] Reason was not, however, to be used to raise 'Objections' that:

> often Occasion Disturbance to weak People; many who may be shocked by the Difficulty, may not be capable of readily understanding the Answers: And therefore thus to raise such Scruples, is to lay a stumbling-Block in the Way of our weak Brethren, and perplex them with Notions and Curiosities, the Knowledge of which is no Way necessary to Salvation.[50]

Put another way, faith required that people reason from what they were told by scripture but not seek to explain by reason what was revealed. In a compelling example in *De Origine Mali*, King argues that knowledge of eternal damnation is the only sure basis upon which to expect people to act for the good, regardless of immediate personal gain. However, he concludes that thought with the observation that:

[I]t does not therefore follow [that] because the Goodness of God has reveal'd to us that the Punishment of the Wicked shall endure for ever, that he is also obliged to reveal why and how that comes to pass.[51]

Swift himself built the argument of his sermon 'On the Trinity' on the assertion that 'Faith is a Virtue by which any Thing commanded us by God to believe, appears evident and certain to us, although we do not see, nor can conceive it'.[52]

For Swift, even more than for Law and King, mysteries were the basis of that 'profound humility, awful reverence, [and] internal piety' that made religion a suitable guide to all matters of social conduct. This idea Swift had advanced in the forceful irony of *An Argument Against Abolishing Christianity*, and in the brazen advocacy of a social faith in *A Project for the Advancement of Religion, and Reformation of Manners*. For Swift, a Christianity built upon divine edict and practiced as a civic duty provided not only a means to breathe life back into the church, but also a mechanism by which to preserve society. And here Swift found an unlikely exemplar in Edward Hyde, Earl of Clarendon, whose 1707 *History of the Rebellion* Swift read four times, completing it for a final time on 18 April 1741.[53]

Clarendon was a committed rationalist, a sympathiser with the latitudinarians, 'more at home in the Renaissance than in the Reformation', as Lewis Curtis reflects in his study of *Anglican Moods of the Eighteenth Century*.[54] Clarendon and his circle were 'concerned more with correct actions than with correct thought', B.H.G. Wormwald explains.[55] This was an attitude with which Swift was profoundly sympathetic, and of Clarendon he would write to Bolingbroke that he should be placed beside Bacon and Shaftesbury, who 'if they had not been so great, would have been less unfortunate'.[56]

For Swift, as for Clarendon, it was 'proper actions' that mattered. How Swift intended to ensure such actions, the conclusion to the sermon 'On the Testimony of Conscience' makes plain:

> [U]nless Men are guided by the Advice and Judgment of a Conscience founded on Religion, they can give no Security that they will be either good Subjects, faithful Servants of the Publick, or honest in their mutual Dealings; and since there is no other Tie thro' which the Pride, or Lust, or Avarice, or Ambition of Mankind will not certainly break one Time or another.[57]

Where Clarendon extolled the virtues of polite society, and where Law sought humility, reverence and piety, Swift sought to prevent their opposites – pride, arrogance and ostentation. It was this essential pessimism that separated him from the rationalism of the latitudinarians. Swift knew 'it is impossible for a man who openly declares against religion to give any reasonable Security that he will not be false and cruel'.[58] In the example of men such as Clarendon, however, Swift could find epitomised a particular concept of Christian sentiment to which he was sympathetic: 'Poised, kind, likely to excuse faults, hopeful, benevolent, empirical, and reverent, they appear to have understood the horror under which man must live'.[59]

One of the men who most firmly represented the latitudinarian wing of the Anglican church was John Tillotson, Archbishop of Canterbury from 1691–94.[60] Tillotson believed 'every man of ordinary capacity . . . can . . . judge [the essentials of religion] for himself'.[61] This was a proposition that horrified Swift, who knew all too well the dangers of letting the individual 'judge . . . for himself'. It was precisely such individual endeavour that allowed Asgil to be taken 'for a Wit, or *Toland* for a Philosopher . . . [and] *Tindal* for a profound Author'.[62] Nonetheless, Swift borrowed from Tillotson's example when it came to writing his sermons. It was Tillotson who had established the technique of telling his listeners what he was going to do and then setting about it with single-minded thoroughness, before finishing the whole with a crescendo of reiteration. Like Tillotson's, most of Swift's surviving sermons begin with a categorical listing of what is to be accomplished, as, for example, the sermon 'On Brotherly Love', wherein Swift outlines his method and proceeds to follow that outline exactly.[63] Most charmingly, perhaps, in his sermon 'On the Martyrdom of King Charles I', Swift concludes part one of his treatise with the abrupt admonition to his congregation that 'This is enough for your information on the first head'.[64] In concluding his thoughts 'On the Trinity', Swift's reiteration makes it quite clear what he believes his sermon has accomplished:

> I have endeavoured to put this Doctrine upon a short and sure Foot, levelled to the meanest Understanding; by which we may, as the Apostle directs, be ready to give an Answer to every Man that asketh us a Reason of the Hope that is in us, with Meekness and Fear.[65]

When the time came, Swift put everything he had learned into his advice to a young would-be cleric – advice Swift thought essential to improving the stature, and so the effectiveness, of the Church of Ireland. By putting the Irish edition in the words of a gentleman, Swift deliberately adopted the voice of the patrons he knew were vital for the church's survival, again seeking to link his cause with the self-interest of other parties. In a country where Anglican landowners accounted for less than fifteen per cent of the population any decay in the social contract so tenuously represented by the Church of Ireland's privileged position immediately threatened the well-being of the lay gentry.

It is Swift's disappointed secular side that begins the *Letter*. His choice of author freed him to castigate those outside the church for many of its troubles without being accused of seeking merely to improve his own lot. The sympathetic aspect of the supposed patron makes regretful, and so unthreatening, the accusation that a committed churchman would need to be on guard against the 'present Dispositions of Mankind towards the *Church*'.[66] In the guise of a friendly letter of advice, Swift quickly and confidently prepares the ground for his continuing critique of the conflict between the church's interest and the selfish ambitions of the new cultural elite.

The *Letter* represents no radical break with any of Swift's previous political and social analyses of his age. Indeed, one of its most striking aspects is how quickly the *Letter* becomes a near-autobiographical account of Swift's own experiences, validating many, if not all, of his earlier activities. What had his time in Kilroot been but a passing of his 'Quarantine among some of the desolate churches . . . where you may at least learn to *read* and to *speak*, before you venture to expose your Parts in a City-Congregation?'.[67] Swift had not shirked his obligations when in his district, and it would not have been hard to notice when one among his very few parishioners was unimpressesd by the sermon, giving 'Notice of whatever [was] amiss either in . . . Voice or Gesture'.[68]

Swift's attitude towards sermons was far more serious than that of many of his contemporaries, as befitted the commitment to plain speaking that pervades the *Letter*. Then, as now, many clerics no doubt gave solid, uninspiring sermons, Sunday after Sunday. Gordon Rupp demonstrates when looking back on eighteenth-century clerics of various stripes that:

> Many preachers were content to read to their flock the sermons of the famous. Hence the incident in the *Spectator* when Sir Roger de Coverley replied to one who asked 'Who preaches tomorrow?' 'The Bishop of St Asaph in the morning and Dr South in the afternoon.' He then showed us his list of preachers . . . where I saw with a great deal of pleasure Archbishop Tillotson, Bishop Saunderson, Doctor Barrow, Doctor Calamy . . . [69]

And, Rupp goes on:

> The young brothers Wesley preached one another's sermons and anybody else's they found suitable. Samuel Johnson wrote sermons for hire . . . Some used notes, others read from manuscripts, though reaction against Puritanism discouraged the extempore and the impromptu.[70]

Swift wrote his own sermons and he understood the dangers of 'the Frequent Use of obscure Terms . . . than which I do not know a more universal, inexcusable, and unnecessary Mistake among the Clergy'.[71] The young gentleman just beginning his clerical work is instructed in no uncertain terms about the dangers of using any of 'several hundred Words [common] in a Sermon of a new Beginner, which not one of his Hearers among a Hundred, could possibly understand'.[72] Swift suggested imitating Clarendon's best friend and the brightest light of that pre-Civil War circle, Lord Falkland, who used his servants to test his vocabulary. This too was a piece of well-tested advice, for Swift is said to have read his own sermons to his servants. Tillotson is also discussed, for although the structure of his sermons was admirable, the language of the published sermons was not to be imitated so readily. The Archbishop of Canterbury, who preached before monarchs and peers, tended to enjoy an audience better educated than most congregations, and in any case, Swift points out, one should not forget 'the many Alterations, Additions, and Expungings made by great Authors, in those Treatises which they prepare for the Publick'.[73] Swift thought it best to learn your sermon well, and, perhaps surprisingly, seems to have been influenced here by the Dutch Protestants, about whom he would have heard from Temple, a former ambassador to the Netherlands:

> I cannot get over the Prejudice of taking some little Offence at the Clergy, for perpetually reading their Sermons; perhaps my frequent hearing of foreigners, who never make use of Notes, may have added to my Disgust.[74]

Swift might even have heard such divines himself; after all, 'sermon-tasting was among the delights . . . in that age . . . Many went the round of the pulpits, from those of the leading Dissenters to the Roman Catholics at the embassy chapels'.[75]

The guidelines for suitably ministering to congregations, established early in the *Letter*, underline the importance Swift attached to instructing the public, by word and example, so that they might learn the civility and manners inherent in good Christianity and vital to society's well-being. Swift was quick to remind the young gentleman that 'a Man's Company may be known by his Manner of expressing himself, either in publick Assemblies, or private Conversation'.[76] This was a corollary of his oft-repeated conviction that manners make the man and hypocrisy is no bad thing, a point he most clearly argued in his 1709 missive to the Countess of Berkeley, outlining *A Project for the Advancement of Religion, and Reformation of Manner:*

> Hypocrisy is much more eligible than open Infidelity and Vice: It wears the Livery of Religion, it acknowledgeth her Authority, and is cautious of giving Scandal. . . . And, I believe, it is often with Religion as it is with Love; which, by much Dissembling, at last grows real.[77]

Concern with conduct underpins everything in Swift's advice to the young clergyman. Warning against 'the moving of the Passions', a practice of the Dissenters, the letter writer advances a position that mediates between Tillotson's faith in each person's ability to judge for himself and King's concerns for the mysteries of religion.[78] Swift acknowledged that 'a plain convincing Reason may possibly operate upon the Mind both of a learned and ignorant hearer', but he stressed that reason should be tempered by the obligation to 'tell the People what is their Duty; and then to convince them that it is so'.[79]

The dependence of Swift's argument on an appeal to social *mores* made it peculiarly pertinent to just about any group wishing to protect a position of privilege in society. One indication of the fundamentally conservative social character of Swift's argument, and the relative absence of theological underpinnings, is the almost identical nature of the arguments made by the Puritan colonists in Massachusetts and Connecticut whenever the protected status of the Puritan church was threatened by Anglican encroachment. In Connecticut in 1718, Samuel Estabrook was making a case his contemporary Jonathan Swift would have had little trouble recognising, even as he would have objected to the mouthpiece. Appealing to the colonial legislature, Estabrook argued for laws to prevent schisms (forgetful of both Puritanism's roots and the founding of Connecticut). It was Estabrook's contention that 'Acquies[ence] in the Judgment of the Churches . . . ought to be Compelled, which would very much Conduce . . . Peace and Quietness'.[80] The similarity of Swift's and Estabrook's arguments is not coincidental. Swift's concern for the welfare of a minority church led him to understand the importance not just of effective dissemination of ideas, but also of codes of conduct (and laws) that would protect that church.

Important although the defence of the church was to any clergyman, Swift was realist enough to advise the young man that 'the frequent Custom of preaching against *Atheism, Deism, Free-thinking*, and the like' was of little practical use.[81] The nearly deserted churches of Kilroot and its united parishes, surrounded by the thriving meeting houses of Antrim, had taught Swift that 'persons under those Imputations are generally no great Frequenters of Churches'.[82] But it was not just the Dissenters who threatened the church's well-being. One reason Swift tried to adopt the persona of a lay gentleman was to criticise more effectively the conduct of those people he thought particularly guilty of exacerbating the Church of Ireland's plight. 'I have above Forty [such people] now in my Eye', he writes, before reproducing a shortened list of the evils besetting the church at the hands of the boorish Irish gentry, who are 'oppressing their Tenants, tyrannizing over the Neighbourhood, cheating the Vicar, talking Nonsense, and getting drunk at the Sessions'.[83] It was a criticism more likely to stick if it appeared to come from within the landed class itself.

William King, a witness of the years 1688–91, understood the problematic position of the:

> Protestants of Ireland [who] are sensible that they have no other security for their estates, religion, liberty or lives but their union to England and their dependence on the Crown thereof . . . and ever will and must whilst there are six or seven Papists for one Protestant in it.[84]

But it was Swift who sought to link that understanding with the argument that the way to ensure the preservation of those bonds was by irreversibly connecting the well-being of the established church with the welfare, social and political, of the gentry. With the secular government in England, and hence in Dublin, no longer sharing that analysis, Swift was preparing the ground for an appeal to the countryside while the church still had the opportunity to reassert its hold among the nervous, minor representatives of the Anglican landed classes.

Indeed, Swift's concluding thought in the *Letter to a Young Gentleman* is a specific and undeniable attack upon the sort of theological investigations at which the Archbishop of Dublin was so adept:

I THINK the Clergy have almost given over perplexing themselves and their Hearers, with abstruse Points of Predestination, Election, and the like; at least, it is time they should . . . [85]

At the same time as he was working on his *Letter to a Young Gentleman*, Swift turned his attention to demonstrating his ability at the one role he had always stressed as important, being, as he would tell Pope in a letter of 10 January 1721, 'a common friend of all deserving persons . . . when they were in distress'.[86] His church and many of its members were in distress, and Swift had every intention of continuing to be their deserving friend. This tract that would once and for all announce his arrival on the Irish stage was *A Proposal for the Universal Use of Irish Manufacture, in Cloaths and Furniture of Houses, &c. Utterly Rejecting and Renouncing Every Thing wearable that comes from England*. Whatever the apparent nature of the work, the *Letter* and *Proposal* were both an integral part of Swift's increasingly public and sustained defence of the people who made up the bulk of his church, and whose very real and everyday distress he could see whenever he ventured out of his front door. The *Letter to a Young Gentleman* was a necessary stage in the transition from political propaganda to social advocacy. In England, Swift had found the justification for his work in the church's interests. In Ireland, that same need to defend the church would find its expression in a defence of the men and women who were its congregants. What had changed was not the motivation, but the arena. The *Letter to a Young Gentleman* completed a transition in attention from the Tories to the plight of Ireland's Anglican citizens, a plight Swift intended to relieve as much for the benefit of the church as for reasons of Christian charity.

CHAPTER FOUR

'Vertue in this deluded people': who will save the Irish?

I

[Query:] How far it may be in our power to better our affairs, without interfering with our neighbours?

George Berkeley[1]

Jonathan Swift warned the young gentleman designing for holy orders that 'moving the Passions . . . will leave few Impressions upon any of our Spirits, deep enough to last till the next Morning, or rather to the next Meal',[2] but his experience as a pamphleteer for the Tories had taught him that much could be accomplished by exciting the political passions of a specific constituency. Such tactics had helped the Tories win the 1710 election, when the Sacheverell trial was used to commingle the country party's agenda with protection of the church's rights. Such tactics and the accusation of Jacobitism had in turn cost the Tories the first Hanoverian election.[3]

In order to create a workable constituency in Ireland, Swift had to find an issue that could be made to suggest a natural link between the church and a significant political power base. He needed an issue upon which at least the Irish-born bishops, a majority of the resident landowners, most of the lower clergy, a sizeable cross-section of the electorate and guild members could be made to see eye-to-eye. Swift came increasingly to believe that the plight of the artisan and trading classes of the Irish Anglicans could be that issue.

Archbishop King had long been moved by the plight of the ordinary Irishman, regularly returning to the Bible for parallels with Ireland's situation. He had written to Gilbert Burnet, Bishop of Salisbury, on 29 January 1697, that:

Ireland is a province and, generally speaking, it has been the fate of all provinces to be under governors who had no interest or concern to seek their welfare . . . [H]ence the wise man tells us, *Eccl[esiastes]* 5, 8: 'If thou seest oppression of the poor and violent perverting of judgement and Justice *in a province* marvell not at the matter', for this is generally the case of all provinces and particularly of Ireland.[4]

Where King found his Christian charity affronted by social conditions, Swift recognised not so much an assault upon the precepts of his religion as a golden opportunity for a new alliance between the people and the church.

King's analysis of the causes of Irish economic distress was, as usual, more accurate than Swift's would usually manage to be, but this did not matter. Swift was interested in the uses to which the distress could be put. If he worried about the causes at all, it was to elaborate upon causes believed by his prospective audience to be the root of their problems, regardless of the actual situation. S.J. Connolly has pointed out that:

measures like the prohibition on the import of Irish cattle to Great Britain, and the ban on the export of wool and woollen goods, were not part of any master plan to cripple the Irish economy; instead, they represented individual surrenders on the part of government to British vested interests. . . . The real source of Ireland's economic difficulties in the early decades of the eighteenth-century was that it was attempting to sell agricultural produce in a predominantly rural Europe.[5]

It was Ireland's situation as a 'province' which left it open to these piecemeal erosions of its trade. Ironically, Swift's plea for a society that was essentially autarkist might have had the short-term effect of off-setting the trading restrictions imposed upon the country. Those benefits would have been accidental, however. Again, though, this was not the issue for Swift: he was simply seizing upon the political opportunity he saw presented at that moment.

After finishing his *Letter to a Young Gentleman*, Swift quickly wrote a tract that would appear on the king's birthday, a timing designed to reinforce its explicit development of the nascent Irish Anglican distinction between court and parliament. It was a distinction King had faulted his friend William Molyneux for failing to make in *The*

Case of Ireland's Being Bound by Acts of Parliament in England. 'I understand no liberty but being governed by our own laws', the then Bishop of Derry had written to Francis Annesley on 16 April 1698 after reading Molyneux's essay. Fourteen days earlier, King had written to a Mr Jackson of Coleraine about the Woolen Bill then nearing passage in the English parliament. This legislation would impose a high tax on exports of Irish broadcloth in return for promised English support of the Irish linen trade. Distressed as he was by the state of Ireland's agriculture, and already distrustful of English claims of good intentions, William King, the bishop of a see surrounded by thriving Presbyterian congregations, would also have been troubled by the fact that Ireland's putative linen trade was concentrated in Ulster, a circumstance which could only have further strengthened the hand of the Dissenters.[6] King's letter to Jackson of 2 April 1698, however, stressed the constitutional and political ramifications of the proposed bill, which would 'alienate the affections of the King's subjects from His Majesty and . . . discourage them from . . . effectually secur[ing] Ireland to England.'[7] King recognised the need to frame the debate in broader terms than those of Irish husbandry alone. It was a technique both he and Swift were to develop further as they struggled to favourably define Ireland's relationship to England.

Having established that the interests of the court coincided with those of the Irish, even when against the wishes of the parliament in London, King admitted the inevitable intellectual conclusion to such an argument in a letter to Annesley on 25 June 1698. It was 'the Parliament of England,' not the court, that would one day come to rue 'these breeches on Ireland'.[8] This distinction between monarch and parliament would become increasingly important as the emerging Irish Anglican political grouping struggled to distinguish demands for legislative freedom from acts of treason. Although Swift's *Proposal for the Universal Use of Irish Manufacture* drew upon earlier Protestant exponents of Irish rights, most noticeably upon Molyneux's *Case of Ireland*, it was the first such appeal directed to an audience which, despite King's earlier private analyses, had not previously been the focus of such tracts – the Irish themselves (or, at least, one small part of that population). Molyneux before Swift, and the next great Protestant Irish advocate after him, Charles Lucas, both avoided 'suggest[ing] a practical method of dealing with England's usurpations' of Irish rights, Robert McDowell reminds us. Instead, 'both appealed to the better nature of Englishmen.'[9] Swift, who had an essential distrust of 'great Ministers', very few of whom 'would ever descend to take Advice',[10] and who remembered Harley's failure to reward him adequately, had no intention of making a similar appeal.[11]

Lucas, a Dublin Dissenter, would take care to distinguish himself from Swift, reverting to the tradition of thinking more of his English than of his Irish audience. Writing anonymously as the editor of the 1758 edition of what was then called *The History of the Four Last Years of the Queen*, Lucas praised Swift's literary abilities but asserted that he had:[12]

> long been hardily singular in condemning this great man's conduct, amidst the admiring multitude; nor ever could have thought of making an interest in a man, whose principles and manners he could, by no rule or reason of honour, approve, however he might have admired his parts and wit.[13]

In the *Proposal*, Swift addresses 'plain honest men', citing the plight of the Irish weavers, Anglicans almost to a man. As so often in Swift, an apparently simple proposal quickly turns out to be about much more than the state of Ireland's wool and linen trades, deftly touching a variety of problems and always echoing, though seldom explicitly, the concerns of senior churchmen who had already expressed opinions about the plight of Ireland. King himself is held up as a model of the new Irishman in a manner that refocuses the question away from England's increasing control over Ireland, directing discussion instead towards Ireland's need to address its own economic woes: 'I have, indeed, seen the present Archbishop of *Dublin* clad from Head to Foot in our own Manufacture', says the anonymous pamphleteer, demonstrating that Irishmen can, and should, set an example for their fellows. But the next clause makes it plain that the wearing of Irish clothes alone cannot solve the country's problems. In bold and stubborn italics, a much more subversive thought follows: '*his Grace deserves as good a Gown, as if he had not been born among us.*'[14] The very fact that King had been born in Ireland and that his wearing of Irish cloth was nonetheless worthy of comment draws attention to the increasingly second-class status of the Irish-born Anglicans. It also underlines the lack of support domestic manufacture was receiving from the majority of those few Irishmen who could afford to choose between imported and domestic material. Where Molyneux had appealed to English reason, Swift's exhortation of, and commiseration with, King could only be read as a challenge to the Irish themselves.

Swift was moving carefully to establish that certain Church of Ireland clerics were setting an example that would have been well imitated by their fellow Irishmen. It is no accident that he gives as an example the conduct of the senior Irish-born cleric. Equally telling is the derivation of what is now probably Swift's most famous aphorism within Ireland, usually, and somewhat inaccurately, recalled as 'burn everything English but their coal'. In fact this remark was not originally Swift's at all. He had heard it from a senior cleric of impeccable royalist credentials, and a recent lord justice – John Vesey, sometime Archbishop of Tuam.[15] Swift was well aware of the sedition laws in Ireland (advisedly so, as it would turn out) and the remark of Vesey which Swift quotes is actually repeated third-hand:

> I heard the late Archbishop of *Tuam* mention a pleasant Observation of some Body's; *that* Ireland *would never be happy 'till a Law were made for* burning *every* Thing *that came from* England, *except their* People *and their* Coals.[16]

Specific reference to the archdiocese of Tuam also intimates a continuation of thought from the exemplary anti-Commonwealth and then anti-Jacobite Vesey to his successor, the resolute, outspoken and also Irish-born contemporary occupant of the episcopal palace, Edward Synge. In addition, the third-hand nature of the report reinforces not only the historical aspects of the problem, but also hints at an emerging currency of such sentiments that would help consolidate a political grouping which the mid-century parliamentary leader, Henry Flood, would christen the Protestant Patriot Party.

Swift's argument would be fully developed in *The Drapier's Letters*, but in his *Proposal* he makes the giant political leap that was the necessary precursor of appeals that would later address the 'Whole People of Ireland'. Simply put, Anglican Ireland's problem was its sheer lack of numerical strength. In the north, the Presbyterians outnumbered the Anglicans, making them a minority within a minority, and across the thirty-two counties as a whole Catholics vastly outnumbered all sects of Protestants combined.[17] Popular mythology continued to cast Protestant–Catholic relations in the light of the bloody revolt of 1641 and the Irish campaigns of James II from 1688–91. The challenge Swift believed faced the Irish Anglicans was to unite the whole people of Ireland in specific opposition to British parliamentary authority and its disregard for the old order, without jeopardising the minority's right to govern from Dublin.

Disillusioned with English politicians and well versed in the demographics of Ireland (his first living, after all, had been in the heart of Presbyterian Ulster) Swift was peculiarly well placed to offer a solution to the problem many of his compatriots could not bring themselves to address. Typical of those reluctant to fully confront the question of Ireland's relationship with England was Archbishop King, who had remained in Dublin throughout Tyrconnell's administration and who had twice been imprisoned in that period. King could never forget the role William's army had played in the campaign, and his memory was close to being institutional among the older Anglican Irish. Writing to John Percival in February 1720, King conceded that despite the moral claims of the Irish 'those on your side have the power'.[18] It was a power King was less inclined to begrudge than was Swift but about abuses of which the senior cleric was no less resentful.

Swift intuitively grasped the need to assemble a coalition broader than anything the Anglicans could muster on their own. Once again, he could find precedent within the church for the required balancing act between the aspirations of the majority and the desire of the governing Anglicans to continue the existing restraints on both Catholics and non-Anglican Protestants. It was a position King had previously established in the Irish House of Lords when, as Bishop of Derry, he had led the minority opposition to the bill ratifying the Treaty of Limerick which codified the terms of Tyrconnell and Richard Hamilton's surrender. When it was finally submitted to the Irish parliament in 1697 the bill differed significantly from the agreement the Catholic generals had signed and it cancelled many of the concessions granted them in 1691. King agreed with several other peers (temporal and spiritual) that innocent Catholic landowners should not forfeit their property. However, he was almost alone in arguing that the treaty submitted for approval was not the treaty James II's generals had agreed to and that it therefore had neither legal nor moral validity.[19] He felt so strongly that after the bill was approved he wrote a moving letter to his friend Bishop Foy, who had stayed away from Dublin, pairing his vote with:

> one who has made use of it to establish inequity . . . and to break the public faith of the Kingdom given in the Articles of Limerick. I much confess I do not know how you'll answer it to God.[20]

The Anglican bishop of Derry, who would become archbishop of Dublin, had emerged as the principal parliamentary defender of the few rights Catholics still enjoyed in Ireland. It was a position he would maintain throughout his life, a position that enjoyed some sympathy from within the Church of Ireland episcopacy.

Yet when the Irish-born churchmen found themselves in direct opposition to the English position, King was often the 'pragmatist', to use Paddy McNally's words.[21] He frequently found an ally in Archbishop Synge, to whom it would at times fall to put the Christian as well as the political argument, as when he explained his and other clerics' opposition to anti-popery legislation in a letter to William Wake of 19 November 1719:

> It is a melancholy reflection that the true Christian way of reducing popery is not much regarded: nor can I but fear that there are too many amongst us, who had rather keep the Papists as they are, in an almost slavish subjection, than have them made Protestants, and thereby entitled to the same liberties and privileges with the rest of their fellow subjects.[22]

This argument about 'slavish subjection' of the Catholics was especially useful when it could be deployed in connection with a discussion of the abject state of Protestant tenant farmers who were increasingly suffering because of the high rents landlords were able to extract from Catholic tenants who had no meaningful legal right to protection from extortion.

Swift sought to build his appeal to the Irish upon this intellectual and political defence of what King and Synge, among others, felt was reasonable but limited repression. Swift proposed, in effect, that all sectors of Irish society support an Anglican Irish government as a counterweight to extremist policies from England. Trying to create, let alone sustain, such a coalition should have been fraught with difficulties; however, Swift's propensity to simplify politics until it became a matter of personality, and his certainty in the rights of the established church, spared him the doubts that bedeviled more sophisticated advocates of the emerging Irish Anglican position.

One of the fundamental differences between the Irish and the English political systems, and therefore between their two internal power structures, lay in the nature of the upper houses of parliament. The Irish House of Lords was smaller than its combined English–Scottish counterpart and had a proportionally larger number of lords spiritual. In 1713, when the size of the Irish peerage stabilised, there were ninety-nine lords temporal and twenty-two lords spiritual.[23] England and Wales, in contrast, had twenty-six bishops entitled to a place in the Lords and more than 250 lay peers.[24] Moreover, Ireland was a smaller country with far fewer practicing Anglicans and the combination of geographic proximity and lessened pastoral obligations allowed the Irish bishops to present themselves in Dublin whenever the need arose. *The Journal of the Irish House of Lords* for the years 1715–25 indicates that an average of between ten and twelve bishops were usually in attendance when the house was in session. The two most regular attenders were Archbishop King and fellow native Edward Synge, Bishop of Raphoe (and, after Vesey's death, Archbishop of Tuam).[25]

The lords temporal were little better represented, with an average of between fifteen and twenty-five usually attending. Chief among those were a number of peers with deeply held emotional attachments to Ireland, most noticeably John Dillon, seventh Earl of Roscommon, James Caulfield, third Viscount Charlemont, and Thomas Bermingham, fifteenth Baron Athenry. Another regular attender was the senior Irish peer, Robert Fitzgerald, nineteenth Earl of Kildare. Fitzgerald's name bore witness to his descent from the Norman settlers. Roscommon, Charlemont and Athenry all had strong Irish roots: each had been born in the country and each was married to an Irish-born woman. To the Irish-born peers and bishops who attended the House of Lords, further erosion of their rights by London was of personal significance.

There was, then, a natural block of votes in the Irish House of Lords that on certain issues tended to coalesce into an 'Irish' grouping, rather than vote along Whig and Tory lines. Swift never fully understood the irrelevance of the sobriquets Whig and Tory when describing Irish politics, but his extended considerations of the last four years of Queen Anne's reign had reinforced his faith in the power of self-interest to provide political benefit to the church. What Swift began to essay in earnest early in 1720 was the creation of a sustainable parliamentary coalition that could further the church's position in the upper house of the Irish parliament. He was hardly alone in this endeavour, but he was alone in seeking to make the interests of the Anglican church a focal point for the various expressions of peers' differing self-interests.

Standing in the way of Swift's ambitions, and of the hopes of the 'Irish party' in the upper house, was the patronage-ridden House of Commons, where self-interest dictated loyalty to the desires of the administration in Dublin Castle with its deep pockets and close contacts with the managers of the rotten and pocket boroughs. The small number of people entitled to vote in Irish elections, and the historical anachronisms of many of the constituencies as a consequence of Anglican population shifts following the upheavals of 1641 and 1688–91, meant that Ireland enjoyed more pocket and rotten boroughs than did England.[26] Examining the composition of the Irish parliament at the end of the eighteenth-century in his *Historical Review of the State of Ireland*, the historian Francis Peter Plowden estimated that, at best, only 128 out of the 300 seats in the Irish House of Commons could be considered freely elected. He thought thirty individuals (almost all absentee landowners) controlled a majority of the seats.[27] The state of affairs in 1720 would have been similar, there having been minimal electoral reform throughout the century. So obsequious to their patrons' interests were the members of the Commons that J.G. Swift MacNeill and others, when seeking to explain the Commons' failure to join the Lords in opposing English encroachments, have all fallen back upon accounts of 'the absence of any approach to the spirit of nationality' to be found in the lower house.[28] Ironically, then, the Irish House of Lords in many ways better represented the sympathies of the Irish Anglicans than did the House of Commons.[29]

The fate of the 1719 Toleration Bill in the Irish House of Lords helps identify some of the characteristics of the emerging 'Irish' bloc. In October 1719 the Privy Council returned to the Lords for final approval a toleration bill already much weakened by King's opposition. Although he had stripped the bill of its most liberal elements, King was nonetheless resolved to try to deny the bill final assent. He and Synge roamed the precincts of parliament lobbying determinedly for its rejection. When it came, the final vote was twenty-six in favour of the bill, twenty-five against. The Lord Lieutenant, the Duke of Bolton, thought seven of the twenty-two clerics present voted with the administration, and fifteen against. Thus, ten of the twenty-three lay peers present must have sided with the majority of the Irish-born bishops against the administration. While it is misleading to presume a perpetual English–Irish divide when the bishops came to vote, the 1719 vote does demonstrate the increasingly divergent nature of the two factions: six of the seven clerics voting for toleration had all been translated from Britain within the previous four years.[30] Roscommon, Athenry and Kildare were among the lay peers voting with King and Synge. Whenever the House of Lords divided along Irish versus English lines, as it was to do increasingly in the 1720s, the change of a vote one way or the other could make all the difference. The challenge to the Irish-born bishops was to attract one or two more lay peers to their side.

Though most of the bishops were reluctant to acknowledge it, they had in the Dean of St Patrick's a man with years of experience in England developing secular ideas that could keep the lay peers on the church's side. Aware of the growing divisions within Irish politics through his day-to-day contact with King, Swift found an opening for his own involvement in the increasingly dire consequences of a series of debilitating economic acts imposed from London after the Restoration. These acts had not stopped with the 1698 English Woolens Act, which built upon 1666 legislation making it illegal to export all beef, pork and bacon from Ireland, on the grounds that such trade was 'unnecessary, destructive of the welfare of the Kingdom [of England] and a public nuisance'.[31] The promised aid to the Irish linen trade not only never came, but, the very next year, the English parliament went so far as to pass legislation banning the export of Irish wool and woollen products, including linen, except to England where homegrown products could be found at a lower price.

The consequence of all this activity was chronic deflation.[32] Among the absentee landlords there was a steady increase of rents as they struggled to preserve their English lifestyles while remaining dependent upon deflated Irish revenues, a practice so prevalent that Maria Edgeworth's annotation of Irish terms used in *Castle Rackrent* left the title itself unexplicated.[33] Swift could see the consequences of these acts every time he walked through the Liberties surrounding St Patrick's Cathedral. His *Letter to a Young Gentleman* had reminded the Irish clergy that 'a Man is known by his Company',[34] and with his reappearance in print eased by the innocuous nature of the *Letter*, Swift took the opportunity of the king's birthday to publish a broadside examining the economic plight of Ireland. He also extolled the company kept by certain of those churchmen whom had also set an example on matters of the church's survival. The *Proposal* acted upon the offer made in the final paragraph of the *Letter*:

> Your Behaviour in the World is another Scene, upon which, I shall readily offer you my Thoughts, if you appear to desire them from me.[35]

It was with this prospectus for an alliance of church and economic self-interest already well under way that Swift wrote again to Charles Ford in April 1720. '[T]he Question is', he told Ford:

> whether People ought to be Slaves or no. It is like the Quarrell against Convocations; they meet but seldom, have no Power, and for want of those Advantages, cannot make any Figure when they are suffered to assemble. You fetter a Man seven years, then let him loose to shew his Skill in dancing, and because he does it awkwardly, you say he ought to be fettered for Life.[36]

It is telling that, reaching for a metaphor to explain the political situation in Ireland, Swift chose an ecclesiastic dispute for his example. What he intended to demonstrate in the *Proposal* was that, whatever its condition, Ireland could cut a figure sufficient to make its own way in the world.[37]

II

I pretend to pity them, but am inwardly angry.
Swift to Bolingbroke, 19 December 1719

The very first sentence of the *Proposal for the Universal Use of Irish Manufacture* distinguishes it as a tract written in and for Ireland:

It is the peculiar Felicity and Prudence of the People in this Kingdom, that whatever Commodities, or Productions, lie under the greatest Discouragements from *England*, those are what they are sure to be most industrious in cultivating and spreading.[38]

This apparently straightforward opening gambit is a far more intricate observation than the assertion of rights and privileges that had been previous expressions of Anglican Irish identity. Swift does not so much take exception to English legislation (although he will do so later) as question Ireland's response to such dictates.

Designed as an appeal to the Irish themselves, the *Proposal* none-theless needed to address English perceptions of Ireland as a country populated by lazy, ill-educated peasants. The *Proposal* counters that assumption immediately, drawing attention to the 'industrious' nature of its citizens' 'cultivating and spreading'. Such assertions of industry are, however, undermined by the recognition of a 'peculiar' propensity for labouring at tasks doomed to be unsuccessful. Distressed by Britain's assumption of certain legislative rights over Ireland, the pamphlet writer is no less concerned by his fellow Irishmen's wilful obstinacy in trying their hand at what it is Britain seeks to regulate. It is a multi-layered critique, for what the British proscribe, and what the Irish nonetheless labour at, are the very staples of a national economy. The author is positioning himself between an implicit appeal to Irishmen to confront their own behaviour, and an explicit condemnation of British policy toward Ireland. The appeal to the Irish themselves distinguishes the *Proposal* from its contemporaries' reliance upon appeals to the British, but the *Proposal* marks Swift's first use of the sophisticated analysis that would increasingly underpin his defence of Irish rights – a defence that was also almost always an attack upon his compatriots' response to the challenges confronting them. It is an argument that would culminate in the uncompromising logic of *A Modest Proposal*.

The appeal of the *Proposal* might have represented a new tack in domestic Irish politics, but Swift's treatise was not without political precedent. The Irish parliament had been prorogued in 1698 and had not met again until 1703. The deflationary consequences of English economic policy towards Ireland had so affected even the proprietors of seats in the House of Commons that when parliament did reconvene resolutions were passed in the lower house in 1703, 1705 and 1707 stating that 'it would greatly conduce to the relief of the poor and the good of the Kingdom that the inhabitants thereof should use none other but the manufactures of the Kingdom'. So harsh were conditions in Ireland by 1703 that even the sceptical MacNeill can find little fault with the Commons, believing the house to have actually acted, unusually so, out of 'a deep sense of the evil state of their country'.[39]

With even the Irish House of Commons supporting domestic manufacture of clothing, and with Archbishops King and Vesey already on the record as advocates of such practices, Swift had an ideal starting point. He wasted little time expanding the terms of the debate, finishing the opening paragraph of the *Proposal* with the observation that British economic policy in Ireland directly contravened the mercantilist principle that 'People are the *Riches of a Country*'. Britain's policy meant that 'the Politick Gentlemen of *Ireland*' had embarked upon the ruinous course of 'depopulat[ing] vast Tracts of the best Land.'[40]

Swift was, of course, writing on the cusp of developments in economic theories, and the traditional mercantile views of earlier generations were already giving way to the theories of wealth that Adam Smith would finally codify. The appeal to mercantilist analysis, however, was not simply the result of Swift's intellectual conservatism. In contrast to later trends, the exodus from Ireland at the time Swift was writing was primarily one of poorer Anglicans moving to the American colonies and the West Indies. In Ulster, there was also a significant movement of Presbyterians away from Ireland. The general demographic trends were so clear that in 1726 Primate Boulter warned officials in England: 'The whole north is in a ferment at present, and people [are] every day engaging one another to go next year to the *West Indies*.'[41]

This sense that it was the people who were the wealth of a country would continue to form a staple of Irish arguments against English economic proposals. In 1738, David Bindon would argue that:

> From Reason and Experience it is certain, that the power and Riches of a Nation depend not upon its having Mines of *Gold* and *Silver*, but upon its having *a numerous and industrious People. Spain* and *Portugal* are rich in Mines of *Gold* and *Silver*, but thin of Inhabitants; and the few they have are idle or luxurious: Therefore neither of them has any great Power; and the Riches their Slaves

dig from the Bowels of the Earth, are yearly sent out for supporting the Idleness and Luxury of their people. On the contrary, *Britain* and *France* have no Mines of *Gold* and *Silver*; but they have Multitudes of People *usefully employed*, and consequently are rich and powerful.[42]

By this analysis, Ireland fell somewhere between Spain and Britain – it had plenty of people, but British policy increasingly prevented them being usefully employed.[43]

In his concentration on the effects on labour of proposed legislation Swift was covering ground King had already identified as a possible source of conflict between the church and Dublin Castle. King's resistance to the toleration of non-Anglican Protestants was not matched by an equal fervour for additional anti-popery laws, and one reason for this was his understanding of the consequences of such legislation. Already in Ireland, 'Protestant landlords preferred Catholic tenants over Protestant ones because they paid more and were more slavish,' Robert Burns notes in his examination of *Irish Parliamentary Politics in the Eighteenth Century*. Any further repression of Catholics, besides being immoral in King's eyes, would only have exacerbated the situation. Burns reports on King's conviction that 'there were more gentle and more effective ways to root out popery "but not being for the present profit of the landlords, they will not hear of them"'. 'What King seemed to be trying to articulate', concludes Burns, reading into the Archbishop's words everything his life could be said to have demonstrated, 'is that social groups depending on hypocrisy, exploitation, and cruelty for their security and prosperity have a past, a present, but no future'.[44]

In extending that argument to the British trade laws in Ireland, Swift's *Proposal* not only drew upon an economic analysis to which its author was favourably inclined, it also posited an economic course of action that improving the prospects of the lower-and middle-class Anglicans, as well as of the landlords, would inevitably improve the prospects of the established church.

Swift was less concerned with pity and charity than with the potential political gains of an alliance with tradesmen he would later accuse of being more willing 'to gain a shilling by cheating you, than twenty in the honest way of dealing'.[45] It was this very impatience that fuelled the *Proposal*. A treatise written expressly to advance the cause of Ireland castigates the Irish for their frequent failures to act in their own self-interest. Taking King's beliefs out of the cathedral and giving them an airing in the wider secular world, Swift had again found an outlet that allowed his personal frustrations to serve his church. But by putting the emphasis firmly upon the Irish response to British law, the *Proposal* became one of the very first tracts to attempt to define a role for the Irish Anglicans that went further than relying on British munificence. Petulant and demanding, the *Proposal* was a major step on the road to shaping a coherent identity out of the disparate groupings within the Anglican Irish community.

The intricacies of creating a single constituency from so many diverse interests necessarily required several implausible moves, and Swift's opening remark that 'Landlords are every where, by *penal Clauses*, absolutely prohibiting the Tenants from Plowing', does not appear too promising a start.[46] Blaming those who represented the Anglican Irish in parliament risks having the *Proposal* immediately dismissed by the very people it needed most strongly to influence. But it was in keeping with Swift's own radical conservatism to shift the blame away from the poor tenants and dependent classes and direct it instead to the newer class of landlord busy making money at the expense of the welfare of the people. It was a tactic Swift had often employed successfully in England.

In the *Proposal*, however, Swift was following a strategy distinctly different from any he had undertaken in England. The landlords who prohibited farming were obliged to do so as a consequence of British law. Their crime was not so much one of venality as of foolish adherence to laws they could have played at least some part in resisting. More people than just the tenants and artisans would benefit from an 'Irish' response to the economic troubles, a response that would have to be led by the very landlords the pamphlet had apparently just castigated in no uncertain terms. Only someone with Swift's combination of practical intelligence and pragmatic disdain for intellectual arguments could have marshalled the irony and ambiguity necessary to blame Ireland for being foolish at the same moment it was singled-out for its loyalty:

> I could fill a Volume as large as the *History of the wise Men of Goatham*, with a Catalogue only of some *wonderful* Laws and Customs we have observed within thirty Years past.[47]

Laws are 'wonderful' for being both unbelievable and mysterious in an almost biblical sense. In Ireland they were observed not just in the modern sense of those who studied them, as the philosophers of a body politic in London were increasingly doing, but in the still current legal sense of being obeyed. Ireland was being punished for its loyalty to the schemes of the Whig ministry in London.

Gratifying though it must have been to Swift to oppose the Whig ministry, the *Proposal's* concern with issues more pressing than a personal objection to Robert Walpole is underlined by the difference in tone between the arrogance of the Tory tracts and the frustration of the *Proposal*, with its appeal to common sense and the need for action on the part of its readers. After his return to Dublin in 1714, Swift had gone into what Joseph McMinn characterises as 'a deceptive retirement', shedding some of his arrogance and adopting at least some of the sentiments required by his office.[48] Swift had written to Ford on 17 Februrary 1716 that:

> I find the turn of Blood at 50, disposes me strongly to Fears, and therefore I think as little of Publick affairs as I can, because they concern me as one of the Multitude . . . and I dare not trust to Fortune as the younger Folks do.[49]

Swift's claim to be 'one of the multitude' was perhaps not wholly without merit, and his experience as a member of a privileged but largely powerless group – the landless Anglicans – helped consolidate Swift's understanding of the need to combine numbers with the clout of the politicised minority to the advantage of both sides. Just one month before the publication of the *Letter to a Young Gentleman*, and six months before he finished the *Proposal for the Universal Use of Irish Manufacture*, Swift wrote to Ford again. 'You live in the midst of the World, I wholly out of it,' Swift wrote, adding an account of his lack of zest for action before pulling off another of his sudden reversals:

> Take this Philosophy in return of your Apology for writing a word of Politicks. But as the World is now turned, no Cloyster is retired enough to keep Politicks out, and I will own they raise my Passions . . . perhaps more than yours who live amongst them.[50]

Safe in correspondence with his oldest friend, Swift served notice about the motivation of an author soon to reappear in the world, ready to give voice to innate good sense and affronted by the stupidity and inaction of those who would claim to be his betters.

Of a different order from the controlled rage and righteous indignation of the London tracts, the humility of Swift as loyal Irishman and private citizen shocked by basic violations of cherished and fundamental rights had first appeared in yet another letter to Ford. A long argument over appellate jurisdiction within Ireland had finally ended up in the Westminster parliament which, on 26 March 1720, passed the

Declaratory Act, claiming absolute authority over Ireland for the British parliament. Swift, writing to Ford immediately after news of the vote arrived in Dublin, noted that, henceforth, Irish politics could be reduced to one question: 'whether People ought to be Slaves or no'.[51] The question was neither so disingenuous, nor so simple, as it might at first have appeared, for, as Swift told Ford in the same letter, Ireland's Anglicans lived in a legally ill-defined country, a nation 'which is no Nation'.[52]

One reason the question 'whether People ought to be Slaves or no' was not as simple as it might have sounded could be found with the bishops, who had used their power in the Irish House of Lords to pursue claims of appellate authority. The bishops pushed their claims to such a degree that, to protect what it believed to be authority granted by a law promulgated in 1495 by Sir Edward Poynings, the British parliament felt compelled to pass the Declaratory Act.[53] The root of the peers' determined march into near legislative oblivion lay, as with so many problems, in land. Ironically, on this issue the English- and Irish-born bishops allied themselves against a coalition of lay peers who felt the church controlled too much land. The agreement of the twenty-two bishops on the question of land rights had resulted in persistent refusals of the Irish House of Lords to recognise the British House of Lords as the final court of appeal for Irish law suits. Law suits between landlords, tenants and the church, which claimed large tracts of land for itself, were a perennial feature of the Irish Sessions. Lay peers, British and Irish, consistently sought to deny the right of the Irish House of Lords to decide land matters, because if it did 'then the bishops of Ireland would [have been] in a position to determine the disposition of every acre of ground in the kingdom'.[54] As a direct result of this impasse Dublin Castle was finally compelled to ask the parliament in Westminster to legislate, thereby granting victory to the lay peers at a cost most Irish-born peers could ill afford, and defeating the English-born bishops with legislation they had themselves often supported.

The Declaratory Act of 1720 held Ireland to be 'subordinate unto and dependent upon the imperial Crown of Great Britain'. In consequence of this, 'the king's majesty [and] . . . parliament assembled, had, hath, and of right ought to have full power and authority to make laws and statutes of sufficient force and validity to bind the kingdom and people of Ireland'. This act made one significant change to Poynings' Law: Ireland was no longer simply subject to the English crown, as Poynings had stipulated, but was now subject to the 'Imperial Crown', and, more importantly, to the parliament in Westminster. The question of freedom, then, became not a matter of claiming rights to self-governance while recognising the Crown's authority – which the Irish Anglicans had never denied – but of obtaining from Westminster certain privileges the parliament there claimed to exercise over Ireland by authority of the monarch.[55]

What Swift sought to accomplish by having the *Proposal* address the economic plight of Ireland, and by having his address coincide with the king's birthday, was to refocus the political attention of the Anglican Irish on affairs they could control themselves. It was a stroke of genius on Swift's part to recognise that in order to succeed in his object so soon after passage of the Declaratory Act he needed to ignore the one item of legislation on which everyone in Ireland had an opinion. The Declaratory Act had come about as a direct consequence of the stubbornness of the clergy in the House of Lords. They had been acting in the interest of their church but against the very landlords and Anglican tenants Swift needed to build his coalition. Any debate on the merits of the Declaratory Act would only have exacerbated the situation. While others railed against Westminster and the administration in Dublin, Swift published a tract which, by 'seem[ing] to lack premeditation [and] by avoiding obvious balance, antithesis, and the common resources of formal rhetoric', as Ehrenpreis describes it,[56] distinguished itself as an ardently nationalist tract which never once addressed the most important piece of legislation to define Ireland's place in the world in more than three centuries.

Swift was not saying anything new in the *Proposal*; indeed, he was careful to hew to a line the Irish houses of parliament had themselves advocated. The *Proposal* cuts quickly to the chase, moving to submerge the debate between the church and the lay peers under the more pressing needs of the nation:

> I SHOULD wish the Parliament had thought fit to have suspended their Regulation of *Church* Matters, and Enlargements of the *Prerogative*, until a more convenient Time, because they did not appear very pressing, (at least to the Persons *principally concerned*) and, instead of those great Refinements in *Politicks* and *Divinity*, had *amused* Themselves and their Committees, a little, with the *State of the Nation*.[57]

Swift's chosen narrator is carefully ambiguous on the matter of the church. He defends it from the recent series of attacks by the Commons and Dublin Castle, but he does not defend it absolutely, suggesting merely that there are better things to do at the moment than challenge the church's prerogative. However, this voice of moderation, which McMinn identifies as a 'favourite note of the pamphlets – a mock-innocent disappointment and surprise',[58] is itself deceptive, for there is a parenthetical defence of the church that is defiantly self-perpetuating of church rights. The becomingly modest thinker, whose modesty cannot overcome his indignant need to contribute to the debate, asserts first that parliament should have 'suspended their Regulation of *Church* Matters . . . until a more convenient Time'.[59] But then he denies them any right to such regulation by specifically attributing to the leading churchmen, those 'Persons *principally* concerned',[60] the wisdom of experience that allows them to determine whether the church-state compact need be reopened. The *Proposal* introduces the church to the debate only to exempt it from those matters which intrude upon its sovereignty. In effect, parliament stands accused of seeking to enlarge its 'prerogative' while its vestiges of sovereign power were being stripped – of fiddling while Rome burned.

Parliament would have been better employed addressing matters over which it still had authority: 'What if the House of Commons had thought fit to make a Resolution . . . against wearing any Cloath or Stuff in their Families, which were not of the Growth and Manufacture of this Kingdom?'.[61] The pamphlet goes on to enquire, 'What if the Ladies would be content with *Irish* Stuffs for the Furniture of their Houses, for Gowns and Petticoats to themselves and their Daughters?'.[62] The House of Commons had in fact passed such resolutions several times in the previous decade, as Swift well knew. The members of the House had, however, failed to act upon its resolutions, as they themselves had been forced to admit in 1707 when they added to a resolution sent to the House of Lords the pledge that this time they would 'engage their honours to each other that they would conform to said resolution'.[63]

The writer of the *Proposal* knew his parliamentary history. The question 'What if [the House of Commons] had sent up such a Resolution to be agreed to by the House of Lords; and by their own Practice and Encouragement, spread the Execution of it in their several Counties?' establishes the framework for a further indictment of the lower house.[64] It also prepares the ground for a later, explicit commendation of certain clergy for acting according to the desires of parliament, thereby setting an example the members of the Commons would have done well to follow, instead of interfering in church affairs. By reiterating the Irish parliament's own resolutions the *Proposal* argues that parliament was enfeebled but that it was the members, not the institution, that was failing the country.

That it was not the institution that was failing Ireland was a critical contention, for if Ireland were to legitimately claim sovereign nation status it would require a functioning parliamentary body. The only conceivable framework for such a body included a monarch at its head, so throughout the *Proposal* there is no criticism of George I. Indeed, the next suggestion in the *Proposal* is specifically designed to quell accusations of treason, denying that Irish parliamentary opposition to English authority was in any way opposition to the sovereign. What Swift suggested was that:

> I hope, and believe, nothing could please his Majesty better than to hear that his loyal Subjects, of both Sexes, in this Kingdom, celebrated his *Birth-Day* (now approaching) *universally* clad in their own Manufacture. Is there Vertue enough left in this deluded People to save them from the Brink of Ruin?[65]

The audacity of this idea is still breathtaking. The pamphlet writer is presuming to voice the sentiments of the monarch, sentiments to which he could not have been privy, and which, though seemingly harmless, would have had unimaginable consequences for the government of Ireland. If the people of Ireland acted on this advice, the king would be faced with a choice: either condemn the Irish people for using the fruit of their own labour to recognise their king, or accept their good wishes and snub his government. Had the Irish people followed the pamphlet's advice, King George I would have been trapped into officially reducing Ireland to the status of a colony or recognising it as a separate kingdom within his domain. Swift was disguising one of the most radical suggestions ever to be made in Ireland as a loyal act of a people taking 'a classic stand against the tyranny of power'.[66]

Swift himself understood the dangers inherent in his position, and he felt compelled to enquire whether there 'Is . . . Vertue enough left in this deluded People to save them from the Brink of Ruin?'.[67] If that virtue were to be found anywhere in Ireland it would be in the Church of Ireland, an institution the *Proposal* intended to promote from victim of a degenerate parliament to role model. This was a manoeuvre Swift had often practiced in England, and the leaders of good and just government had been regularly presented as near paragons of virtue. Bolingbroke, Harcourt, Oxford, Somers, Sancroft and others had all been praised for their devotion to the established church, even if circumstances had at times later required reappraisal. What distinguishes the *Proposal* from Swift's work in England is the reversal in the relationship of church and government. Where earlier the argument had developed along the lines that because Oxford was a true friend of the church he was therefore best suited to govern, Swift now argued that the native Church of Ireland people were the true friends of Ireland, and therefore best suited to govern. The church had gone from partnership to leadership.

As early as 1697, when still Bishop of Derry, William King had grasped the necessity of setting the Church of Ireland on a footing that claimed for it a special role in society. In King's view, the church was in a fundamental sense above the laws of the land and should have been outside the interference of other institutions, a point he made clear in a complaint to Sir Robert Southwell about the refusal of London and Canterbury to sanction a convocation of the Church of Ireland. The language of King's complaint is remarkable for its resemblance in theme to later, broader discussions of Irish rights. 'The first article of the magna carta', King wrote on 21 December 1697:

> is that the church of England shall be free, and that freedom can consist in nothing but in choosing the ecclesiastical constitutions by which she is governed in convocations, and to give the king a power to call a certain number of divines and counsellors and by them to make or repeal canons for the church is . . . contrary to her liberty . . . If the church once come to have her constitutions altered without convocations, which are her legal representatives, she is no more free but an absolute slave . . . [68]

It was King who, in February 1720 in another letter to Southwell, made the connection between the Church of Ireland's rights and privileges and those of Ireland itself. King reminded Southwell of his opposition to the Declaratory Act and warned that he could not 'value anything that I hold at the mere will and pleasure of another; that is the title of slaves'. Swift was not alone in explicitly asking 'whether People ought to be Slaves or no'.

From convocation to parliament, King had been in the forefront of the battle to preserve Irish rights and, specifically, the rights of the Church of Ireland. His arguments had been legalistic and constitutional. With the economic situation in Ireland now convincing everyone of the importance of that debate, Swift moved in the *Proposal* to promote the arguments of King and his colleagues to the status of national sentiment. For the sake of his church, Swift set about building a consensus that would remake Ireland's body politic. He built upon an idealistic conservatism that reached back to fundamental precepts of

English legal philosophy, but in so doing he sought to separate Ireland from English political dominion forever.

Leadership alone would not be enough and Swift is careful to suggest that Irish-born clergy were not just leading the defence of Ireland's rights, but were also at the forefront of those feeling the ill-effects of English policy. Embattled and losing ground, the native-born churchmen were symbols of both resistance and warning:

> I think it needless to exhort the *Clergy* to follow [King's] good Example, because *in a little Time, those among them who are so unfortunate to have had their Birth and Education in this Country will think themselves abundantly happy when they can afford Irish Crape* . . .[69]

The challenge to the Irish was to make it possible for the senior Irish-born cleric to wear Irish-made clothing 'as good . . . as if he had not been born among us'.[70] It was a programme that would benefit the Irish workmen and artisans who laboured to make such goods and which would secure the church the respect it deserved.

All the ingredients for the grandest of alliances were now in place and the full scope of the *Proposal's* intentions could be revealed. Swift built upon the warnings about Ireland's plight, and upon Vesey's repetition of the advice to burn 'every Thing that came from England, except their People and their Coals',[71] to turn the *Proposal* from a simple economic tract into an appeal for the creation of a distinct Irish culture. 'I should not be sorry if [the English] would stay at home', says the writer, glossing Vesey. English migration to Ireland was an issue important to all Irish-born churchmen concerned about the increasing control of the hierarchy by such English imports as Bishops John Evans of Meath and William Nicolson of Derry, who were soon to be joined by Hugh Boulter as Primate of Ireland on his promotion to Archbishop of Armagh.[72]

The conservative nature of the *Proposal's* reaction to English encroachments on Irish church and parliamentary rights is linked with a radical proposal for Irish economic self-sufficiency. For the first time, a writer on Irish affairs commingled narrow appeals for the preservation of a particular Irish group's rights with an appeal to the welfare of the Irish nation as a whole. So unprecedented was the nature of this appeal, Swift was forced to interpret the myth which served as one of his central metaphors in a highly unorthodox manner. The story of Arachne and Pallas is a commonplace tale of mortal hubris punished by divine retribution. For the pamphlet writer it is something else entirely, with Ireland cast in the role of Arachne, an innocent victim of

England's Pallas-style arrogance. As recounted in the *Proposal*, Pallas finds herself 'almost equalled in her own Art' and 'stung with Rage and Envy, knockt her rival down'. The metaphor is developed with Arachne condemned, like Ireland, to '*spin* and *weave* for ever, *out of her own Bowels*, and *in a very narrow Compass*'. The writer continues:

> I confess, that from a Boy, I always pitied poor *Arachne*, and could never heartily love the Goddess, on Account of so *cruel and unjust a Sentence*; which, however, is *fully executed* upon *Us by England*, with further Additions of *Rigor* and *Severity*. For the greatest Part of *our Bowels and Vitals* is extracted, without allowing us the Liberty of *spinning* and *weaving* them.[73]

The first few pages of the *Proposal* move from subject to subject, from group to group, suggesting that all of Ireland's native-born people share a common discomfort. In the second half, Swift sets out to argue that an economic response alone is not sufficient. Ireland needs an indigenous Anglican cultural identity to secure it against further English encroachments. Swift knew economic interests on their own could not preserve forever the alliance he sought to build. In arguing that the economic erosion of Ireland's identity was on a par with other English encroachments, Swift sought to multiply the causes upon which the Anglican Irish could agree.

'The Scripture tells us', the writer says, quoting Ecclesiastes 7:7, '*Oppression makes a Wise Man mad*',[74] and in Ireland the evidence for that was not hard to find. 'It is wonderful to observe the Biass among our People in favour of *Things*, *Persons*, and *Wares* of all Kinds that come from *England*'.[75] One telling example could be found in the man who:

> for thirty Years past, hath been the *common Standard of Stupidity in England*, where he was never heard a Minute in any *Assembly*, or by any *Party* . . . yet, upon his Arrival hither . . . talked . . . without either *Gracefulness*, *Propriety*, or *Meaning*; and, at the same Time [was] admired and followed as the Pattern of *Eloquence* and *Wisdom*.[76]

It was behaviour such as this, just as much as the increasing poverty of Ireland, that resulted in 'some *Ministers* . . . from their *high* Elevation. . . . look[ing] *down* upon this Kingdom, as if it had been one of their *Colonies* of *Out-casts* in *America*'.[77]

Swift was again building his argument upon ground already cleared by others, but it was left to him to make the necessary connections for the population at large. Complaints about English fools coming to Ireland mirrored the very arguments that King had been most consistently levelling against the Englishmen transferred to Irish bishoprics. His criticism was encapsulated in a furious letter, 17 June 1721 to Arthur Charlett, Master of University College, Oxford, characterising the translated Englishmen as being far from 'the brightest generally speaking'. Timothy Goodwin, Bishop of Kilmore, had reported to William Wake in early 1718 that Synge thought 'there are enough [English-born bishops] already and [he] suspects that we lay schemes for bringing over more'. Goodwin appeared genuinely stunned that Synge 'seems to think it hard that English Bishops should take the best Bishopricks here'. His amazement suggests that King was indeed right to suspect the intelligence of his English-born counterparts. Swift himself would later refer to the English party in the Church of Ireland as a bunch of 'worthless bishops, all bedangled with their pert illiterate relations and flatterers'.[78] *A Proposal for the Universal Use of Irish Manufacture* both adumbrates future campaigns of the 'present *Dublin* faction on the bench', which Hugh Boulter urged he be allowed 'to break [lest] it . . . be impossible for me to serve his Majesty further' on his accession as Primate of All Ireland[79] and echoes earlier complaints of the one body in Ireland the author thought capable of leading that country out of the abyss.

The penultimate paragraph of the *Proposal* returns to the question of the landlords' behaviour – reiterating the argument that the Irish have themselves to blame and possess their own means of salvation:

> I would now expostulate a little with our Country Landlords; who, by unmeasurable *screwing* and *racking* their Tenants . . . have . . . reduced the miserable *People* to a *worse Condition* . . . so that the whole *Species* of what we call *Substantial Farmers*, will, in a very few Years, be utterly at an end.[80]

Among the victims of such behaviour were the bishops, whom the landlords sought to prevent 'from letting their Revenues at a moderate half Value, (whereby the whole *Order* would, in an Age, have been reduced to manifest Beggary)'.[81] But while relief of the church should have been reason enough for the landlords to change their ways, the ultimate appeal is to their self-esteem and self-interest:

> I have heard *great* Divines affirm, that *nothing is so likely to call down an universal Judgment from Heaven upon a Nation, as universal*

Oppression; and whether this be not already verified in Part, *their Worships* the Landlords are *now* at full Leisure to consider.[82]

Hardly a modest man, Swift had no doubt that if, in light of the *Proposal*'s arguments, the landlords did stop to consider their conduct, *'Oppression* would, in Time, teach a little *Wisdom* to *Fools'*,[83] fools who would recognise their own role in creating a society where:

> Whoever travels this Country, and observes the *Face* of Nature, or the *Faces*, and Habits, and Dwellings of the *Natives*, will hardly think himself in a Land where either *Law*, *Religion*, or common *Humanity* is professed.[84]

The *Proposal* is a useful tract for demonstrating one linguistic distinction of the period not unique to Swift but exploited by him with perhaps greater finesse than others managed – the occasional distinction between the word 'Irish' and the word 'native'. 'Irish' could mean just about whatever an author wished of it and was a powerful word precisely because of its inherent ambiguities, but 'native', when used by the Anglican Irish, could only mean 'Catholic'. It was an important distinction to Swift and his ilk, who knew full well that they were sitting upon appropriated lands, possession of which they sought to derive political rights from, while at the same time they had to be careful to ensure that those rights were not extended to the dispossessed former owners of that land. His final use of the word 'native' makes it clear that however broadly Swift might have hoped the word 'Irish' would be interpreted, this is a tract aimed squarely at the Anglican Irish community, a community whose self-interest would, coincidentally, benefit others. Like King, like Synge, Swift's position was that Catholics were already repressed enough. To extend their degradation was to undermine the whole society, Protestant and Catholic alike. Swift was not advocating a common politics, but he did count Catholics as members of society, albeit as ones with very limited, very specific, bounds set upon their participation in that society.

At least from the period of Henry Grattan's quest for Irish parliamentary independence, the *Proposal* has been one of the easiest texts to use to support claims for Swift's inclusiveness. However, that argument has been frequently disproved, perhaps most eloquently as early as 1816 by Francis, Lord Jeffrey, then editor of *The Edinburgh Review* and a virulent Whig who would later become a senior Scottish law officer. Jeffrey was taking aim at the Swift edition prepared by his former friend Sir Walter Scott, an edition at least partly used to lend 'historical' weight to Scott's argument that Britain was almost inevitably becoming a pluralist multinational democracy. Rubbish, wrote Jeffrey, pointing out that:

> a single fact is decisive upon this point. While [Swift's] friends were in power, we hear nothing of the grievances of Ireland; and to the last we hear nothing of its radical grievance, the oppression of its Catholic population. His object was, not to do good to Ireland, but to vex and annoy the English ministry. To do this, however, with effect, it was necessary that he should speak to the interests and the feelings of some party who possessed a certain degree of power and influence. This unfortunately was not the case in that day with the Catholics . . . [85]

Jeffrey was absolutely right about one thing: Swift's political writings were forever seeking to 'speak to the interests and the feelings of some party who possessed a certain degree of power'. He was wrong to attribute that to a desire to annoy the English. Swift's agenda was far more complex and positive. He may have avoided any discussion of Catholic rights because that community had no power, but Swift had another reason for avoiding making claims on their behalf: advocacy of Catholic rights was, by its very nature, inimicable to the advancement of the cause of the Church of Ireland as the established church, and that was Swift's major aim whenever he put pen to paper for a political purpose.

Swift intended to appeal to what he saw as the rights of the Irish Anglicans but for him that second word was self-evident, and if that meant that, on occasion, others might mistake particular appeals for a broader plea so be it. Swift was a believer in shifting alliances, but it would never have occurred to him that civil rights of any but the meanest sort could be enjoyed by any but those professing the religion of the established church.

Jeffrey's broadside pointed out that the Catholics' lack of political power 'gave them only a stronger title to the services of a truly brave or generous advocate [but] was sufficient to silence Swift'.[86] Swift's 'silence' on the subject of Catholic rights is not grounds to deny his bravery or generosity in the political realm, but it does serve to highlight the distinction between his broad words and his specific intentions.

The *Proposal* draws upon earlier theories of Irish sovereignty but develops them to demonstrate that the solution to Ireland's problems lay in redefining Ireland's relationship with England – a redefinition that needed to originate within Ireland and which would have had the church playing a leading role. It was an opening move in what Swift knew would be a long campaign, a campaign King and Molyneux, among others, had made possible. In the *Proposal*, Swift is careful to suggest that 'some Body' be found 'who can write Sense, to put [these promises] into Form'; 'some Body' who was to find his voice when one of the tailors' own emerged on the scene with his *Letter to the Shop-Keepers, Tradesmen, and Farmers, and Common-People of Ireland*, signing his name M.B. Drapier. But there was to be a four-year hiatus before the message of the *Proposal* could be further developed in the light of circumstance. In the interval, other events in Ireland once again required Swift to divert his attention from the plight of the Anglican poor and concentrate instead on his and the church's own immediate needs.

CHAPTER FIVE

A 'bubble . . . sufficient to do our business': the economy of a province

I

Britain may be described as a political culture in which theories
of revolution are invented but never put into practice.

J.G.A. Pocock[1]

While the *Proposal for the Universal Use of Irish Manufacture* was the
most detailed foray into economic theory Swift had yet undertaken, its
thesis was predicated upon traditional mercantilist assumptions. In
the first half of the eighteenth century, when the intellectual assumptions
underlying theories of wealth, property and prosperity were in a
significant degree of flux, the newer ideas that would come to dominate
the field were still the property of an intellectual minority for whom
Swift had little sympathy. However, while his personal commitment to
mercantilist precepts was genuine, Swift's sympathies here coincided
with ideas which the majority of the Anglican population of Ireland
would have agreed with – and, more importantly, which they would
have thought they understood.[2]

Swift was naturally sympathetic to the traditional assumptions
underlying theories of wealth and prosperity and that is hardly
surprising, but his sympathy would not have translated into what are
effectively published defences of such theories had he not thought to
gain some other advantage from their appearance. The *Proposal* draws
heavily upon contemporary analyses of events in Ireland being made
by a circle loosely gathered around Archbishop King. The political
instincts of King's circle, and their social standing, offered Swift
precisely the examples he needed to remind people of the positives to

be gained from a sustained coalition between church and populace. It might seem surprising, then, that once he had completed the *Proposal* Swift abruptly curtailed his essays on Irish affairs. The tracts did not dry up completely but the exuberance and urgency of the *Proposal* were not to resurface until the series of letters purporting to come from the pen of M.B. Drapier began appearing in 1724. However, this near silence was not wasted time, nor was it without precedent in Swift's career. The economic debate of most urgency in Ireland in the years immediately after 1720 was that of whether Ireland needed a national bank. Swift had clear views opposed to the plan, but, as with the debate over Dunkirk's fortifications, discussion of a national bank left him essentially indifferent, unable to see in the debate much that could be turned to the church's advantage.

In any case, Swift had a more personal matter to resolve that would occupy some considerable part of 1720 and much of the first half of 1721. The administration of Ireland had recognised the potential consequences of the *Proposal*'s appeal for expression of Irish loyalty to George I. The response was quick. Unable to prove that Swift was the author, the administration instead detained Edward Waters, the printer of the *Proposal*, and charged him under the sedition laws. Swift immediately engaged himself in trying to get Waters released.

For much of the time Waters was in jail, the Lord Lieutenant, the Duke of Grafton, was absent in England on business. The prosecution of the case against Waters was left up to Chief Justice William Whitshed, who despised Swift with a fervour returned by the dean.[3] The jury in the case refused to be impressed by either Whitshed's pleas or by the judge's instructions and returned verdicts dismissing the case no fewer than nine times. Finally, in the spring of 1721, Whitshed realised the implications of continuing with the retrials and decided to wait until the return of the Duke of Grafton. Swift had even gone to the length of interceding on his printer's behalf with Robert, Viscount Molesworth in the summer of 1720. Despite his differences with Swift, Molesworth, who had opposed the Declaratory Act in the British House of Lords, had thought briefly of reprinting the *Proposal* in England under his protection. Nothing had come of that, but he had agreed to help on Waters' behalf.[4] Swift had also written to Sir Thomas Hanmer, Speaker of the British House of Commons, describing the *Proposal* as 'a weak hasty Scribble', hardly worthy of the government's attention.[5]

It was not until August 1721, eighteen months after the *Proposal* had first appeared, that Grafton bowed to pressure from London, accepted the judicially inescapable and issued a grant of *noli prosequi*.[6] Loyally working to help Waters, Swift avoided any extended public consideration of Ireland's situation. He wrote a few poems, among them 'An Excellent New Song on a Seditious Pamphlet', with its refrain:

> We'll buy English silks for our wives and our daughters,
> In spite of his Deanship and journeyman Waters.[7]

He expressed some concern for the author's own fate and implicitly accepted authorship of the *Proposal* (if doing so in an anonymous poem can be called 'accepting authorship'):

> . . . as for the Dean,
> You know whom I mean,
> If the printer will peach him, he'll scarce come off clean.[8]

After the *Proposal* appeared, it is often claimed that 'Protestant Ireland saw that it had a new voice, experienced, resolute and sympathetic'.[9] In fact, much of Protestant Ireland would only come to this realisation in retrospect, but the *Proposal* had in it everything that Swift, and others, would relentlessly develop to their various conclusions.[10] Swift would concentrate on the worsening economic plight of Ireland, while King and the parliamentarians developed the legal and political claims necessary to complement analyses such as Swift's. Having publicly begun the task of distinguishing Irish rights from those of the English, as King had been urging in private for so long, Swift was obliged to wait until his political allies could develop something approaching a coherent rationale for further action. In the debate over the bank, Swift failed to distinguish any particular position that would advance the claims he sought to make for the benefit of the church.

This need to bide his time not only allowed Swift to concentrate on Waters' case but also left him free to turn his attention to his own affairs – affairs now greatly complicated by changes in his relationship with Vanessa, resident at Celbridge, 11 miles from Dublin. By the summer of 1720 this relationship was again vexing him severely, this time at least as much because of the illness of her sister, Mary, as because of Vanessa's own demands upon him. On 4 August 1720 Swift apologised for not having written to Vanessa earlier, observing that 'I was in great Apprehension that poor [Mary] was worse, and till I could be satisfied in that particular, I would not write again'.[11] Mary died on 27 February 1721. Genuinely distressed, Swift was equally concerned about the effect her death would have on Vanessa's demands on him. 'For Gods sake get your Friends about you', he advised in his letter commiserating on Mary's death, but he made no effort to go immediately himself.[12] By July, he felt compelled to seek to warn her off:

> Cad[enus] [i.e. Swift] assures me he continues to esteem and love and value you above all things, and so will do to the End of his Life, but at the same time entreats that you would not make your self or him unhappy by Imaginations.[13]

Swift had also been unwell throughout the summer of 1720. He had thought of going to Aix-la-Chapelle to recuperate, but 'the most mortal Impediment to all Thoughts of travelling', he had told Charles Ford, was that 'I should dy with Spleen to be in such a Condition in strange Places'.[14]

The belief that he could let others engage in political debate without him must have been something of a relief to Swift. The *Letter to a Young Gentleman* and the *Proposal* had reintroduced him to the public, but, along with more pressing matters, Swift had for some time been exercised by one other personal concern – years of anonymous authorship had left him liable to be identified with articles he had not, and would not, have written. In 1718 there appeared *A Dedication to a Great Man*, a pamphlet praising George I and finding fault with the Anglican clergy for not sufficiently appreciating him. Swift had adopted various personae throughout his political authorship, many seemingly opposed to his own sympathies. However, an assault upon the Anglican Church as a body, rather than upon individual clerics, even though ironically intended, was not something Swift would ever have risked. Nonetheless, he soon found himself credited with the *Dedication's* composition. The next year, a reply appeared in the form of *A Letter to the Reverend Mr Dean Swift*. Its author wondered that Swift, 'whose affection to the church was never doubted, though his Christianity was ever questioned', should now have chosen to praise King George. On reflection, however, he recognised that:

> as it is well known you never were a slave to constancy and principle, we can easily account for this your behaviour, and in defence of it say, That in this instance, you have put off prejudice, and resumed your understanding.[15]

Swift was eager to answer such accusations and, early in January 1721, he undertook to do just that.

Swift began a long defence of his recent career in a letter addressed to someone he believed would judge him fairly. 'I had rather chuse to appeal to you than to my Lord Chief Justice Whitshed, under the situation I am in', he wrote to Alexander Pope.[16] The letter was never sent and it stands beside Swift's unpublished defences of himself and the Tories written between 1714 and 1720. Unlike those retrospective validations of his activities, however, Swift's letter to Pope overflows with urgent matters he felt needed immediate clarification. The heart of Swift's complaint is that of a man unfairly deprived of the freedoms of English law and so, as McMinn stresses, the letter 'defends [Swift's] integrity as a writer abused and threatened by tyrannical laws'.[17] Swift's complaint is that of one English writer to another, of a man who has done his duty, kept his peace for six years and then been harassed for a pamphlet he believes to be consistent with everything for which he had struggled in England.

'I came to my station here', Swift says, 'where I have continued ever since in the greatest privacy'.[18] So jealously had he maintained this privacy that Swift claims to 'neither know the names nor number of the family which now reigns, further than the Prayer Book informs me'.[19] Recently, however, he reports:

> I have written in this kingdom, a discourse to persuade the wretched people to wear their own manufactures instead of those from England. This treatise soon spread very fast, being agreeable to the sentiments of the whole nation.[20]

Swift is concerned with two things: his own reputation as an author and the travails imposed upon him by supposed 'party' loyalties. In this private correspondence, Swift recounts the events following the publication of the *Proposal* in a tone notable for its restrained indignation and reliance upon the evidence, although he cannot refrain from claiming that even Whitshed found 'not a single syllable of party in the whole treatise'.[21] Swift sets the *Proposal* firmly in the context of his earlier life and work – conducted in England. His defence of a tract that rhetorically and politically was designed to distinguish Ireland from England argues that its appeal is strictly within the traditions of English political debate. Appeals to 'liberty', to the evils of 'party', are the appeals of an English author distressed by 'that scheme of politics . . . of setting up moneyed interest in opposition to the landed'.[22] There is nothing in the letter to Pope to distinguish it as 'Irish'.

Ultimately, Swift's complaint is that of an author, not of an aggrieved nationalist: 'I have been much concerned . . . to see how ill a taste for wit and sense prevails in the world', he tells Pope, a consequence of all that 'politics and South Sea, and Party, and operas and masquerades have introduced'.[23] What angers Swift the most is the attribution to him of pamphlets that are possessed of neither his wit, nor his manner. 'Writings' have been 'ascribed . . . to me, of which any man of common sense and literature would be heartily ashamed', he complains, adding that he cannot avoid saying a few words upon the *Dedication*:

> [T]here is one circumstance which makes it impossible for me to have been the author of a treatise, wherein there are several pages containing a panegyric upon King George, of whose character and person I am utterly ignorant, nor ever had once the curiosity to inquire into either, living at so great a distance as I do, and having long done with whatever can relate to public matters.[24]

Defence of himself and consideration of the role of party aside, Swift continues to see the events of 1714 as the defining period of his life. Of all those events with which he was involved only one seems in retrospect worth recording:

> I only wish my endeavours had succeeded better in the great point I had at heart, which was that of reconciling the ministers to each other. This might have been done, if others who had more concern and more influence would have acted their parts; and if this had succeeded, the public interest of both Church and State would not have been the worse, nor the Protestant succession endangered.[25]

However radical the practical consequences of the *Proposal's* suggestions might have been, Swift saw nothing particularly revolutionary about them. Although others might have blanched at a recipe which still put the church before either the state or the Protestant succession, for Swift the *Proposal* was just the latest in a series of rearguard actions designed to protect the rights and privileges he had sought to foster throughout his career.

The pernicious nature of a government willing to ignore a verdict of not guilty nine times, simply to prosecute a mere printer, underlined the gulf that had opened between traditional legal protections inherited from England and the conduct of the English administration in Ireland:

> I could never discover the necessity of suspending any law upon which the liberty of the most innocent persons depended: neither do I think this practice hath made the taste of arbitrary power so agreeable as that we should desire to see it repeated . . . [T]hose

diligent inquiries into remote and problematical guilt, with a new power of enforcing them by chains and dungeons to every person whose face a minister thinks fit to dislike, are not only opposite to that maxim, which declares it better that ten guilty men should escape, than one innocent suffer, but likewise leave a gate wide open to the whole tribe of informers; the most accursed, prostitute, and abandoned race that God ever permitted to plague mankind.[26]

'These', says Swift, 'are some of the sentiments I had ... while I was in the world', and while he denies necessarily holding them now, that denial is fallacious. By his own admission, Swift is 'too much a politician to expose my own safety by offensive words'.[27]

The still-tentative nature of Anglican Ireland's opposition to English rule is apparent in this careful defence which deliberately establishes grounds for Irish action based upon English precedent. Swift was not yet willing to grant Ireland the status of independent nation, but he could build upon English tradition and the rights claimed by Anglicans in England to argue that it was just, proper and in keeping with legal tradition for the Anglican Irish to resist arbitrary rule. This defence of himself to Pope is most interesting for what it doesn't mention anywhere: rights belonging to Irishmen as a consequence of being Irish. It was Swift's refusal to distinguish the rights of the Anglicans in Ireland from those in England that made the *Proposal* so powerful a document. As English policy moved ever further away from what he had always seen as desirable and necessary, Swift employed rhetorical skills honed in England to drive a wedge between the placemen of Westminster and Dublin Castle and his own exemplars of civic conduct whom he found within the Church of Ireland. And it was this division, based upon a reactionary defence of old values, that would finally give Anglican Ireland a distinct identity in Swift's writings.

Swift was able to defend himself to Pope and to deal with other personal issues precisely because the economic debate he had so carefully co-opted in the *Proposal* was outside the emerging fight over the proposed national bank and its related schemes. Others in Dublin were not as constrained as Swift by the single-minded question of 'what's in it for the church?'. As the economic plight of Ireland worsened Archbishop King returned to work on a document that he had first circulated privately in 1716. *Some Observations on the Taxes pay'd by Ireland to Support the Government* sought to draw a connection between the English perception of Ireland's condition and the resulting legislative oppression of the province. *Some Observations*, whose wide circulation among King's supporters and friends Ferguson discusses,[28] represented a further crucial step in distinguishing Ireland's identity from that of England. As before, King shied away from making a direct appeal to the Irish and he chose to address the English. Indeed, he specifically sought to detail how Ireland's tax revenue surpassed the demands it made upon English coffers. However, in making *Some Observations* King could not refrain from suggesting that if English lawmakers would only recognise the return they were already getting from Ireland and stop aggravating the situation, Ireland could get on with rectifying its own affairs. In short, argued King: 'The people of Ireland do find, that the greatest inconveniences which happen to the Kingdom, arise for the most part from the Misrepresentations of the State & Condition of it'.[29]

From a variety of directions, Anglican Ireland's political and clerical leaders were all converging upon a position that required them to take matters into their own hands and to cease relying upon English munificence. In an almost unbelievable coincidence of ill-considered timing, the Westminster parliament was busy in 1720–21 arranging to provide the Irish parliament with precisely the goad it needed to shift the entire debate from a theoretical disquisition on Irish rights to outright action, but until those plans came to fruition Swift had time on his hands.

While the Anglican Irish leaders in parliament continued to develop the theoretical justifications of their right to self-determination, Swift seized the opportunity of this hiatus in public debate of interest to him to begin work on the book that would ultimately secure his reputation. Finally published in 1726, *Gulliver's Travels* is remarkable for many reasons, but one of its most troubling aspects is the complete lack of any religious programme in its pages. This absence, however, provides a powerful insight into Swift's own attitudes toward religion. More than any other work he wrote, *Gulliver's Travels* offers a diversity of contexts from which to examine the nature of society. Gulliver visits several types of society and his commentary upon each of them, what he says and does not say, allows Swift the opportunity to examine a variety of possible societies.

Montag explores these various commentaries, and the unifying force behind them all, in his excellent study of 'Quarrels with nature', the concluding chapter of his penetrating *The Unthinkable Swift*. Among the various points he makes, perhaps the most pertinent when it comes to explaining Swift's reasons for omitting the church from this extended study of man and his world is the thought that:

> *Gulliver's Travels* manifest[s] not a set of arguments against but rather a refusal, a denial . . . of the various doctrines of nascent liberalism . . . This denial or refusal is of course a defence: a defence of doctrines no longer regarded as valid from within an institution that is itself an island separated by great gulfs from the world around; an island in time – in, but in an important sense not of, early capitalist Britain.[30]

That institution was the Church of Ireland. The point is that Gulliver's first three voyages explore societies that are in all in some manner corrupt. At best, Swift could have invented corrupt religious institutions to place in these corrupt civil societies, but to what end?

Montag demonstrates that while Swift 'favours a minimal state', he also imagined 'one in which authority was primarily exercised outside the state'.[31] This was an authority which Swift imagined should be, and had once been, vested in the spiritual apparatus of the church–state compact. The state made and policed policy, but it was policy guided by the principles of the church. In the ideal world, 'institutions appear necessary . . . only to counter external threats and the ever-present possibility of "unnatural" rebellion'.[32] Look, for example, at the lack of institutions and of a state structure in the land of the Houyhnhnm. But, of course, as *Gulliver's Travels* makes clear, the world is corrupt. The institutions explored in the first three voyages are as corrupt as they are because of society's falling away from the ideal, but Swift disdains from identifying any church as somehow involved in that corruption. Indeed, when he does touch on the church, as in chapter eight of the voyage to Laputa, where he offers '*A further Account of Glubbdubdrib. Antient and Modern History corrected*',[33] the attack is too easy and too brief to allow for any possibility of the reader elliding church corruption with other institutional failures. Concluding his lengthy examination of the comparison of ancient and modern 'heroes' in the presence of those ancients who 'seemed to be an Assembly of Heroes and Demy-Gods; the other a Knot of Pedlars, Pick-pockets, Highwaymen and Bullies',[34] Gulliver calls up 'a Dozen or two of Kings with their Ancestors', only to be disappointed to find 'an *Italian* Prelate' in one royal lineage and 'an Abbot, and two Cardinals' in another.[35] This is hardly a sophisticated attack upon any of the churches of Europe.

Perhaps more indicative of Swift's own attitude toward religion is the final book, for if the author of *Gulliver's Travels* believed in the divine, or even sublime, nature of religion, then Houyhnhnm society would surely boast the most compelling portrait of religion Swift could imagine. Instead, there is to be found no suggestion that the

Houyhnhnms have any discourse with the divine, or even a belief in some eternal truth. The Houyhnhnms have one compelling trait that spares them the need for an organised religion: 'Houyhnhnm imagination . . . instinctively recoils from thoughts which vitiate rather than enhance life', notes DePorte and, again:

> The Fourth Voyage is . . . less a fantasy of pure rationality than a fantasy of psychic harmony . . . Houyhnhnms represent the possibility of imaginative 'wholeness'. . . . Small wonder, Swift should have Gulliver report that the root meaning of the word 'Houyhnhnm' is *'the Perfection of Nature'*.[36]

For Swift, a society perfectly able to regulate itself through reason, experience and discourse would have no need of a religion to encourage, cajole and coerce good conduct. In England and Ireland, however, there was more than enough imagination to ensure the need for an established church.

It is no less true in *Gulliver's Travels* than in *The Battle of the Books* or in his various poems on the subject of the ancients and the moderns that Swift's heroes of the ancient world do not need a church in order to dictate their proper behaviour. It is only in a world fallen away from the ideal that the influence of the church is important. Caesar could destroy the liberty of the Roman people because there was no authority 'outside' the state to preserve it, but, as with the apple in the Garden of Eden, who was to know of what was absent until sin was introduced into the world? '*Cæsar* freely confessed' to Gulliver 'that the greatest Actions of his own Life were not equal by many Degrees to the Glory of taking it away',[37] but regicide, or even Caesaricide, was not to be undertaken lightly. The peace of the land, as Swift knew and as Anglican doctrines of passive obedience taught, was protected by everyone in society agreeing on certain religious principles, or if not agreeing on them at least not challenging them. Where established religion is mentioned in *Gulliver's Travels* conformity is valued and it is the king of Brobdingnag who:

> laughed at my odd Kind of Arithmetick (as he was pleased to call it) in reckoning the Numbers of our People by a Computation drawn from the several Sects among us in Religion and Politicks. He said, he knew no Reason why those who entertain Opinions prejudicial to the Publick should be obliged to change, or should not be obliged to conceal them. And, as it was Tyranny in any Government to require the first, so it was Weakness not to

> enforce the second: For, a Man may be allowed to keep Poisons in his Closet, but not to vend them about as Cordials.[38]

It is in this sense that the church is 'outside' the state. Whatever one's personal beliefs (and these were free to be held by each person), certain doctrines had to be expressed in public because otherwise society itself was in jeopardy.

The established church (any established church)[39] remains outside the tale of *Gulliver's Travels* because the story is an exploration of the decline of states that have fallen from their ordained condition and which are not protected by any authority outside that state. Ireland (and England, only more so) were well on the way to being a mixture of Lilliput, Brobdingnag and Laputa (in particular), and other countries in Europe (Spain and France especially) were further along still, but in Ireland, at least, there remained the possibility that the established church could confer protection against the arbitrary abuses of civil power from which the states were increasingly suffering.[40] It is the absence of any demonstration of the church's decline and fall, in contrast to the careful and detailed demonstration of the corruptibility of civic institutions, which renders *Gulliver's Travels* an implicitly respectful account of the powers of established religion.

Swift was a man who believed the church the guardian of social morality. He was deeply conservative and orthodox not because of any great and guiding spiritual certainty, but, as he would say so many times in his sermons, because of the need to preserve the peace. Swift's religion was situational. In short, Swift feared the consequences of a failure of established religion more than he rejoiced in the certainty of faith. He was specific about this in his sermon 'On the Martyrdom of King Charles I', when he argued that it was 'necessary . . . for those in power to curb, in season, all such unruly spirits as desire to introduce new doctrines and discipline in the church, or new forms of government in the state'.[41]

Swift's own political instincts led him to promote the church whenever the opportunity presented itself. In Ireland after the publication of his *Proposal for the Universal Use of Irish Manufacture* events took a course that left Swift unsure how best to advance the cause of the church by involving himself in political debate. The machinations of the British and Irish parliaments left him essentially uninterested, unable to see any reason to join the fray. Swift was free, therefore, to enjoy himself and to give vent to the literary and satirical amusements with which his early years in England had allowed him to experiment. It was this side of his character which had earned him the friendship of men such as Pope and Arbuthnot – friendships which had ignored religious and political differences. Angry and powerless in Dublin, Swift took the opportunity to divert his energy into a more amusing endeavour.

By 1720, Swift had spent the better part of twelve years promoting the welfare of the Church of Ireland, and so of Ireland. It was a task he had undertaken because he believed absolutely in its importance, but he was never a monomaniac, as his continuing correspondence with numerous friends illustrates. Busy though he was defending Waters from authority, justifying himself to Pope and restraining Vanessa's demands upon him, Swift nonetheless seized the opportunity presented by the turn of events in Irish political debate to begin writing his vast satire of human failing. For a while, at least, Swift believed himself free of the political demands of the collapsing church-state compact, believed himself free to expend his energy in other areas.

It was a freedom he would be able to enjoy only so long as the debate going on around him offered little immediate possibility of benefit to the church. Luckily for us, the various component parts of the eruption in Irish political life that would eventually lead Swift to pen *The Drapier's Letters* had each first to establish themselves within the currency of debate. The manner in which that happened is as vital to understanding the events that culminated in *The Drapier's Letters* as it was essentially uninteresting to Swift himself. We must understand the debate that he was basically content to leave to others if we are to recognise the nature of Swift's dramatic re-emergence in 1724, this time in the guise of M.B. Drapier.

II

> Blest paper-credit! last and best supply!
> That lends Corruption lighter wings to fly!
> Gold imp'd by thee, can compass hardest things,
> Can pocket States, can fetch or carry Kings;
> A single leaf shall waft an Army o'er,
> Or ship off Senates to a distant Shore.
>
> Alexander Pope[42]

It is too easy to forget that the work Swift undertaken in the guise of M.B. Drapier was begun only when the matter it addressed was all but resolved. The drapier's attack on English proposals to introduce a copper half-penny coin to Ireland followed a hiatus of a little more than three years from the appearance of the *Proposal*. However, by the time of the *Drapier's Letters* more than just the half-penny debate had come to a head. Swift had remained on the sidelines throughout a series of debates that had each in turn further prepared the ground for the culminating indignation he would use to separate forever Irish aspirations from English claims to parliamentary authority.

The debate over the patent granting William Wood the right to mint coinage for Ireland was actually the final part in a protracted argument that had begun at the same time that the Declaratory Act was passing the Houses of Parliament in Westminster. From the Declaratory Act to direct rule from London was only a tiny intellectual step, but the Irish parliament still had one particular power that required its continued existence: Irish tax revenue had to be approved by the Dublin parliament. Whig managers in England could find no way to justify removing this right without advocating union between Ireland and Britain, something they opposed. The legislative authority of parliament in England had been won by a series of concessions forced on the crown, concessions that, crucially, denied the ability to raise taxes to anyone other than parliament. It was Poynings' Law, which had just led to the need for the Declaratory Act, which now offered protection to the Irish parliament. Poynings had only added English laws then existing to Irish statutes; he had not denied the authority of the Irish parliament.[43] In 1720, Ireland still officially remained a separate political entity even though ultimately subject to British authority. To deny the Irish parliament the authority to tax was to question the relationship of monarch, ministry and legislature.

There was, however, an alternative. The battle that would at last define the legislative limits of the Irish parliament – and define them, to everybody's surprise, in Ireland's favour – began when the English ministry took its first steps towards implementing that alternative. The labyrinthine parliamentary process required after passage of the Declaratory Act slowed progress to a crawl on the proposal for 'a *Thing* they call a *Bank*', which Swift dismissed in a paragraph of his *Proposal*.[44] But when Grafton arrived in Ireland on 28 August 1721 he was equipped with a memorial summarising a series of meetings that had taken place in London in the summer of 1720. These meetings had discussed ways to 'make the government of Irelan d self-supporting and free of financial dependence on the Irish parliament'.[45]

What the Declaratory Act had begun, this action would have made absolute. The Irish parliament was not governed by the Septenniel Act which required regular meetings of, and elections for, the Westminster parliament. If some way could have been found to secure sufficient monies to operate the Irish administration independently of Irish tax sources, the Irish parliament could have been prorogued and placed on permanent leave.[46]

For a brief while this idea actually appeared to be a political and economic possibility. Burns recounts with detail and clarity the whole sequence of events, as well as the continuing Irish opposition to the Declaratory Act which encouraged London to try to prorogue the Irish parliament as quickly as possible and for as long as possible. Simultaneously, there was a fortuitous convergence of 'flourishing . . . Irish revenues' with the submission of two proposals to the government, fees from which could have been used to balance the Irish budget. Meanwhile, Britain worked to eliminate the relatively paltry £80,000 discrepancy between 1719's operating costs and non-tax generated revenue. One of the proposals submitted to Westminster called for the chartering of a fire insurance group for Ireland, with the backers of this scheme offering the government £100,000 for a charter. The other proposal called for the creation of a Bank of Ireland, and here there were two competing groups petitioning for the charter, each offering the government £50,000. The government was thus looking at a windfall of at least £150,000, and when it combined this with a plan to reduce and restructure the British army's Irish garrison, there was an anticipated administrative surplus of £10,000 per annum, with £150,000 or more set aside for contingencies.[47] All these circumstances meant that in July 1720 the English government believed it had a very real chance of effectively being able to abolish the Irish parliament.

The bills required for such plans had been under discussion throughout 1720, and in Dublin the administration had already begun to discuss what acts of patronage would be required to secure passage of the insurance and bank bills. Then, as with so much that happened in 1720 and 1721, the puncture of the South Sea Bubble intervened. The Bubble had been created when a trading conglomerate, the South Sea Company, had effectively offered to assume the national debt in return for exclusive trading rights across half the planet. At first, the scheme seemed to be working successfully and shares rose from 129*d* each to 1,100*d* in seven months; anyone with either a line of credit or cash on hand invested in the stock. Then, in three weeks in August 1720, the bottom fell out of the market and shares collapsed precipitously to 185d. Besides bankrupting thousands and straining the emerging credit economy to dangerous limits, the bursting of the South Sea Bubble shattered the British government's financial plans.

One consequence of the precarious financial situation after the collapse of the South Sea Company's stock, and of the Westminster parliament's immediate need for cash, was that schemes which earlier had been devised to render the Irish parliament financially irrelevant became vitally necessary tools as the government scrambled to refinance itself. The scheme to prorogue the Irish parliament indefinitely was put on hold, but plans for a fire insurance company and for a bank became even more attractive. Now, though, the £150,000 raised from the charters would go directly into the coffers at Westminster.

Word of plans in London had not been kept completely from the Irish. When Grafton arrived in Dublin in 1721 he brought with him legislation for the bank and insurance company that was destined to be met with stone-faced opposition. Grafton's situation was complicated by the British ministry's own confusion over the consequences of the Declaratory Act. After nearly a year of debate the government had only just decided that the bills needed to begin their passage into law in Dublin. Grafton arrived, then, with bills written in England, opposed by the Irish who believed them a further degradation of Irish power, and now supported in England in order to bail out the British government. Suddenly, money bills, which had usually passed both Irish houses of parliament almost unanimously, were a bone of contention.[48]

While still in England, Grafton had begun to move to secure passage of the bill authorising establishment of a national bank and, in January 1721, Lords Midleton and Connolly had urged approval of the bank in their capacity as lords justice. In light of later arguments, it is significant that their appeal was based on the 'general want of specie and decay of trade in Ireland'.[49] Their justification for the bank was couched in exactly the same language that William Wood's supporters would use in the debate over the half-penny. The bank debate now beginning and the next great financial argument in Ireland were to be inextricably connected. Lack of specie, and the increasingly pitiful state of much of the Irish economy, would be a constant source of propaganda on both sides throughout the ensuing years. Plans for the bank were neither new nor unknown, as Swift's dismissive reference to the scheme in his *Proposal* indicates, and Archbishop King was on the attack even before Midleton and Connolly had given their blessing. Raising the cry of the nascent patriotic party, the archbishop warned on 30 September 1720 that the scheme would 'put it in the power of the few to cheat the whole kingdom, and bring . . . paper credit to the ruin of the nation'. Quick to join King in his opposition were his old allies Synge and Stearne.

Once the South Sea Bubble had burst and with the legislation finally before parliament in September 1721, King was able to help organise some sort of co-ordinated opposition to the scheme. One of the main arguments against the whole concept was that a central bank would concentrate money in the hands of a wealthy few, diminishing the influence of the cash-poor but land-rich, among whom could be numbered both a significant percentage of the bishops of the Church of Ireland and, crucially, many members of the lower house. Another complaint was that the low interest rates the bank would charge (about five per cent was the promise) threatened the rather more lucrative returns solvent landlords were getting from loaning money to their more impecunious peers. One or other of these arguments was likely to appeal to just about any member of either house. As with many economic issues few people really understood the arguments on either side, but there was growing opposition to the idea. This sentiment was encouraged by recent experiences in France and England with charter companies which had offered to support the government in return for monopolistic trading rights. As far as many could see, the charter for the Bank of Ireland and its plan to sell shares once the business was up and running was simply another such scheme. 'France had its Mississippi bubble and Britain its South Sea bubble', King wrote to Stearne on 5 October 1721. 'It is thought', he added mischievously, 'this Bubble will be Sufficient to do our business'. When the subject came to a vote in the lower house, the most notable performance was, in Burns' description, that of Clotworthy Upton who 'gave a long rambling incoherent presentation [against the bill] which few could follow and no one bothered to answer'.[50] And so the plan was defeated in the lower house.

In November, the House of Lords made clear its view of the subject, resorting to one of its favourite turns of phrase in resolving that the whole idea was 'Prejudicial and of Extream ill Consequence to this kingdom'.[51] In the course of the debate various curious pronouncements followed each other closely, not the least of which was Lord Midleton's discovery of 'an affair . . . of a pernicious nature', which turned out to be the bank itself.[52] A reversal of such a momentous nature could hardly be opposed by lesser placemen and the House of Lords sealed the fate of the scheme – a scheme in support of which an Irish-born rising star of the church, George Berkeley, privately distanced himself from his fellow clerics. More important, however, was that the two houses of parliament in Dublin had acted with consensus on a matter universally agreed to be of great importance to the administration in England. It was a crucial moment in the recovery of Irish parliamentary authority, the House of Commons having made the rare decision to put aside cronyism in favour of independent action.

Despite a year and a half of planning and the backing of the government in London, the bank bill had died in both Irish houses in less than three months. Having taken the bold step of opposing Westminster, Thomas Brodrick, brother of Lord Midleton, and Midleton's son, St John, both leading members of the House of Commons, were now compelled to work with Midleton to ensure their own future prosperity. For the first time, the anti-English bloc in the House of Lords had an effective conduit to the lower house. Disagreements would, of course, remain, but so powerful was this alliance to become that when the court did finally rid itself of Midleton as Lord Chancellor it made sure not to repeat the mistake of giving the job to another Irishman.

The bank bill fiasco cost Grafton his job and brought Lord Carteret over to Dublin as Lord Lieutenant. These developments were to define the terms of Swift's later involvement with the debate over Wood's patent. These terms were the re-emergence of the authority of the Irish parliament on fiscal matters; the forced recognition on Dublin Castle's part of the influence on parliament of the landlords and Anglican merchants, and the replacement of Grafton by a redoubtable politician whom Swift and others remembered from earlier administrations in England and in whom they were willing to place some trust. More importantly, the bank battle brought the arcana of specie and exchange rates into the public arena. Terms obscure even to many of those engaged in the debate were suddenly in daily use on both sides. Pamphleteers struggled to elucidate the almost incomprehensible; that they might not properly understand such things themselves did not much matter. The currency of arcane terminology combined with conventional ideas about land and power to provide Swift with an ideal environment in which to launch his later attack on the British half-penny.

The economic views espoused by Swift were firmly grounded in the theories of the seventeenth century and recapitulated ideas that had been shaped in a different economic climate. One of the more famous of Swift's near-contemporary commentators on economic theory is John Locke, now best remembered for his political and philosophical treatises. But as Patrick Hyde Kelly explains, economic theory for Locke was part of an overall philosophical consideration of moral precepts.[53] It is important, Kelly stresses, to remember that:

> The unquestioning assumption of earlier scholars that sixteenth-, seventeenth-, and early eighteenth-century writers were simply grasping with greater or lesser success after the categories which came to dominate [modern economic theories] . . . has given way

to a realisation that there is a radical discontinuity between the two forms of discourse.[54]

Writing on the cusp of that discontinuity, Swift instinctively looked back. Suspicious of new ideas, he shared a temperamental affinity with those who saw economic questions as a branch of moral philosophy, and so as quite distinct from the emerging mathematics based science of economics.

Swift's understanding of economics was not as simplistic as the above remarks suggest. Exactly how sophisticated his understanding of economics was is discussed at some length in James Kelly's essay 'Jonathan Swift and the Irish Economy in the 1720s'. What is most telling is the political line-up with which Swift's published ecomonic tracts sided. Coinage, as Swift knew but would overlook in *The Drapier's Letters*, was in short supply in Ireland, but mercantilist theory did not necessarily need to address that fact and both Molesworth, who was active in the British parliament on behalf of Irish interests, and Francis Hutchinson, Bishop of Down and Connor, among others, delivered lengthy analyses of the situation which came down to questions of how to employ the untapped labour pool in Ireland, a classic mer-cantilist position. Neither of them addressed issues of capital but both concentrated on the development of fisheries and the exploitation of natural resources.[55] Molesworth's *Some Considerations for Promoting the Agriculture of Ireland and Employing the Poor* (1723) and Hutchinson's *A Letter to a Member of Parliament Concerning the Imploying and Providing for the Poor* (1723) both considered the question of beggars and itinerants. As labour was the wealth of the nation in a simplified mercantilist theory, this concentration on the unemployed poor is not as surprising as it might seem. Molesworth thought it best to deport them, rather as modern economic theory would advocate shutting down loss-making industry or destroying counterfeit bills in order to increase total wealth – another fine example of how one man's moderation in one area does not necessarily make him a moderate in others. Hutchinson thought this extreme and suggested badging them instead, limiting their begging to their home parish, and finding them work on public projects. Swift would later support Hutchinson's plan to badge beggars, but in *The Drapier's Letters* he would address Molesworth in the third letter and describe *the Considerations* as 'an excellent discourse' in *Some Arguments Against Enlarging the Powers of the Bishops, in letting of Leases, with* Remarks *on some* Queries *Lately published*.[56]

Swift did understand many of the ramifications of the shortage of coin in Ireland, and in some of his analyses he demonstrates more sophistication than he was willing to admit to in the debate over the bank or Wood's half-pence. His instincts were conservative and backward looking, even as the evidence of his own eyes demonstrated to him the everyday hardships of the poor and trading classes. For the debate on the bank and the later *Drapier's Letters*, however, Swift was not principally engaged upon an economic argument, and his rhetoric would simplify the issues so that they could be better grasped by his intended audiences. In any case, Swift was still growing into the arguments that would shape his two most sophisticated economic arguments, *The Intelligencer* numbers 15 and 19.

The writers who were developing the fundamental assumptions that characterise modern economic theory found little they wished to preserve in the mercantilist works of Locke and his colleagues. Indeed, 'in referring to Locke's pamphlets on money, Harris, Massie, and Steuart, all spoke of the incoherence and lack of organisation in his work, despite flashes of insight'.[57] If Locke was deemed 'incoherent' by the advocates of the nascent science of economic theory, it is not surprising that the majority of contributors to popular debate on economic matters hardly began to understand the issues with which they were grappling. In Ireland's case, and fortuitously for Swift, popular understandings of mercantilism were based on precisely the sort of 'incoherence and lack of organisation' that could be readily adapted for popular political pamphlets. 'Mercantilism was far more a defensive system than a positive prescription for economic growth', dedicated to an 'apparently obsessive concern with increasing the national stock of precious metals', writes Kelly:

> Its assumptions . . . had grown out of perception of the depressing effects of inadequate monetary circulation in times of crisis, manifested in collapsing prices, labourers laid off, bankruptcies amongst merchants, and resultant poverty and weakness in the state.[58]

In effect, the mercantilists argued against change not because the existing system was perfect or perhaps even perfectible but because the alternatives were guaranteed to be catastrophic.

Such hard-headed acceptance of reality and rejection of wishful theorising appealed to Swift, and in Ireland such sentiments were more fiercely held than in England because history had regularly reminded the Anglicans of what happened when the rules of mercantilism were ignored. Indeed, Ireland's situation was even used in Britain as a model of what happened when mercantile precepts were flouted. In *Some Considerations of the Consequences of the Lowering of Interest, and Raising the Value of* MONEY, *In a Letter sent to a Member of Parliament, 1691,* Locke had specifically cited Ireland under James II's administration. 'The *quantity* of pure Silver separable from the Alloy, makes the real *value* of Money', Locke asserts, and he provides a proof that would haunt Ireland far into the eighteenth century:

> If it does not, Coin Copper with the same Stamp and denomi-nation, and see whether it will be of the same value. I suspect your Stamp will make it of no more worth, than the Copper-Money of *Ireland* is, which is its weight in Copper, and no more. That Money lost so much to *Ireland,* as it passed for above the rate of Copper. But yet I think no body suffered so much by it as he, by whose Authority it was made current.[59]

It is not hard to spot in Locke's example the complaint of King in his *State of Protestants in Ireland* that James II had designed his actions to deprive Protestants 'of their estates and improvements and send them to die or beg'.[60] Swift was so impressed by this argument that he used it in the second of *The Drapier's Letters* when considering what would happen if debased coinage were in circulation:

> The *farmers* must *rob* or *beg,* or leave their *country.* The *shopkeepers* in this and every other town, must *break* and *starve;* for it is the *landed man* that maintains the *merchant,* and *shopkeeper,* and *handicraftsman.*[61]

Anglican Ireland did not need to search far to find financial ruin and the threat of the Stuarts behind schemes for paper money and base-metal coinage.

For Swift, an added attraction of the mercantilist position was its fundamental intertwining of money, morality and natural law. Kelly makes it clear that:

> [t]he case which Locke advances for maintaining the existing monetary standard . . . rests partly on ethical considerations (par-ticularly the fraud resulting from the invasion of contract) and partly on technical ones. . . . [E]thical and technical considerations reinforce each other in the context of natural law.[62]

In addition to common sense and popular opinion, then, Swift was able to deploy righteous indignation against those who would overturn the basis upon which a nation's prosperity was built. The pamphlets of the bank opponents would allow Swift to present his own, later appeals to the 'Whole People of Ireland' with the economic debate already suitably simplified for public consumption.

There were a considerable number of tracts published on either side, but the leading pamphlet writers in the debate over the Bank of Ireland were Henry Maxwell, a potential governor of the bank, in favour, and Hercules Rowley, MP for Londonderry, opposed. Maxwell was handicapped by his unapologetic honesty, Rowley by a style that bordered on the incoherent and the apocalyptic. Ultimately, this contrast in styles left Rowley with a considerable advantage, for what Maxwell gained in clarity and coherence he lost to a popular imagination well acquainted with the ever present threat of catastrophe. Additionally, Maxwell was ahead of his time, perhaps the first writer on Irish economic affairs to move beyond the prevalent mercantilist certainties. He did, though, understand some of the political necessities of debate, and his *Reasons Offered for Erecting a Bank in Ireland* initially address the many Irish landowners who were in debt. Under the terms of the proposed charter, Maxwell stresses, the bank would be obliged 'not to tackle more than five per cent interest for lending or discounting'.[63]

The backbone of Maxwell's treatise is that lower interest rates would make it 'better husbandry to improve than purchase' land.[64] Such improvements would lead to flourishing trade and growth in the artisan sectors as the demand for goods and services increased. In time, Maxwell argues, 'our poor would have full employment, our country would be populous, and our inhabitants industrious'.[65] Maxwell was committed to Ireland's improvement, but it is indicative of the still indeterminate nature of economic theory that while he put development of industry and trade ahead of land values, he defended that approach with mercantilist analyses of population and land use.

Unfortunately for his cause, Maxwell would appear to have been a man unable to let a good idea alone once it had reached its most pertinent political simplification: 'Erecting a bank could and would lower interest rates' across the board because 'the interest taken by the bank will govern the interest of the nation *without a law*'.[66] If Maxwell's disarmingly honest development of the consequences of having a strong central bank was well grounded in economic theory, it was also precisely the type of political argument that could only further alarm Irishmen who already had grave doubts about English intentions. It was to this fear of further English encroachment that Rowley devoted most of his attention, concerning himself hardly at all with economic matters.

Rowley early on invoked Ireland's relationship with England, beginning his *Answer to a Book Entitled 'Reasons Offered for Erecting a Bank in Ireland'* with a profoundly cynical remark that has nothing to do with economics and everything to do with political sentiment:

> If the intended *Bank* prove advantageous to us by increasing our trade and encouraging our manufactures – and should in the least interfere with or hinder the trade of *England*, then we may expect they will procure a Repeal of the Charter, and so cramp our trade and discourage our manufactures as to render them impracticable. If it happens to impoverish us, and drain our little substance into *Great Britain*, then indeed we may be sure of a continuation.[67]

While it was bad enough that Ireland's future was inextricably to be linked to England's whim, there was worse to come. Irish law, Rowley argued, meant '[t]he Papists cannot purchase lands and are at a loss how to lay out their money', and so '[t]hey will buy Bank Stock and get control of the Bank to the weakening of the Protestant interest'.[68] Rowley well knew his audience when he combined Anglican Ireland's resentment of English encroachment with their great fear of Catholic power. It did not matter that the sum total of Catholic wealth in no manner approached even a fraction of the capital of the proposed bank.

Rowley's one attempt at economic reasoning well demonstrates the mercantilist position from which Swift would later build his own opposition to Wood's monetary schemes:

> Whenever the importation of consumable commodities destroyed at home exceeds the exportation of the manufactured or unmanu- factured products of any country, then it must be daily impov- erished. Lessening our Importations and encouraging our manufactures would feed the hungry, clothe the naked and relieve the oppressed.[69]

It would also obviate the need for schemes such as Molesworth's and Hutchinson's for dealing with the poor. This had been the implication behind Swift's arguments in his *Proposal for the Universal Use of Irish Manufacture*. It would be the basis of much of the rest of his 'Irish' works, and is perhaps best encapsulated in his 1728 essay, *A Short View of the State of Ireland*, which depends upon the observation that:

The first Cause of a Kingdom's thriving, is the Fruitfulness of the Soil, to produce the Necessaries and Conveniencies of Life; not only sufficient for the Inhabitants, but for Exportation into other Countries.[70]

Swift's one significant contribution to the bank debate came in the form of *A Letter from a Lady in Town*, which appeared 'by a satisfying coincidence . . . on the very day the Irish Houses defeated a bill to introduce the bank'.[71] This was not the first time Swift had published a pamphlet once the outcome of the debate was already known, seeking to link his work with events already determined. But Swift's delay was not just a consequence of his own preoccupations. The bank matter did to some extent confuse him. Despite his earlier dealings with the vicars choral, Lord Abercorn, a proposed governor of the bank, was a staunch friend of the Church of Ireland, and Bishop Evans, whom Swift despised above all other transplanted clerics, was as staunchly against the bank as was King. In addition, Swift's own doubts about the ability of the Irish to fight for their best interests were steadily increasing. 'I hear you are likely to be the sole Opposer of the Bank', he had written to King on 28 September 1721. '[Y]ou will certainly miscarry', he continued, because 'Bankrupts are always for setting up Banks: How then can you think a Bank will fail of a Majority in both Houses?'.[72] The next week, King reported to Stearne that Swift had 'offered to lay me five guineas . . . the bill would pass, for a good natural reason . . . that it was for private advantage and public mischief'.[73]

King's opposition to the administration in Dublin Castle had been so consistent it could no longer be ignored, so when the Duke of Bolton left Ireland in late 1720 he omitted King from the appointments to lords justice. In a letter of May 1721 to Chetwode, Swift had reported that 'few persons have less credit with the present powers than the Archbishop'.[74] Swift's pessimism was by now considerable. Even allowing for some degree of dissembling, his letter to Chetwode after the bill had been killed is noticeable for its lack of presumption that he had had much to do with defeating the idea. In fact, Swift wrote with scathing sarcasm that 'I thought a bank ought to be established and would be so because it was the only ruinous thing wanting to the kingdom, and therefore I had not the least doubt but that the parliament would pass it'.[75] Much of the credit for the defeat, Swift suggested, should go to Rowley who produced the best pamphlet on the matter, 'though he was not thought to have many talents for an author'.[76]

Besides the *Letter from a Lady*, Swift's most extended consideration of the matter was a poem, 'The Bank Thrown Down', also published after the project had been defeated. Several anonymous pamphlets written about the bank have been attributed to Swift at some time or another, but it is indicative of his profile throughout the debate that most of those pamphlets wrongly attributed to Swift were published after the conclusion was apparent.[77] One of the pamphlets attributed to Swift was the *Subscribers to the Bank Plac'd according to Their Order and Quality*. Whoever the author, its analysis provides the clearest contemporary example of just how far the realignment in Irish politics had proceeded. Published in December 1721, when the bank had already failed, the analysis is typical of Swift, justifying opposition to the bank by an appeal to traditional values. The whole is essentially a listing of the position and titles of those supporting the bank. It must have been with some excitement that the writer realised he could begin with the following list of supporters of the scheme:

Arch Bishops	0
Marquisses	0
Earls	0
Bishops	2[78]

This was exactly the sort of analysis guaranteed to appeal to someone more interested in defending traditional social assumptions than in defeating the bank on its merits. Importantly, the *Subscribers to the Bank* cements the link between the church, commitment to the land and the general welfare of the people of Ireland. After establishing the identity of all but twenty-eight of the 201 subscribers to the bank, all but a handful of whom were merchants or speculators rather than landowners, the writer reminds his readers that there are 2,000,000 people in Ireland and 16,800,000 acres of land.[79] The implication is clear: those closest to the land and therefore those best suited to protect the welfare of the country, were firmly opposed to the bank. Pamphlets such as *Subscribers to the Bank* helped cement in the public mind the link between church, land and opposition to English encroachments. Opposition to credit and, by implication, to base coinage by an analysis not of wealth but of labour was precisely the framework Swift would build upon to forge the consensus he sought in the debate over Wood's copper coinage. Yet it was not until after the debate was won that Swift could safely seek to turn the political victory of an emerging Anglican Irish identity into a conservative's trumpeting of traditional values.

Even as he opposed most of what men such as Connolly and Midleton stood for, Swift waited for an opportunity to adopt their language to build a broad coalition for his own schemes. In the aftermath of the success of parliamentary opposition to the Bank of Ireland, however, the secular interests in parliament turned their attention back to their old quarrel with the church over who should set rents and define land-use policy. Just as a coalition Swift could have welcomed seemed to be forming, the church–Commons stand-off returned to dominate domestic Irish politics. Luckily for Swift, and perhaps for the church as a whole, the government in England had already embarked on yet another scheme that would unite the various Irish factions. This time, the debate would last long enough, and be pressing enough to the Anglican tradesmen and artisans, for Swift to be able to manipulate the rhetoric to create his most accomplished defence of the church's rights and privileges under the guise of an appeal to secular interests. In doing so, he would draw heavily upon the various arguments against the bank with which the public was now familiar.

CHAPTER SIX

'The struggle for control of rents': the Commons takes on the church

I

[T]he Man that studies to oppress the whole World in Servitude, and Bring it under the Power of that Nation to which he belongs, this Man is truly wicked and unworthy of Success, however he may veil his Ambition, Pride, and Fury in some particular Instances, under the specious pretence of Clemency and Love of his Country.

Archbishop William King[1]

It was a peculiar felicity of the government in London during the first decade of King George I's reign that whenever it was about to conclude a particularly unpopular item of restrictive legislation concerning Ireland it would choose that time to introduce a new and even more restrictive legislative proposal to the Irish. Just as the bank scheme had followed hot on the heels of the Declaratory Act, so even as the bank proposal was suffering defeat the government in London was preparing to bless a plan to allow William Wood, a Midlands ironmonger, to coin a new, base-metal half-penny for use in Ireland.

Yet the Whig ministry was culpable more of cowardice than of either venality or anti-Irish sentiment on the matter of the patent to be granted to Wood. In 1718 Wood had made the acquaintance of the Duchess of Kendal, whose chief attribute in his eyes was her illicit but widely acknowledged relationship with George I.[2] What Wood wanted was simple: to profit from Ireland's need for coinage. His proposal, based as it was on greed, was of exactly the sort that Irishmen feared motivated all English business dealings with Ireland. For a substantial fee, Kendal agreed to use her influence to get Wood the patent to coin copper money for Ireland. She approached the First Lord of the

Treasury, the Earl of Sunderland, who was the son-in-law of the Duchess of Marlborough and who had been the first Hanoverian Whig appointed Lord Lieutenant of Ireland. He in turn saw an opportunity to bolster his own tottering ministry and assented to Wood's request for a patent.[3]

The irony of what would later ensue is that few people denied Ireland's legitimate need of coinage. Midleton and Connolly had both defended their initial support of the bank scheme by highlighting Ireland's want of specie. Johnston provides graphic, and at times harrowing, accounts of the consequences of the Irish fiscal crunch in his introduction to *The Querist*.[4] In Ireland, as in much of Europe, coinage from various countries was accepted as legal tender and Portuguese, Austrian and Dutch coins all circulated freely in Swift's time, their value dependent on metal content and occasionally defined by legislative action. Unlike most countries, however, Ireland did not have its own mint and so had no way of efficiently ensuring a useful mix in the coinage available at any time. An additional misfortune was that the value of gold coins was greater in Ireland than in many other countries, leading to an influx of gold. Silver went the other way, for it was more valuable abroad than in Ireland. The problem with such arrangements was that gold coins could not be used for small, day-to-day transactions because of their relatively high value. Consequently, credit was already a staple of much Irish business – the very principle to which the opponents of the bank scheme had objected most strongly. During the debate over Wood's patent, the reliably Whig English newspaper, *The Postboy*, would remind its readers that before the patent was granted:

> there was the utmost Necessity for Copper Money . . . ; so that some Gentlemen who employ hundreds of the Poor [in Ireland], were forc'd to tally with their Workmen, and give them Bits of Cards with their Seal on one Side, and their Names on the other.[5]

Johnston's analysis of rents in Ireland at that time shows that a Trinity College, Dublin-owned estate in Co. Carlow was let for 4s 5d per acre in 1705.[6] Thomas Prior's *Observation on Coin* (1729) noted that with silver and guineas exported to England, Ireland was 'reduced to moidores [a Portuguese gold coin], the most inconvenient coin of all'.[7] The moidore was valued at £1 10s. In other words, you could rent about four acres of farmland in Co. Carlow in exchange for the *coin* most widely circulated in Ireland. No wonder small transactions required IOUs.

Another measure of the steady depletion of Ireland's currency reserves comes in Swift's own 1727 reflections, *A Short View of the State of Ireland*. Setting aside the irony of the fact that three years earlier he had made his name opposing plans that were only possible because of the shortage of specie, the tract is perceptive in its recognition that Ireland's trouble lay in:

> *Bankers* . . . who, for their private Advantage, have sent away all our Silver, and one Third of our Gold; so that within three Years past, the running Cash of the Nation, which was about five Hundred Thousand Pounds, is now less than two; and must daily diminish, unless we have Liberty to coin, as well as that important Kingdom the Isle of *Man*; and the meanest Prince in the *German* Empire . . . [8]

Ireland's financial worries were not always appreciated in England. One reason for persistent English assumptions of Ireland's prosperity in this period was the vast amount of currency from Ireland in circulation in England. The weakness of Ireland's economy meant that there was a consistent gap between the value of coins in Ireland and in England. Irish landlords resident in England were obliged to collect an ever-increasing number of coins in rent in Ireland, simply to preserve their standard of living in England. Actually a consequence of devaluation, this seemingly ready supply of money nonetheless implied prosperity to those unable, or unwilling, to consider the economic reality behind the appearance. In addition to the outflow of silver, the British East India Company sought to acquire from Ireland as much foreign coinage as it could – coinage it then reused in the country of origin or in colonial trade at a favourable exchange rate. Even as Irish merchants struggled to find tender small enough to make change, and as workmen were paid in IOUs, English merchant houses and banks were often awash in coins from Ireland.

So vague was the English understanding of Ireland's plight, Swift was obliged to remind Adrian Drift, secretary to the recently deceased Matthew Prior, that accounts of Irish subscriptions to Prior's verse were in local currency, where 'a guinea is one pound three shillings', a discount rate of thirteen per cent.[9] Swift also promised in the same letter (3 February 1722) to 'gather up the money [owed] as fast as I can, and have it sent as specie by some friend'.[10] So tenuous was Ireland's financial situation, Swift felt it necessary to reassure his correspondent that the money he received would be in a form exchangeable for its precious metal content.[11]

By the time of Prior's death, the mercantile system in England had already been largely overwhelmed by the increasing reliance of the country upon credit secured by anticipated income. Public policy was increasingly directed toward establishing what we can now recognise as a modern economic system. A booming export trade had been fostered by a series of laws which included those that restricted Ireland's commerce. At the same time, there had been significant growth in both private companies conducting this trade and, as a result of European wars, a marked increase in public credit. D.W. Jones provides an extensive overview of the precipitous growth in English trade, and in public debt, following William III's accession. Jones argues that England's explosive growth was largely fuelled by overseas military adventures.[12] A prolonged domestic peace and the coronation of George I, who brought with him the military alliances entered into while he was Elector Palatine in Hanover, only accelerated the pace of economic growth. Thomas Horne's examination of why Sir Bernard Mandeville held mercantilism in contempt notes that the amount of capital invested in publicly traded 'companies increased . . . from £4 million in 1695 to £20 million in 1717 to £50 million in 1720'.[13]

At the same time, investors had begun to push schemes for fire and, later, marine insurance companies. Lorraine Daston records both the emergence of schemes that have survived to modern times and the frenzy of activity around what we would now consider gambling.[14] Modern insurance schemes grew out of the reorganisation of the mathematics of probability in the seventeenth century. The first fire insurance scheme was proposed in 1680, Daston notes, and 'the Amicable Society for mutual insurance of lives was established in 1706'.[15] One major supporter of such schemes was Defoe, who envisioned a world in which 'all the Contingencies of Life might be Fenc'd against by this Method (as Fire already is) as Thieves, Floods by Land, Storms by Sea, Losses of all Sorts and Death it self'.[16]

The need to pay for wars in Europe, and the growth of the new merchant and trading classes, led to an enormous shift in land ownership in Britain between 1680 and 1740, with the largest land-holders benefitting at the expense of the smaller ones.[17] 'The taxes levied by the government . . . fell most heavily on land and on those who drew their entire income from rents', says Horne, highlighting one of the principal strains within the economic system of the period. Consequently, the larger landowners, who could also derive income from government positions or from other sources, fared better than the smaller landowners. This trend was reinforced by the growth in both private joint stock companies and the government's enormous offerings of public credit at a secured rate of about six per cent. It was this stress in Britain's economic system that had won the Tories the 1710 election (with help from the Sacheverell trial), but the overall trend was unstoppable: that election had been the last gasp of an already over-extended squirearchy. Land was no longer the principal source of income for those driving the economy; rather, possession of large tracts of land was now a way of demonstrating sufficient income from other sources to support such holdings.

In Ireland, however, economic change on this scale had yet to arrive. On his return to Ireland, Swift found a society still largely operating along lines he had yearned to recreate in England. Land was still the source of wealth, the principal employer of labour, and the basis of what indigenous political power remained. But changes in British law, driven by the need to protect trade, were increasingly undermining what remained of Ireland's economic life. Following the ideas which had earlier sought to prevent agricultural competition between Ireland and England, legislation now denied Irish businessmen the opportunity to invest in many of the industrial and trading opportunities that had led to economic growth in England. They could, at best, become middlemen, supplying raw goods to England. The Irish were compelled to try to make mercantilism work in the face of a trading partner with monopolistic claims on their trade and with access to their money. This could only weaken a system which, as Robert Ekelund and Robert Tollison have demonstrated can, at its heart, be identified as driving a 'rent-seeking society'.[18] Irish political interests were increasingly confronting each other over control of a steadily shrinking pie, a confrontation temporarily set aside each time Westminster unveiled some new economically egregious proposal for Ireland.

It was against this backdrop that the proposal to grant William Wood a patent to mint copper coinage quietly began its life in 1718. It was reinvigorated in 1721 when the British government, stunned by the collapse of the South Sea Bubble, turned to Robert Walpole. Walpole, who needed Kendal's support as he tried to build a government from the wreckage of the Bubble, rediscovered the deal struck with Sunderland on Wood's behalf and found himself obliged to pursue the patent.[19]

There was much wrong with Wood's proposal, not the least of which was its venality, but the idea of minting base-metal coins was not new. Such coins existed in many countries in Europe, but were not exportable, and had surfaced from time to time in England and Ireland. In England, the growth of paper money and paper credit had increased acceptance of the idea that money could exist with a face value not related to its metal content so long as that money was backed by a trusted holder of sufficient silver and gold supplies. Ironically, however, there was so much specie in England in the early eighteenth century there was no need for base-metal coins. That this was not the case in Ireland did not necessarily make it palatable to the Irish that they should have thrust upon them from England a debased coinage. The reasons for opposition were several, but they would boil down to this: Ireland required precious metal for purchases of all its imports. Because of British trade sanctions and Ireland's dependence upon land rather than manufacture, most of the goods in everyday use had to be imported. As a result, there was a legitimate fear that an oversupply of copper, while useful for domestic trade, might beggar the country as importers carried the remaining gold and silver away, further denuding Ireland of the precious metals it needed to buy its wares.

What Walpole and the other English ministers could little understand was that economic changes in England had not also occurred in Ireland. What they were about to discover was that debate over the patent could not be manipulated along traditional 'English' versus 'Irish' party lines. The terms of debate were going to be dictated by economic principles and, given the state of Ireland's economy, there was little English politicians could have done to help their cause. Indeed, even England's staunchest supporter in the Irish House of Commons, William Conolly (no relation to Lord Connolly of the bank scheme), would prove unable to control his parliamentary faction despite almost unlimited access to patronage.

Conolly seems to have understood the situation from the start. His political fortunes were entirely dependent upon English goodwill, for unlike Lord Midleton and the rest of the Brodrick family, Conolly was from a poor background and had no domestic political base upon which to fall back. He could not himself oppose the patent, but he was in a position to operate behind the scenes to try to kill the idea before he had to vote on it. One of the first steps required to secure passage of the newly resurrected scheme was a report from the Irish Commissioners of the Revenue, who were responsible for overseeing the money supply. The commissioners were appointed by Westminster but were effectively the hand-picked choices of Conolly, as dependent upon him as he was upon Dublin Castle. They hired no less a person than Humphrey French, confidante of Archbishop King, as agent to represent them in London. Working through appointees of the crown, Conolly secured the services of a friend of the most vocal of all the 'Irish' party men, a man who had a voice not only in the pulpit and in the House of Lords, but also in the Privy Council.

It is an indication of how little regard the English administration then paid to Irish affairs that Walpole failed to notice that his chief ally in Ireland was siding, albeit discreetly, with one of his most powerful opponents. Even Conolly could not bring himself to support a scheme so potentially ruinous to an economy which no longer bore even a theoretical resemblance to Britain's. Sinecures and patronage aside, Conolly was not about to jeopardise an estate estimated at £15,000 per annum in 1724.[20] Nor was he willing to endanger the fortune with which he was building what would be the first of the Irish 'big houses', a house Berkeley had described to his patron Sir John Percival in 1722:

> The most remarkable thing now going on is a house of Mr Conolly's at Castletown. It is 142 feet in front, and above 60 deep in the clear, the height will be about 70. It is to be of fine wrought stone, harder and better coloured than the Portland . . . The plan is chiefly of Mr Conolly's invention, however, in some points they are pleased to consult me. I hope it will be an ornament to the country.[21]

Preening and a certain braggadocio notwithstanding, Conolly was investing in Castletown because that was where he thought to find financial security.

Wood's patent was destined to encounter resistance because of its challenge to the value of land and so to most of the wealth in Ireland. This was something Swift understood only too well, and it was an issue that would clearly cross party political lines. But this golden opportunity would be forced to await Swift's attentions until it was all but over, for the dean of St Patrick's was occupied with another land-use debate, one that grew from the very heart of mercantilist theories. It was a debate that would lead to a temporary alliance at least as unlikely as the Conolly–King understanding. In an argument over the regulation of church-land leases, Swift was just about to find himself siding with Bishop Evans of Meath and opposing William King. The debate of 1722 and 1723, which kept Swift's attention away from the question of Wood's patent, was very much concerned with those vital church interests that would later lead him to join the assault on Wood. In his battles of 1722, 1723 and 1724, Swift reached the climax of his defence of the established church. The logic of his opposition to King on church leases would lead him naturally to join that same archbishop's ardent opposition to William Wood's plans for Ireland.

II

> For my own part, I entirely agree with your Grace, that a free
> Man ought not to confine his Converse to any one Party;
> neither would I do so, if I were free.
>
> Jonathan Swift to Archbishop King, 28 March 1713

It is now often forgotten that even during the flurry of activity surrounding the Declaratory Act and then Wood's patent, the Irish parliament was also employed legislating on domestic affairs. The House of Commons in Dublin was controlled by a handful of individuals who, whether they lived in Ireland or in England, relied upon the land for a large portion of their income. It was a situation that had inevitably led throughout the years to a series of skirmishes between the controllers of the Commons and the largest landholder in Ireland, the Church of Ireland. This had been directly responsible for passage of the Declaratory Act.

The Church of Ireland, like its established counterparts elsewhere in Europe, relied upon two principal sources of income – tithes and rents. Crucially, two factors distinguished the Church of Ireland from its English counterpart. Irish bishops did not have the access to other investment opportunities, or to government sinecures, that had allowed the Church of England bishops to steadily diversify the sources of their income. Additionally, in one of those historical accidents that combined cultural identity with legislative oversight, the Church of Ireland's rights as a landholder were far greater than the corresponding protections granted the Church of England. For hundreds of years, Anglican establishment in Ireland had been an essential social as well as legislative counterweight to Catholic Ireland's assertions. The Church of Ireland, therefore, had been protected from some of the social pressures that had eroded the Church of England's position in society. This erosion was inevitably escalated by the presence after 1707 of a second established church, the Scottish Presbyterian Kirk, within the United Kingdom. In Ireland, laws of Charles I designed to protect the established church were still on the books in 1720.

The most important function of these laws, as far as both the church and its civil opponents were concerned, was the protection of the value of church-owned land. In *Swift and the Church of Ireland*, Landa gives a clear summary of that protection:

> The statute of Charles I – the 'great Magna Charta for our Church
> Revenues', as Swift's enemy, Bishop Evans of Meath called it –

contained two valuable clauses. One of these prevented bishops and ecclesiastical corporations from giving leases for a period longer than twenty-one years. Its intention was to prevent a greedy prelate from injuring a successor by a long lease . . . In such a transaction the incumbent bishop, who received the [steep fee associated with such long leases] naturally profited;[22] but if the lease extended into the incumbency of a successor that successor suffered, being saddled with a lease of low annual return . . . The second clause of the statute . . . provided that see lands be leased at not less than one-half their real value at the time the lease was made . . . [I]t meant that the Church as owner of lands always participated in the rise in value of those lands.[23]

Landa reminds us that the second of those two clauses was more often observed in the breach than in the practice, and even the first clause was not strictly adhered to, but 'the statutes [were] a comfort to clerical landlords'.[24] At times, the statutes could also provide legal recourse for the clerics.

The dependence of the upper echelons of Irish civil society upon land for their income ensured constant friction between church and secular powers, even as the big landholders who rented from the bishops promptly re-rented that land one, two or even three times at steadily increasing rents, *'screwing* and *racking* their Tenants all over the Kingdom', as Swift noted in his *Proposal for the Universal Use of Irish Manufacture*.[25] Indeed, Swift's lobbying for remission of the First Fruits and Twentieth Parts had been based on the Church of Ireland's need to use those revenues in order to establish a trust fund for the restoration and improvement of church property. One cause of the need for that trust fund was the Irish House of Commons' steady refusal to provide the Church of Ireland additional glebes and small holdings attached to the churches in order not to further increase church control over the land. To restore the physical infrastructure, the Church of Ireland had been compelled to turn to the monarch for relief and Swift had been one of its envoys to London. Fifteen years later, he was again to find himself busy protecting the right of the church to secure its financial well-being.

With the bank scheme now securely dead and Wood's patent still making its painful way through the English parliamentary machinery, the Irish House of Commons turned its attention to its members' desire to rid themselves of those bothersome statutes of Charles I. There had been a series of minor skirmishes in the years leading up to 1723 – skirmishes which Archbishop King had been able to win in the

Privy Council. However, in 1723 the dam broke and the House of Commons introduced a bill disingenuously designated an 'Act for the Preservation of the Inheritance, Rights and Profits of Lands belonging to the Church and Persons Ecclesiastical'. The cornerstone of the proposed legislation was designed to turn the most crucial of Charles I's acts upon its head, citing the 'pernicious' nature of a law which meant that every twenty-one years a landholder could suddenly find his rent increased by any amount necessary to raise the rent to at least half its current real value.

Instead, the Commons proposed, bishops should be permitted to reset the rent at no more than the highest annual rent set anytime in the preceding twenty years. This would effectively freeze rents and prevent the church from sharing in the benefits of increasing land values. Furthermore, the Commons suggested, bishops should be allowed to set leases for longer than the current twenty-one year limit. In return for this, the bishop setting the lease could receive a far greater fine than current practice allowed. The upshot of this, as the clerical bench in the House of Lords realised to a man, would be devastating to church interests. If a venal bishop decided to set a long lease and pocket a high fine for his own benefit, a successor cleric thirty, forty or more years later could find himself not only with an income from the land far below its actual value, but also obliged to renew the lease at that level. Twenty-one year leases were traditionally set on a graded scale, with rent for the first seven years being less than for the next seven, and the final seven years of the lease being the highest. The Commons' plan would have meant that the renewed lease could at no stage be for a higher rent than one that had been asked in the preceding twenty years.[26]

It is important to recognise the particular danger the church understood in this bill, and also to appreciate the cynicism of the Commons. The church would have been compelled, in fairly short order, to rely upon the generosity of the state for its operation, whereas in 1723 it was still a self-sufficient organisation supporting itself from its rental and tithed income, unlike its English counterpart. In addition, the bill would have meant very real reductions in rental income because there was no suggestion that the fixed rent would take account of inflation; that is, a rent set at £100 per annum in 1723 could have been renewed at no more than £100 when it next came up for renewal – not the equivalent of £100 in 1723 terms, but the actual face value. As a last straw, there were to be no equivalent restrictions upon the rents, or their duration, which could be levied by those subletting the land they held from the church. So as church income fell, the margin accruing to those who rackrented the land would increase. The members of the House of Commons would inevitably gain in wealth as the churchmen became steadily poorer.

It was, as Landa notes, a bill designed to appeal to the 'cupidity of the present bishops by offering them the opportunity . . . of pocketing large fines'.[27] That the bishops resisted this temptation to a man does not mean that the House of Commons might not have been justified in expecting this appeal to succeed. Wondering why he should bother to become Bishop of Derry, William Nicolson, then the Bishop of Carlisle, had written on 31 January 1717 to Wake, dwelling on the financial attractions of the see. He noted that it would be worth £2,400 per annum 'beside fines', and admitted that the money was important, because:

> The circumstances of my poor family do indeed call (loudly enough) for a better support than I can afford them. I have four daughters unmarried, the youngest whereof is in her sixteenth year; and I am sometimes troubled (God forgive me!) that I cannot furnish . . . portions proper for their respective settlements in the world.[28]

Nicolson's reluctance was not so much financial as it was concerned with his age, but expressions of monetary interest such as this gave the House of Commons hope that at least some bishops might support its bill. And as the events culminating in the Declaratory Act had demonstrated, on matters of land rights the Commons could count on the support of an overwhelming majority of the lay peers.

It was not just Nicolson's concern with money that gave the Commons reason to hope that the bishops would succumb to personal greed. They could find plenty of evidence of such greed in the actions of Bishop Evans himself, actions which were promptly magnified by the propaganda efforts of clerical opponents such as Swift and King. Evans recorded in a letter of 23 May 1718 to Wake that he had arrived in Meath to find the value of his land 'double . . . what it was thirty years ago', but the rent unchanged. Evans sought to raise the rent on land which had previously been leased to Henry St George (coincidentally a relative of Swift's old friend, St George Ashe) at £200 per annum for 13,000 acres. St George refused to pay another penny and Evans began legal proceedings against him after first finding a willing tenant, pending St George's eviction. Evans was acting in full compliance with the law, but part of the deal he cut with St George's would-be successor was payment of a substantial fine. It was not hard for others to see in Evans' actions the machinations of a greedy man.

Evans lost the case in court, thanks to a jury stacked against him by friends of St George, but in late April 1722 he was able to secure victory by virtue of a decree from Ireland's chief legal officer (appointed, of course, by Westminster). It was against this background that the House of Commons moved in 1723. Despite precedent, they probably hoped for at least the acquiescence of William King, who had been pursuing his own policies as a landlord – policies designed to keep the English out of Irish bishoprics.

King was famous within Ireland for letting his entailed land at far less than it could have commanded. He did this, at times, that better husbandry might be encouraged. Swift would acknowledge this in his 1727 'Excellent New Song upon His Grace Our Good Lord Archbishop of Dublin', noting that 'firmness to the public good . . . / Has lost His Grace for ten years past ten thousand pounds'.[29] King had long understood that the anti-Popery laws which prevented Catholic ownership of land had the unwelcome consequence of making Catholic tenants preferable to Protestant ones, for, he had told Samuel Molyneux in a letter of 25 August 1718, Catholics 'live more frugally and meanly than [Protestants] can do [and] are able to pay greater rents'.[30] But King's intention was not just to protect Anglican tenants. He saw in the deliberate suppression of rent a way of discouraging English clerics from accepting Irish positions. Evans, complaining to Wake about King's lack of support for his case against St George, 'notwithstanding plain law, reason, and Acts of Parliament', reported that King had said:

> he might have increased the yearly revenues of Derry and Dublin, but that he would not do it, lest Englishmen should be his successors . . . and that he agreed with some of his brethren not to advance the revenue of the sees for the aforegoing reason, but to be contented with fines.[31]

King typically took a fine equivalent to eighteen months' rent and put much of that money into church property or relief of the indigent, being, as he told Wake on 23 March 1720, shocked by the extent of poverty in Dublin. 'I was of the opinion before that ($^1/_3$) of this city needed Charity, but . . . enquiries have assured me that at least one-half are in this lamentable state'. 'The truth is', he added, 'it is so great a grief to see so many miserable and not be able to relieve them that I can hardly think, speak or write of anything'.[32] Swift reports that King's stewards would secure the rents before 'my lord should send it all into the poor man's box'.[33]

Whatever his motivation, and however justified his increasing despair over English transplants, King's actions ran directly counter to all economic common sense in a society where realised land values were the driving force of economic growth. No wonder the House of Commons decided to codify practices that Ireland's leading archbishop already appeared to espouse. Unfortunately for them, they had confused cause and effect. King understood only too well the long-term repercussions of the Commons' proposal, which would set the Church of Ireland on the same footing as the Church of England where, King reminded Southwell on 26 December 1723, 'the bishoprics are so reduced that they can't maintain the bishops'.[34]

King's opposition to the Commons' plans, however, was tempered by his own concerns over intraparliamentary negotiations. King and Evans controlled a sufficient number of votes in the House of Lords to make passage of the Commons' bill difficult, at best. Additionally, both were members of the Privy Council and were fairly confident of their ability to overturn the bill there, if necessary. However, there was a series of housekeeping bills concerning the Church of Ireland just beginning passage through the Irish parliament in the upper house. King was greatly concerned that these would suffer defeat in the lower house if the Commons was not in some manner mollified. Early in the discussion about the bishops' response he advocated limited compromise, if only to ensure that some co-operation be preserved between the two houses.

Evans had his own reasons for opposing compromise, but he also had on his side the undeniable fact that with the entire bench of clergy in the upper house in agreement the Commons' bill would be lucky to survive debate in the House of Lords, unless more lay peers than usual bothered to present themselves in Dublin. King's suggestion of compromise struck Evans as ill-considered, and the clerics once more split into two camps. For Swift, the issue was clear and his characteristic expedient absolutism in defence of the church drove him into co-operation with Evans. So sure was Swift that land and power were interchangeable, and so implacably opposed to compromise was he, he unhesitatingly put aside antipathy to Evans to join those advocating outright opposition. Just as he had with his 1708 *Letter Concerning the Sacramental Test*, Swift broke ranks with those with whom he had come to be so closely associated because he would brook no compromise on so fundamental an issue of church rights. His siding with Evans was entirely consistent with his political activities until that time. Everything Swift believed indicated that this time the church truly was 'in danger', and he was not simply seeking to score points when he sided with those he believed to be its best friends at that particular moment.

In November 1723 King actually tried to introduce a compromise bill in the upper house. Aware of King's intentions, Swift sought to force the issue in late October 1723, just prior to the first vote on the matter in the House of Commons, when he published *Some Arguments Against Enlarging the Powers of the Bishops, in letting of Leases, with* Remarks *on some* Queries *Lately published*. Although he published it anonymously, Swift was immediately acknowledged as the author, surprising the Whig, English bishops as much as anyone. Nicolson would even suggest that Swift's work be 'allow'd to atone for a multitude of bypast Transgressions'.[35]

Swift's work should have come as no particular surprise, and he must have been relieved to be able to demonstrate again the sincerity of his opinion 'that a free Man ought not to confine his Converse to any one Party; neither would I do so, if I were free'.[36] *Against Enlarging the Powers of Bishops* has at its heart the modest assumption that 'those . . . who profess themselves Members of the Church established, and under the Apostolic Government of Bishops, do desire the continuance and Transmission of [that church] to Posterity, at least, in as good a Condition as it is at present'.[37] As before, however, there is a subtext informed by Swift's sense that he is raising an issue that could do greater damage to the church's opponents than they understood. With the bill to restrict the bishops' ability to set rents originating from the very landholders whom he thought depended upon the church's protection against Catholic aspirations, Swift narrows the appeal of his argument to members of 'our Party', i.e. those moderates who supported the bill but who still professed a concern for the church.[38]

The pamphlet specifically excludes Catholics and Dissenters from its appeal as neither group had any possible interest in standing beside the church on this issue, and neither had, in any case, representation in parliament. Informed by his own convictions, Swift wrote with the potentially staggering assumption that English-style Tories among the Irish landowners would not determine their own economic interest to be best served by weakening the church's control of rents. What Swift sought to do was drive a wedge through the ranks of the Commons, separating churchmen from the others. Swift's strategy in 1723 was identical to that of his 1712 *Letter to a Whig Lord*, wherein one moderate appealed to others on behalf of the church. It was a deft move, made possible at least in part by the Commons' disingenuous selection of a title for their bill. Swift was able to launch his counter-offensive under the very rubric that would best gain him an audience from those he most urgently needed to address.

King and a reluctant Stearne were working to arrange a show of strength sufficient to compel the Commons to accept their lordships' compromise proposal, while Evans and Nicolson co-ordinated a campaign of correspondence to rally the Church of England and the English Privy Council to their aid. Also on this side of the divide was the Primate of Ireland, Boulter, for whom Swift had little time and *vice versa*, yet on this issue they agreed. Boulter was always an advocate of improving the living conditions of his clergy, partially because that would attract a better level of cleric, both from Ireland and from England, but also because, as he explained in a letter of 7 May 1730 to the Duke of Newcastle:

> the number of papists in this kingdom is so great, that it is of the utmost consequence to the protestant interest here to bring them over by all Christian methods to the church of *Ireland*. In order to do this, we are labouring to increase the number of Churches and of parsonage houses . . . the greatest part of the livings here having neither house nor land belonging to them.[39]

Without secured, long-term prospects of income from lands, this plan would have failed.

Simultaneously, Swift sought to recast the debate along lines at which he was so adept, sidestepping the obvious questions of what would happen to the church's and the laity's wealth – the classic political question, 'What's in it for me?' – and instead launching into a history lesson specifically designed to raise the spectre of popish success and Irish upheaval. The question Swift sought to address in his quest to scuttle the bill was: 'What of Ireland's interest?'. By which, of course, he meant 'Anglican Ireland' and its establishment and privileges.

Against Enlarging the Powers of the Bishops begins by stressing the essentially beggared nature of the church compared with its rightful claims:

> [I]t be now near 200 Years since almost three Parts in four of the Church Revenues have been taken from the Clergy: Besides the Spoils that have been gradually made ever since, of Glebes and other Lands, by the Confusion of Times, the Fraud of encroaching Neighbours, or the Power of Oppressors, too great to be encountred.[40]

But this was not to be another of Swift's complaints about the ravages wrought by loss of 'possessions of which the church had been robbed by Henry VIII'.[41] The final item of the dirge shifts the complaint away from rapacious lay landowners, raising instead the far more powerful image of a Catholic administration, similar to that of Tyrconnell's, seizing church lands.

The argument that if disposition of church lands remained the provenance of the bishops Anglican Ireland would be protected might seem far-fetched. However, the essential mercantilist equation of land and power gave Swift's argument a validity he could prove by drawing on another lesson from history. Swift reminds his readers:

> About the Time of the Reformation, many *Popish* Bishops of this Kingdom, knowing they must have been soon ejected, if they would not change their Religion, made long Leases and Fee-farms of great Part of their Lands, reserving very inconsiderable Rents, sometimes only a Chiefry . . . By these Means, Episcopal Revenues were so low reduced, that three or four Sees were often united to make a tolerable Competency.[42]

The implication that only an idiot, or papal sympathiser, would behave in this manner could not advance Swift's argument much further, but it did him no harm to suggest that the established Anglican church, so vital to governing Ireland's sense of identity, would have been denuded of all vitality were it not for the restorative actions of James I, Charles I and Charles II. In demonstrating the validity of his thesis, Swift begins to shift his argument onto grounds he understood to be vital to his church's survival: that the Irish economy needed land, and that the Church of Ireland was at least as good a guardian of that land as any other person or body. And make no mistake about it, Swift tells his readers, it is land that matters because there is no other bulwark against 'the perpetual Decrease in the Value of Gold and Silver', a statement he makes twice in as many pages.[43] Swift chooses to give as evidence Evans' own situation and in so doing he makes it clear that this particular appeal is not concerned with questions of national origin, but with the church as a whole. The See of Meath was valued at £400 per annum at the time of Charles II's act protecting church rent. What, Swift asks, would have become of it by 1723 if that were still its income?[44] Whatever his friends and foes might have made of this apparent change in sympathies, it was his integrity and commitment to the established church that determined the nature of Swift's *Arguments*.

Because the danger was that Swift's 'Way of Reasoning may seem to bear a more favourable Eye to the Clergy, than perhaps will suit with the present Disposition',[45] the body of the *Arguments* seeks to demonstrate that if the bill were to pass, '[t]he present Bishops will, indeed, be no Sufferers'.[46] After all, the incumbent bishops could reasonably expect to die before the long-term leases began to lose their intrinsic value. This was an argument the sponsors of the bill had relied on to appeal to at least certain of the bishops. In Swift's analysis, however, the principal consequence of driving down the value of the leases would only be to discourage 'Men of Credit and Consequence' from seeking Irish translations, so that the appointments would be left entirely to the 'Disposal of a chief Governor, who can never fail of some worthless illiterate Chaplain'.[47]

These lesser transplants would continue to hold seats in the House of Lords and, in some cases, in the Privy Council. It was usual, too, to have at least one of the four archbishops serving as a lord justice, even if the behaviour of King and Stearne had resulted in their recent exclusion from the post. Significant political power would, then, remain with the upper clergy regardless of the value of their lands, but as that value fell there would be a commensurate decline in the quality of the bench of bishops, a decline that could only further damage the prospects of all Irishmen. Weakening the church, for whatever reason, would ultimately benefit no one at all. The corollary here is that a strong church was needed to ensure a politically competent, and selfless, bench of bishops.

Swift's steadily increasing pessimism about England's attitude to Ireland served him well. Unlike King, he did not believe that depressing the income of Irish bishoprics would prevent English translations. Swift was convinced some Englishman could always be found to serve in preference to a native-born cleric whenever the English so desired. The only effect of driving down income would be to lessen the quality of the men translated to Ireland. That Swift already believed the quality of the English-born bishops pitiful was beside the point. The nature of clerical transplants affected all Irishmen, not just those with careers within the church. Landowners and lay members of both houses of parliament would do well to reflect upon the consequences to them of a clerical 'Bench . . . composed of mean, ignorant, fawning Gown-men, humbling Supplicants and Dependents upon the *Court*'.[48]

Swift's analysis was designed specifically to appeal to members of the Commons who still relied upon Irish revenues for their income, as opposed to those who voted with the Court and English government in return for pensions and sinecures. Those members of the Commons who had sided with the nascent Irish bloc in the House of Lords over matters such as the Bank scheme, and who opposed further English encroachments upon Irish economic rights, were well advised to consider their prospects if the House of Lords became a rubber stamp for Dublin Castle. The strains within the Irish economic system, and the current ability of the upper clergy to rely upon revenues from the land, meant that those about to vote on a bill designed 'for the Preservation of the Inheritance, Rights, and Profits' of the church would do well to consider the long-term consequences to themselves of not properly protecting that church. Once again, Swift deployed economic self-interest to try to craft a broad coalition in defence of his church.

Against Enlarging the Powers of the Bishops also considers the broader question of how landowners ought to conduct themselves. As the struggle to protect Irish rights became ever more intricate, Swift increasingly sought to link in the public mind the idea that the general well-being of the people was bound up with the continued ability of the bishops to shape public policy by example, as well as by legislation. So it is that Swift's tract, which has so carefully begun by appealing to the self-interest of the wealthier Irish Anglicans, spends some considerable part of its second half considering the conduct of landlords. By and large, writes Swift, bishops 'liveth as piously and hospitably', as any lay landlord and, in fact, tend to treat the tenants better, for:

> [I]f they be his immediate Tenants, you may distinguish them, at first Sight, by their Habits and Horses; or if you go to their Houses, by their comfortable Way of living.[49]

Here, whatever their differences on this particular matter, Swift must have had the example of King in mind. Unfortunately, many of those 'immediate Tenants generally speaking, have others under them, and . . . a Third and Fourth . . . till it comes [to the last] who sits at rack rent, and lives as miserably as an *Irish* [i.e. Catholic] Farmer'.[50] Defending the bishops, Swift argues for the preservation of an effective, regulated mercantilist system. Fair rents would continue to enable bishops to reside in their sees, where, after all, they are 'bound, in Conscience . . . [to] keep Hospitality'.[51] What is most notable in this impassioned plea is the increasingly antagonistic position the pamphlet takes towards the very persons it is seeking to influence – the secular landlords here accused of renting out their own leases without due regard for proper husbandry. In *Against Enlarging the Powers of Bishops*, Swift has a difficult time reconciling various competing interests and he inevitably finds himself developing a critique at least partially dependent upon national sentiments. Appealing to those Anglicans who would vote on the future of the church, Swift also finds it useful to address the increasing number of poor Anglicans forced to live 'as miserably as an *Irish* farmer'. Attempting to side with Evans and the other English bishops, Swift makes a final plea that he hopes will forever intertwine the Irish body politic with the Church of Ireland.

As control of the land became increasingly important because other economic avenues were closed to the Irish, the reconciling of competing claims to land became ever more problematic. Ironically, these tensions offered a writer of Swift's nature greater opportunities than would a more tightly defined debate. The rational basis of his *Arguments* having been developed as far as possible, Swift lets loose a salvo of indignation that bypasses the House of Commons and appeals directly to tenants and other Anglican Irishmen, further eroding the distinction between the country's interests and those of the Church of Ireland:

> Has *the Nation been thrown into Confusion*? And have *many poor Families been ruined* by rack-Rents paid for by the Lands of the Church? Does *the Nation cry out* to have a Law that must, in Time, send their Bishops a begging? But, GOD be thanked, the *Clamour* of Enemies to the Church is not yet the *Cry*, and, I hope, will never be the *Voice* of the Nation . . . The Bishops, *at least*, are not to answer for the Poverty of Tenants.[52]

The position Swift ultimately had to take in the *Arguments* was dictated by the chasm that had opened between his intricate identification of the church's welfare with economic practice and moral law as represented in mercantilist theories, and the reality of Irish politics as determined by English authority.

Opposition to the 'Act of Parliament . . . *For the Preservation of the Inheritance, Rights and Profits of Lands belonging to the Church, and Persons Ecclesiastical*; . . . was grounded upon Reasons that do still, and must for ever subsist', says Swift in concluding his lengthy re-evaluation of the Church of Ireland's position in the body politic.[53] Those reasons were the inalienable, and to Ireland vital, sanctity of the Constitution in Church and State and the fundamental equating of wealth and land. Ultimately, the Commons' bill would die in the Privy Council, as would King's compromise, but even before that occurred word of William Wood's plans was all over Ireland. Copper coinage could fatally cripple the economic foundations upon which Swift had only just finished constructing another justification of the church's privileges.

What the inherent contradictions of the *Arguments Against Enlarging the Powers of the Bishops* had made abundantly clear was that only if all of Anglican Ireland had a single legislative agenda could the Church of Ireland be protected against the encroachments of those who should have been its friends. The audaciously venal and evidently badly thought-out nature of Wood's patent was exactly the opportunity Swift needed to clarify, and so to strengthen, the connection between the church's welfare and that of the whole of Ireland. William Wood, Swift would argue in the second *Drapier's Letter*, was nothing but another of those 'High-way Men' who regularly sought to denude Ireland of its wealth.[54] In the *Arguments*, he had already railed against paying a thief in advance as an inappropriate way to 'prevent the Sin of Robbery'.[55] It was Wood who would give Swift the opportunity he finally needed to unequivocally link the strength of his church with the moral and economic welfare of his country.

'The vandals of the present age': the Dean's ironic legacy

I

The body of the People are generally either so dead that they cannot move, or so mad that they cannot be reclaimed.
George Savile, Marquis of Halifax[1]

The four year gap between major 'patriotic' writings, from the *Proposal* to *The Drapier's Letters*, makes no particular sense if examined for evidence of Swift's Irish patriotism. Similarly, Swift's writings in the years from 1708 to 1714 are filled with contradictions if we ask when Swift became a 'Tory' and stopped being a 'Whig'. However, if we give Swift credit as a man possessing some essential integrity (albeit an integrity obscured by a difficult and at times deliberately opaque personality), and if we acknowledge his commitment to a radically conservative analysis of the church's role in society, a much more convincing account of the years 1710–24 emerges. Swift made the transition so smoothly from church envoy to polemicist for a rearguard action because he thought he had found a cultural nostalgia for his own agenda in Ireland's economic woes.

From the exploratory writings of the post-1714 exile to the urgent appeal of *A Proposal for the Universal Use of Irish Manufacture*, and hence to *Some Arguments Against Enlarging the Powers of Bishops*, was a logically consistent, and politically sophisticated, progression. With the fortuitous emergence of Wood's half-penny on centre stage Jonathan Swift became an Irish patriot, not by design but because his own determined loyalty to his church found an opportunity for expression in his country's plight.

It is perhaps the greatest irony of Swift's work that the circumstances which led this backward-looking, legalistic and conservative churchman

145

to add his considerable polemical talents to the nascent national party in Ireland were the very circumstances which thereafter denied him any further room for manoeuvre. The successful opposition to the Bank of Ireland scheme and then to Wood's patent, both so soon after the Declaratory Act which should have permanently crippled parliament, gave the Irish House of Commons a sense of its own power that it preserved until at last, in 1800, Westminster finally succeeded in buying Anglican Ireland's capitulation.[2]

Swift had aligned himself with the winning side in the argument over Ireland's future, and in so doing he had shown the lay members of parliament that they need fear neither Westminster nor the Irish House of Lords. The self-interest of those members meant that economic reform within Ireland became the principal issue of state and the pressure on the nation's largest landholder, the Church of Ireland, steadily increased.

Swift was reduced to castigating the Irish parliament for making all the wrong decisions; but whereas in England he had always had an opposition party to seek to rally to the church's cause, in Ireland he had nothing. After the fight over Wood's patent, political debate in Ireland evolved into a struggle between pro-independence and pro-union with Britain factions, neither of which held much of a brief for the Church of Ireland. Out of this disappointment grew Swift's final bitterness, until at last he branded the Irish House of Commons 'that kingdom's bane' and its members: 'Biennial squires',

> Who sell their souls and votes for naught;
> The nation stripped, go joyful back,
> To rob the church, their tenants rack.[3]

The success of *The Drapier's Letters*, which was only possible because of the skill with which Swift had conducted himself from 1710–24, helped secure the 'present age' the Dean would henceforth rail against. By creating a sense of Irish independence, *The Drapier's Letters* made it possible for the Irish House of Commons to consider at length the welfare of its members and constituents. The Church of Ireland, deprived on King's death in 1729 of leadership in the House of Lords that was other than a mouthpiece for Westminster, could no longer influence the debate. In the end, Swift would ask only that his friends' lines:

> In praise of long departed wit,
> Be graved on either side in columns

More to my praise than all my volumes;
To burst with envy, spite, and rage,
The vandals of the present age.[4]

Jonathan Swift's work, and silence, throughout the years 1710–24 were a necessary precursor to the angry appeal of *The Drapier's Letters*, those great invocations of Irish rights that had for their premise no particular patriotic purpose. Instead, Swift sought to claim for his church the leadership of Irish society. The assumption that *The Drapier's Letters* were born of anger and frustration at what Swift saw outside his door each day denies the full depth and intricacy of the motivation behind the letters. The anger and the frustration were there all right, but there was both something more noble and something more opportunist mixed in with the indignation. *The Drapier's Letters* did not spring fully formed from the pen of a suddenly reinvigorated polemicist. There was something much more measured, something much more inevitable and something much more intricate about them.

Using his experience and political skills, Swift produced in 1724 a work that too often has been assumed to stand alone, marking some sort of pinnacle of genius. It is a tribute to Swift that *The Drapier's Letters* have so well withstood that demand. It would do him more justice if we understood the motivation for those letters to be the product of something more than just a historical accident.

There is a context to Swift's 'Irish' work that, while firmly grounded in events in Ireland, has to do with far more than Ireland itself. It is a context that irreducibly connects Swift's English work and his middle years of near silence with his appeals on behalf of the Irish. It is a context defined by the role he believed should be played by the institution to which he devoted more than half his life – the Church of Ireland.

Notes

The correspondence of William King quoted in this text can be found in the King collection held at Trinity College, Dublin. References are provided below where the letters have been published and are easily accessible.

PROLOGUE

1 Enright, D.J. (1986), 'Swift, Fielding, and Bad Taste', *The Alluring Problem: An Essay on Irony*. Oxford: Oxford University Press, p. 75.
2 Douglas, A., Kelly, P. and Campbell Ross, I. (eds) (1998) 'Introduction: Locating Swift'. *Locating Swift: Essays from Dublin on the 250th Anniversary of the Death of Jonathan Swift 1667–1745*, Dublin: Four Courts Press.
3 Higgins, I. (1994) *Swift's Politics: A Study in Disaffection*, Cambridge: Cambridge University Press, p. 11.
4 Fabricant, C. (1995) 'Swift as Irish Historian'. *Walking Naboth's Vineyard: New Studies of Swift*, Notre Dame, IN: University of Notre Dame Press, pp. 43–4.
5 Hill, C. (1985) 'Censorship and English Literature'. *The Collected Essays of Christopher Hill. Vol. 1: Writing and Revolution in Seventeenth Century England*, Amherst, MA: The University of Massachusetts Press, p. 33.
6 The best recent overview of writings about Swift is to be found in Aileen Douglas, A., Kelly, P. and Campbell Ross, I., 'Introduction: Locating Swift,' the introductory chapter of the essay collection *Locating Swift*.
7 See especially his sermon 'On False Witness'. In Davis, H. (1939–68) *Prose Works on Jonathan Swift* 14 vols, Oxford: Basil Blackwell, vol. IX, pp. 180–9.
8 As this work was nearing completion, interest in King suddenly blossomed. A significant new study, Philip O'Regan's *Archbishop William King (1650–1729) and the Constitution in Church and State*, will be in print before this work and it promises to redefine almost everything we think we know about King. Additionally, Joseph Richardson at the National University of Ireland, Maynooth, has just completed a lengthy doctoral examination of King's philosophy.
9 Mant, R. (1840) *History of the Church of Ireland from the Reformation to the Revolution*, 2 vols, London, vol. I, p. 1.
10 Phillips, W. (ed.) (1933) *History of the Church of Ireland from the Earliest Times to the Present Day*, 3 vols, London: Oxford University Press, vol. I, p. v.
11 Two far more recent studies of the Church of Ireland provide excellent discussions of both the Church's relationship with the Church of England and also of its own sense of its place in Irish society, a sense often at odds with that of the majority of the Irish. They are Acheson, A. (1997) *A History of the Church of Ireland, 1691–1996*. Dublin: Columba, APCK and Ford, A., McGuire, J. and Milne, K. (eds) (1995) *As by Law Established: The Church of Ireland since the Reformation*, Dublin: Lilliput Press.
12 Montag, W. (1994) *The Unthinkable Swift*, London: Verso, p. 17.

13   DePorte, M. (1993a) 'The Road to St Patrick's: Swift and the Problem of Belief'. *Swift Studies* 8, p. 14.
14   Ibid., p. 13.
15   Said, E. (1969) 'Swift's Tory Anarchy'. *Eighteenth-Century Studies* 3, (Fall) p. 50.
16   Montag, W. (1994) op. cit., p. 41. Swift would not be the last towering Irish literary figure to recreate himself out of an 'imaginary solution' to pressing social tensions. Edna Longley, for example, demonstrates how William Butler Yeats anticipated the events leading up to the creation of the Irish Free State by 'found[ing] a one-man sect' ('Louis MacNeice: "The Walls are Flowing"' in Dawe, G. and Longley, E. (eds) (1985) *Across a Roaring Hill: The Protestant Imagination in Modern Ireland. Essays in Honour of John Hewitt*, Belfast: Blackstaff, p. 120), remaking Ireland in a manner that still permitted him a role. Yeats dodged the need to determine one's identity, however wilful that identity, by opting for a variety of masks that mediated the violent disturbances of the everyday. Swift's approach was not dissimilar.
17   Montag, W. (1994) op. cit., p. 41.
18   Idem.
19   Breandán Ó Buachalla's body of work demonstrates the prevalence of Jacobite imagery in Irish literature, particularly in poetry and songs, in the years following James' flight from Ireland. That Swift at least knew of some of this literature is probably beyond question. That it interested him is another matter. Irish Jacobitism was Catholic. Swift's Jacobite friends were high church and Protestant. The two movements had little common ground.
20   Nokes, D. (1985) *Jonathan Swift, a Hypocrite Reversed*, Oxford: Oxford University Press, p. ix.
21   Fabricant, C. (1992) *Swift's Landscape*, Baltimore: Johns Hopkins University Press, p. 7.

CHAPTER ONE

1   Pascal, B. (1941) *Pensées*. Translated by W.F. Trotter, New York: Modern Library.
2   The Anglican church as finally constituted by Elizabeth I is the parent of the worldwide Episcopalian congregation, whose various national organisations are self-governing. 'Anglican' now strictly refers only to the Church of England. I use it to describe the Church of Ireland in Swift's time because many of its senior clerics viewed it as a part of the Church of England, and also to underline the complex inter-relationship of the two churches.
3   The case in Scotland was somewhat different. There, the Presbyterian Kirk was established, but both the church's structure and the demands of Anglican communicants in Scotland placed the Kirk on a separate footing from the Churches of England and Ireland. Just to make matters more confusing, the Church of Scotland is the Presbyterian church's official name. The Episcopalian Church in Scotland is the sister congregation of the Church of England. More confusing still is that thanks to policies of some Scottish monarchs, most notably James VI (James I of England), the Church of Scotland was for some parts of its history prior to 1690 actually a church with an episcopacy. Wales was treated as part of England as far as legislation and its church were concerned. The Church in Wales (as it is now known) was disestablished in 1920 when a separate province of six dioceses was created.
4   Pope, A. (1940–69) *The Poems*. Edited by J. Butt, 11 vols, London: Methuen.

5 'Ireland', lines 1–2 from Rogers, P. (ed.) (1983) *Jonathan Swift: The Complete Poems*, New Haven: Yale University Press.

6 Williams, H. (ed.) (1963–65) *The Correspondence of Jonathan Swift*, 5 vols, Oxford: Clarendon, p. 373.

7 Queen Anne died on 1 August 1714; Swift did not tarry long in England, arriving in Ireland on 24 August.

8 Rogers, P. op. cit. 'In Sickness', lines 3–8.

9 Writing about early eighteenth-century Anglican Irish political activity is to risk getting embroiled in a debate over terms which were never clearly defined and which, in many cases, did not appear in regular use until well into the nineteenth century. Two such terms are tempting and perhaps apposite, but I have in the end decided to avoid them. Those terms are 'Anglo-Irish', generally taken to mean the Anglican Irish of English descent who increasingly distinguished themselves from the Anglican English; and 'Ascendancy', a socio-political term defining the political ruling class in pre-1922 Ireland. Swift would have been a member of both groups, and his political discourse certainly helped shape their later identities. At the risk of appearing either simplistic or cowardly, I refer to the Irish-born Anglican grouping as Anglican Irish, a better reflection of the still tentative political alliances that would evolve into the Anglo-Irish and Ascendancy society.

10 Berkeley, G. *The Irish Patriot or Queries upon Queries* No. 350 in Johnson, J. (ed.) (1970) *Bishop Berkeley's Querist in Historical Perspective*, Dundalk: Dundalgan.

11 Ehrenpreis, I. (1962–83) *Swift: The Man, His Works and the Age*, 3 vols, Cambridge, MA: Harvard University Press, vol. III, p. 830.

12 Downie, J.A. (1984) Jonathan Swift: Political Writer, London: Routledge & Kegan Paul, pp. 333–4.

13 For a delightfully idiosyncratic and cheerful appreciation of Swift and his reputation within political circles, see Michael Foot's essay (1981) 'Round the Next Corner', in *Debts of Honour*, London: Picador, pp. 181–212. Leader of the British Labour Party from 1980–83, Foot's unapologetic socialism combines with a spirited breadth of learning to produce a series of essays that make obvious, in being the exception to the rule, the current dearth of learning among so many politicians – a trend Swift thought he detected in his time and which he found both abhorrent and dangerous. In discussing William Hazlitt's celebration of Swift, Foot reminds us that Swift's reputation has often been highest in the very circles he would have most despised.

14 Hayton, D. (1981) 'The Crisis in Ireland and the Disintegration of Queen Anne's Last Ministry'. *Irish Historical Studies* XXII (March) p. 196.

15 Idem.

16 Ibid., p. 207.

17 Walpole's ruthlessness as head of the Committee of Secrecy was in marked contrast to the Earl of Oxford, who had a long-standing argument with Bolingbroke over how far the Tories should go in excluding Whigs from government. As Lord Treasurer, Oxford's power had been immense; however, in keeping with tradition his six-person cabinet had included Whigs. Oxford fell from power on 27 July, four days before Anne's death. On 30 July, the Duke of Shrewsbury replaced Oxford. Bolingbroke, who was neither in the Privy Council nor one of the designated Regents, was unable to use Oxford's downfall to his own advantage. Additionally, he seems not to have had a particular programme in mind beyond ensuring his own faction's advancement. For an excellent summary of what went wrong for the Tories, and an account of the four readily identifiable factions within that party, see Chapters 6 and 7 in

Speck, W.A. (1977) *Stability and Strife: England, 1714–1760,* Cambridge: Harvard University Press.

18   Ehrenpreis, I. op. cit., vol. III, pp. 6–7.

19   Ehrenpreis argues convincingly that the actual sender of the packet, the chaplain to the Duchess of Ormonde, would not have mailed the parcel without the Duke's approval. Ehrenpreis, I. op. cit., vol. III, p. 15.

20   For the problems of exactly dating this and other sermons by Swift, see Daw, C. (1970) 'An Annotated Edition of Five Sermons by Jonathan Swift'. Dissertation. University of Virginia.

21   Davis, H. (ed.) (1939–68) *Prose Works of Jonathan Swift,* 14 vols, Oxford: Basil Blackwell, vol. IX, p. 180.

22   Ibid., vol. IX, p. 181.

23   Ibid., vol. IX, pp. 181, 185. In contrast to Swift's adept conduct stands that of his good friend Thomas Sheridan. Sheridan lost his own living when, without due care and attention, he chose for the text of his sermon to be delivered on the King's birthday, the biblical thought that 'Sufficient unto the day is the evil thereof' (Matt. 6.34).

24   Ibid., vol. XI, p. 191.

25   Downie, J.A. (1984) *Jonathan Swift: Political Writer.* London: Routledge & Kegan Paul.

26   Elias, A.C. (1982) *Swift at Moor Park: Problems in Biography and Criticism.* Philadelphia: University of Pennsylvania Press.

27   Davis, H. (1939–68) op. cit., vol. IX, p. 185.

28   Robinson (1650–1723) was a cleric initially lacking any conspicuous patronage who served as chaplain to the English diplomatic mission to Sweden for more than twenty years. He was eventually transferred to a living and given a prebendary. Later he rose to be Bishop of Bristol (1710), Lord Privy Seal (1711) and, finally (with the Earl of Oxford's advocacy), Bishop of London (1714). For more on Robinson, see Hatton, R.M. (1955) 'John Robinson and the *Account of Sweden'. Bulletin of the Institute of Historical Research,* xxviii, pp. 128–59.

29   Lock, F.P. (1980) *The Politics of Gulliver's Travels.* Oxford: Clarendon. Lock has adapted the phrase 'Cato complex' from Johnson, J.W. (1967) *The Formation of English Neo-Classical Thought,* Princeton: Princeton University Press. Johnson, in turn, borrows the phrase of Joseph Addison's 1713 play *Cato.*

30   Quoted in Klein, L.E. (1994) *Shaftesbury and the Culture of Politeness,* Cambridge: Cambridge University Press, p. 147.

31   In *Sentiments,* Swift draws upon the image of 'the latter Cato' to argue that 'before Things proceed to open Violence, the truest Service a private Man may hope to do his Country, is by unbiasing his Mind as much as possible, and then endeavouring to moderate between Rival Powers' (Davis, H. (1939–68) op. cit., vol. II, p. 2), a task he would imagine himself undertaking as he fancied himself struggleing to reconcile Oxford and Bolingbroke as their administration collapsed around them.

32   Davis, H. (1939–68) op. cit., vol. II, p. 18.

33   Ibid., vol. II, p. 14.

34   Berkeley, G. (1970) op cit., no. 28.

35   Hunter, J.P. (1990) *Before Novels: The Cultural Contexts of Eighteenth-Century English Fiction,* New York: Norton.

36   Leavis, F.R. (1953) 'The Irony of Swift'. *The Common Pursuit,* London: Chatto & Windus, p. 86.

37   Ibid., p. 87.

38   Davie, D. (1978) *A Gathered Church: The Literature of the English Dissenting Interest, 1700–1930,* New York: Oxford University Press, p. 26.

39 Rogers, P. (1983) op. cit., 'Verses on the Death of Dr Swift D.S.P.D.', lines 55–8.
40 Kierkegaard, S. (1989) *The Concept of Irony, with Continual Reference to Socrates*, H.V. and E.H. Hong (ed. and trans.) Princeton: Princeton University Press.
41 Halifax, Marquis of (1989) 'Of Alterations'. *Miscellaneous Thoughts and Reflections*. M.N. Brown, (ed.) 3 vols. vol. 1, Oxford: Clarendon, p. 469.
42 Rosenheim, E.W. (1963) *Swift and the Satirist's Art*, Chicago: University of Chicago, p. 227.
43 Kramnick, I. (1968) *Bolingbroke and his Circle: The Politics of Nostalgia in the Age of Walpole*, Cambridge, MA: Harvard University Press.
44 Rosenheim, E.W. (1963) op. cit., p. 25.
45 Quoted in Smith, E. (1999) 'Mad Poet's Society'. Review of Alan Wall, *The Lightning Cage*, London: Chatto & Windus, p. 14.
46 Joseph Addison described himself as an 'Englishman born in Dublin' and thought no more of the location of his birth than would have someone from Bristol. Jonathan Swift, responding to what must have been the identical question, answered that he was 'an Englishman born in Ireland'.

CHAPTER TWO

1   Smedley, J. (1728) *Gulliveriana: or, A Fourth Volume of Miscellanies*. London.
2   The First Fruits and Twentieth Parts were an ecclesiastic levy and tax, respectively, initially returned to Rome but, after the Reformation, claimed by the Crown. The First Fruits was a sum nominally equal to the annual value of the benefice, paid by the incumbent as he assumed his living. The Twentieth Parts originally required an incumbent to surrender one-twentieth of the annual income of a benefice. Over time, a fixed sum levy had replaced the initially proportional assessment.
3   Boyer, A. (1719) *Political State*, London, vol. VII, p. 183.
4   Letter to William Wake, Archbishop of Canterbury, 18.5.1713.
5   Quoted in Carpenter, A. (ed.) (1974) *Letters to and from Persons of Quality*. Dublin: Cadenus, p. 28.
6   Idem.
7   Absenteeism was not restricted to Ireland, nor was it a vice only of the lower clergy. Benjamin Hoadly, the leading exponent of Church of England recognition of state authority, toleration and the legitimacy of the Dissenting churches, rose to be Bishop of Bangor. He failed throughout his tenure of office to visit this foremost of all the Welsh sees even once.
8   Swift, J. (1948) *Journal to Stella*. Sir Harold Williams (ed.) 2 vols. Oxford: Clarendon.
9   Williams, H. (ed.) (1963–65) *The Correspondence of Jonathan Swift*, Oxford: Clarendon, vol. I, p. 178.
10 Landa, L. (1965) *Swift and the Church of Ireland*, Oxford: Clarendon. Landa's book remains the best guide there is to Swift's ecclesiastical career. The introduction contains much material that helps clarify both the extent of the dismay over Swift's appointment as dean and the reasons behind it.
11 On the other hand, Swift was not exactly slow about attacking Godolphin and on the same day he wrote to Stella he began 'The Virtues of Sid Hamet the Magician's Rod', a savage poetic attack on Godolphin. See Williams' note in *Journal to Stella* and *Poems* pp. 109–12.
12 Williams, H. (1963–65) op. cit., vol. I, p. 173.
13 Ibid vol. I, p. 189.

14 Idem.
15 Ibid., vol. I, p. 245.
16 Swift continued to seek recognition of his role and applying in 1716 to the Trustees of the First Fruits Board for money to buy some additional glebe land at Laracor, Swift suggested that a clause be included in the deed to the effect that it was he who had secured the remission and so made possible the creation of the Board. The idea was rejected out of hand. See Landa, L. (1965) op. cit., pp. 65–6.
17 For a jaundiced but not entirely unjustified commentary on Harley's promotion to Earl of Oxford and Mortimer, see 'Green, D. (1970) *Queen Anne*, New York: Charles Scribner's. 'One sees, with St John, expediency triumphant,' writes Green. On 29 May 1711, 'Harley was rewarded with the Lord Treasurership and an earldom; and to judge from the preamble to his patent of honour one would suppose him to have rescued the nation from daylight robbery . . . Because his claim to the earldom of Oxford was disputed by the Berties, Harley was allowed to add "and Mortimer" to his title. If the Bertie claim succeeded (regrettably it did not), he could always fall back on the alternative' (pp. 248–9). In *The Conduct of the Allies* Swift does, of course, suggest that the Peace of Utrecht did indeed 'rescue the nation from daylight robbery'. See Davis, H. (ed.) (1939–68) *Prose works of Jonathan Swift*, Oxford: Basil Blackwell.
18 Williams, H. (1963–65) op. cit., vol. I, p. 49.
19 Davis, H. (1939–68) op. cit., vol. II, pp. 109–25. It is in this tract that Swift makes his most famous reference to Daniel Defoe, Dissenter, novelist, and sometime employee of Harley. Attacking those who supported repeal of the Test Act, Swift writes of 'One of these Authors (the Fellow that was *pilloryed*, I have forgot his Name) [who] is indeed so grave, sententious, dogmatical a Rogue, that there is no enduring him' (p. 113). Richard Cook's *Jonathan Swift as a Tory Pamphleteer* has an insightful chapter on the relationship between Swift and Defoe. See Cook, R. (1967) *Jonathan Swift as a Tory Pamphleteer*. Seattle: University of Washington Press.
20 Schochet, G.J. (1996) 'The Act of Toleration and the Failure of Comprehension: Persecution, Nonconfirmity and Religious Indifference'. In D. Hook and M. Feingold (eds) *The World of William and Mary: Anglo-Dutch Perspectives on the Revolution of 1688–89*, Stanford: Stanford University Press, p. 181.
21 Williams, H. (1963–65) op. cit., vol. I, p. 80.
22 Davis, H. (1939–68) op. cit., vol. II, p. 116.
23 The Junto was the group of Whig peers perceived as exercising a collective influence over the government of the day. They were the Earls of Halifax, Orford, Sunderland and Wharton, and Lord Somers, to whom Swift dedicated *A Tale of a Tub*.
24 Landa, L. (1980) 'Not the Gravest of Divines'. *Essays in Eighteenth-Century Literature*, Princeton: Princeton University Press, p. 73.
25 Williams, H. (1963–65) op cit., vol. I, p. 123.
26 For an appraisal of, and introduction to, the Non-jurors, see Rupp, G. (1986) *Religion in England 1688–1791*, Oxford: Clarendon, pp. 5–28. Among other useful works for placing the Non-jurors in context are Bennett, G.V. (1975) *The Tory Crisis in Church and State*, Oxford: Clarendon; Douglas, D.C. (1951) *English Scholars, 1600–1730*, London: Eyre and Spottiswoode and Wand, J.W.C. (1951), *The High Church Schism*, New York: Morehouse–Gorham. Cornwall, R.D. (1993) *Visible and Apostolic: The Constitution of the Church in High Church Anglican and Non-juror Thought*, Newpark: University of Delaware Press, provides a

summary overview of questions of doctrine. It is useful in seeking to make connections between high church and Non-juror thought; however, in putting the ecclesiological questions above all others, Cornwall more often than not loses sight of the political and social contexts upon which their arguments were all in some sense dependent. His primary bibliography is extensive and invaluable for anyone wishing to pursue contemporary exchanges of pamphlets between the high church/Non-juror wing of Anglican thought and the whig/latitudinarian party. The Irish Non-jurors were relatively fewer in number than their English counterparts but included two of the most prominent Non-jurors anywhere in the two islands: Charles Leslie and Henry Dodwell, though both were primarily resident in England. William Sheridan, Bishop of Kilmore and Ardagh, was a Non-juror; he seems to have had the support of almost all the other Irish bishops. A 1697 bill to impose an oath of abjuration was virulently opposed by Bishops Thomas Lindsay (Killaloe), William Lloyd (Killala) and William King (Derry). All four archbishops, Michael Boyle (Armagh), Narcissus Marsh (Dublin), John Vesey (Tuam) and William Palliser (Cashel) also opposed the bill. 'These prelates,' says R.H. Murray, 'were men who cared for the moral nature of the Church, and . . . the Non-juring movement was a powerful witness to this nature' (See Phillips, W.A. (1993) *History of the Church of Ireland*, London: Oxford University Press, vol. III, p. 165).

27 Williams, H. (1963–65) op. cit., vol. I, p. 8.
28 Davis, H. (1939–68) op. cit., vol. VI, p. 130.
29 The War of Spanish Succession (1702–14) was principally concerned with who should succeed the heirless Charles II, King of Spain. The Hapsburg emperors in Austria were related through several generations to the Spanish monarchy and most recently by the marriage of Charles II's sister Margaret Theresa to Emperor Leopold I. France claimed the throne by right of Louis XIV's marriage to Marie Therese, older sister of Charles II. On his death, Charles II willed Spain to Louis' grandson, Philip, Duke of Anjou, and Louis lept at this arrangement despite pre-existing agreements with various European monarchs that Spain should be divided. Upon his grandson's arrival in Madrid, Louis XIV remarked that 'there are no longer any Pyrenees', and the rest of Europe, looking at the map, girded for war
30 King, W. (1731) *Essay on the Origin of Evil*. London.
31 Carpenter, A. (1974) op. cit., p. 31.
32 Ibid., p. 18.
33 Ibid., pp. 44–5.
34 King, W. (1976) *Sermon on Predestination* ed. by A. Carpenter, Dublin: Cadenus, p. 32.
35 Ibid., p. 77.
36 Ibid., p. 79.
37 Idem.
38 Ibid., p. 19.
39 Davis, H. (1939–68) op. cit., vol. IX, p. 77.
40 Ibid., vol. IX, p. 151.
41 Idem.
42 Williams, H. (1963–65) op. cit., vol. I, p. 254.
43 Nokes, D. (1985) *Jonathon Swift, a Hypocrite Reversed: A Critical Biography*. Oxford: Oxford University Press, pp. 86–7.
44 Williams, H. (1963–65) op. cit., vol. I, p. 262.
45 Ibid., vol. I, p. 253.

46 Ibid., vol. I, p. 253.
47 Carpenter, A. (1974) (ed.) op. cit., pp. 30–1.
48 Halifax, Marquis of (1989) *The Character of a Trimmer* ed. by M.N. Brown. Oxford: Clarendon, p. 243.
49 Davis, H. (1939–68) op. cit., vol. IX, p. 179. It was no coincidence that the topic of this sermon echoed Henry Sacheverell's notorious 1709 sermon 'The Perils of False Brethren'. Preached on 5 November 1709 before the Lord Mayor of London, this was the sermon that led to Sacheverell's trial and the consequent Tory victory in the 1710 election. Clive Probyn rightly calls Sacheverell's sermon 'vituperative and intolerant'. Probyn, C. (ed.) (1979) *Jonathan Swift: The Contemporary Background*, New York: Barnes and Noble, p. 61. For a full account of the affair see Holmes, G.S. (1973) *The Trial of Doctor Sachervell*, London: Methuen.
50 Davis, H. (1939–68) op. cit., vol. IX, p. 178.
51 Ibid., vol. IX, pp. 230–1.
52 Idem.
53 Halifax, Marquis of (1989) (ed.) M.N. Brown op. cit., pp. 205–6.
54 King, W. (1731) op. cit., p. 198.
55 Johnson, S. (1905) *Lives of the English Poets* ed. by G. Birkbeck Hill, Oxford: Clarendon, pp. 57–8. The problematics of Swift's charitable dealings are discussed in an essay by Landa, 'Jonathan Swift and Charity' in Landa, L. (ed.) (1980).
56 Quoted in Beckett, J.C. (1971) 'Jonathan Swift as an Ecclesiastical Statesman'. In Donoghue, D. (ed.) *Jonathan Swift: A Critical Anthology*. Harmondsworth: Penguin, p. 146. Much later, A.N. Wilson, one of Britain's leading lay-commentators upon the contemporary state of religion, would touch upon the questions of bishops and faith with this exchange in one of his novels: '"Either you believe in God, or you don't", and if you don't believe in God, you shouldn't be a bishop'. *Essays in Eighteenth-Century Literature*. Princeton: Princeton University Press, pp. 49–62. '"Oh, but it's less simple than that!" screamed some woman, whom I have never seen since [in reply to Godfrey Tucker]'. (Wilson, A.N. (1993) *Daughters of Albion*, New York: Norton, p. 2).
57 Johnson, S. (1905) ed. G. Birkbeck Hill op. cit., pp. 52–3.
58 Chandler, T. B. (1767) *An Appeal to the Public, in Behalf of the Church of England in America*, New York. Once any component of the church-state compact is open to discussion or rejection, so must all the parts of that compact be. The Church of England was founded upon a radical political rethinking of assumptions about that compact and so the Church's political footing was always potentially in trouble. At times, however, it could be theological rather than political integrity that sought to jettison the compact. Pondering the future of the Church of Ireland should James II have prevailed in the war with William III, King found it easy, Carpenter demonstrates, to foresee his church retaining theological justification without royal assent, for if the '"good correspondence" between church and state is endangered by the bad behaviour of either [the crown or the church], the other may break the establishment' (Carpenter, A. (1972) 'William King and the Threats to the Church of Ireland During the Reign of James II', *Irish Historical Studies*, XVII, p. 24). In more recent times, the Primate of the Norwegian Church, Eivind Berggrav, led six other bishops out of the state half of the compact during the Nazi occupation of his country, resigning 'what the state has committed to my charge' but continuing to claim that 'the spiritual calling which has been ordained to me at the altar of God remains mine by God and by right' (quoted

in Cross, F.L. and Livingstone, G.A. (eds) (1997) *The Oxford Dictionary of the Christian Church*, Oxford: Oxford University Press p. 191). This is essentially the position the Non-juring clergy took and that King was willing to entertain when contemplating the possibility of James' continuing reign. It is not surprising so many clerics sympathised with the Non-juror position even while choosing to take the oath of abjuration. For Berggrav's account of his and his church's struggle against Quisling's puppet government and the Nazis, see Berggrav, E. (1943) *With God in the Darkness*. London: Hodder and Stoughton.

59 Davis, H. (1939–68) op. cit., vol. IX, p. 224.
60 Speck, W.A. (1977) *Stability and Strife: England 1714–60*, Cambridge MA: Harvard University Press.
61 From 'To a Dead Todmordian' by Will Healey, quoted in Healey, D. (1990) *The Time of My Life*, London: Penguin.
62 Williams, H. (ed.) (1948) *Journal to Stella* by Jonathan Swift, Oxford: Clarendon, vol. I, p. 24
63 Williams, H. (1939–68) op. cit., vol. I, p. 105.
64 Idem.
65 Ibid., vol. I, p. 106.
66 Ibid., vol. I, p. 108.
67 Ibid., vol. I, p. 120.
68 Davis, H. (1939–68) op. cit., vol. VI, p. 76. Swift here derides the Whig Party in exactly the same manner he had earlier used to mock the 1707 Act of Union joining Scotland and England as a 'monstrous alliance with those who profess Principles destructive to our Religion and Government' (*The Examiner* 29 [22 February 1710]). Such a union would, he thought, 'of necessity fall to Pieces':

> Whoever yet a union saw
> Of kingdoms, without faith or law.
> Henceforward let no statesman dare,
> A kingdom to a ship compare;
> Lest he should call our commonweal,
> A vessel with a double keel:
> Which just like ours, new rigged and manned,
> And got about a league from land,
> By change of wind to leeward side
> The pilot knew not how to guide.
> So tossing faction will o'erwhelm
> Our crazy double-bottomed realm.

From 'Verses Said to be Written on the Union', lines 11–22, from Rogers, P. (ed.) (1983) *Jonathan Swift: The Complete Poems*, New Haven; Yale University Press.
69 *Torism and Trade can never Agree* (1713) London, p. 16.
70 Davis, H. (1939–68) op. cit., vol. VI, p. 78.
71 Tyrconnell was James's most competent commander and cut a dashing, cavalier-type figure throughout the campaign against William III. Outnumbered and outgunned, Tyrconnell combined the best of both irregular and regular warfare tactics. He was particularly successful in Ulster until the numbers and the skills of his lieutenants finally let him down. He was the youngest son of an old English family and had fought in Ireland with the Catholic and royalist Confederation of Kilkenny forces during the Confederate War that coincided with the Civil War in England. Later, he saw service with French

and Spanish armies during the interregnum, where he fought alongside the Duke of York (later James II). At first, Tyrconnell explored the possibility of a settlement with William III, but he ended up attempting to secure Ireland for James. Less dishonest than many officials, he was almost unique among the nobility of that period in being faithful to his wife, Frances Jennings, the sister of Sarah, Duchess of Marlborough. Tyrconnell was an Irish patriot, albeit with distinct old English sympathies, whose distrust of, and lack of respect for, James II did not prevent him siding with the ousted monarch in an attempt to establish a free, independent, Catholic nation with James as its king. Unfortunately, James was interested only in returning to London. Whatever King and later Protestants might have said about him, Tyrconnell was a noble and ultimately tragic character. (Adapted in part from Connolly, S.J. (ed.) (1908) *The Oxford Companion to Irish History*, Oxford: Oxford University Press.) In late 1688 Temple's son, John, had been instrumental in convincing the authorities in London to release another significant Irish general, Richard Hamilton, in the hope that he would convince Tyrconnell to surrender. Instead, Hamilton joined forces with Tyrconnell and John Temple was so distraught he committed suicide by jumping off a boat in the Thames. For more on Tyrconnell and other of James's commanders see Simms, J.G. (1969) *Jacobite Ireland 1685–91*, London: Routledge and Kegan Paul and Doherty, R. (1998) *The Williamite War in Ireland, 1688–91*, Dublin: Four Courts Press.

72   King, W. (1768) *The State of the Protestants under the Late King James's Government.* London, p. 183.

73   Ibid., p. 43.

74   Davis, H. (1939–68) op. cit., vol. X, p. 8.

75   Ibid., vol. VI, pp. 133–4.

76   Ibid., vol. VIII, p. 82. Swift's continuing loyalty to Oxford himself after the latter's fall from grace, a loyalty that went beyond self-justification, has troubled his biographers. One possible bond between Swift and Oxford might be found in a brief comment in the *Journal to Stella*: 'Did I ever tell you that lord treasurer hears ill with the left ear, just as I do? he always turns the right; and his servants whisper him at that only'. This poignant remark is made even more tragic by Swift's lonely observation that 'I dare not tell him, that I am so too, for fear he should think I counterfeited, to make my court' (vol. I: p. 353). The sympathy of a silent fellow-sufferer can forge bonds that last a lifetime.

77   Williams, H. (1963–65) op. cit., vol. I, p. 389.

78   Ibid., vol. I, p. 426.

79   Idem.

80   Nokes, D. (1985) op. cit., p. 194.

81   Ehrenpreis, I. (1962–83) *Swift: The Man, His Works, and the Age*, Cambridge MA: Harvard University Press, vol. II, p. 688.

82   The animosity that separated Swift and Steele had been steadily increasing and by April 1713 they were no longer on speaking terms. Swift thought Steele owed him some regard because he believed 'my Lord Treasurer has kept [Steele] in his employment [as commissioner of the stamp office] upon my intreaty and intercession', as Swift wrote in a letter to Addison, seeking the latter's help in remonstrating with Steele. Steele was using his position as editor of *The Guardian* to assault Swift on a regular basis, harping on his association with *The Examiner*, which Swift was no longer editing, as he reminds Addison in Williams, H. (1963–65) op. cit., pp. 347–8.

83   Lock, F.P. (1983) *Swift's Tory Politics*, Newark: University of Delaware Press.

84   Ehrenpreis, I. (1962–83) op. cit., vol. II, p. 691.
85   Rogers, P. (1983) op. cit., 'The First Ode of the Second Book of Horace Paraphrased', lines 1–2.
86   One reason Defoe had a tricky time defending the Tory ministry was because he inclined to the opinion that the fortifications should not be dismantled at all. Rather, he thought the city should remain in English hands, as it had been at various times before, and that it should be used as a trading port and defensive citadel on the Continent. See Moore, J.R. (1950) 'Defoe, Steele, and the Demolition of Dunkirk'. *Huntington Library Quarterly*, 13 , pp. 279–302.
87   Davis. H. (1939–68) op. cit., vol. VIII, p. 5.
88   Idem.
89   Ibid., vol. VIII, pp. 9–10.
90   Ibid., vol. VIII, p. 12.
91   Ibid., vol. VIII, p. 21.
92   Ibid., vol. VIII, p. 25.
93   Ibid., vol. VIII, p. 76.
94   Williams, H. (1963–65) op. cit., vol. II, p. 32.
95   Davis, H. (1939–68) op. cit., vol. VIII, p. xxiii.

CHAPTER THREE

1   Williams, H. (ed.) (1963–65) *The Correspondence of Jonathan Swift*. 5 Vols. Oxford: Clarendon, vol. II, p. 127.
2   Ibid., vol. II, p. 133.
3   For a full account of these years, and everything else Swift undertook within the church, Landa remains the best source. Ehrenpreis has an excellent summary in *Swift: The Man His Works, and the Age* (1962–83), Cambridge, MA: Harvard University Press, Chapter 2 (pp. 32–58).
4   A vicar choralship was generally held in conjunction with some other living and was a first rung on the ladder of a cathedral's hierarchy. Hook. W.F. (1871) in *A Church Dictionary* defines a vicar choral's responsibilities as being those of an 'assistant or deputy of the canons or prebendaries of collegiate churches . . . especially, though not exclusively in the duties of the choir or chancel, as distinguished from those belonging to the altar and pulpit'. More important than the functions within the cathedral were the various gifts and leases that the vicars choral as a body often controlled.
5   Williams, H. (1963–65) op. cit., vol. I, p. 427.
6   Speck, W.A. (1985) 'Swift and the Historian'. In H.J. Real and H.J. Vienken (eds) *First Munster Symposium on Jonathan Swift*, Munich: Wilhelm Fink, p. 260.
7   Davis, H. (ed.) (1939–68) *Prose Works of Jonathan Swift*, 14 Vols, Oxford: Basil Blackwell, vol. VII, p. xxxv.
8   Williams, H. (1963–65) op. cit., vol. II, p. 112.
9   So well known was Bolingbroke's attitude to Christian teaching, Samuel Johnson made use of it to indulge his own political sympathies when defining 'Irony' in his *Dictionary of the English Language*: 'A mode of speech in which the meaning is contrary to the words: as, *Bolingbroke was a holy man*'.
10   Williams, H. (1963–65) op. cit., vol. II, p. 102.
11   Ibid., vol. II, p. 111.
12   Idem. Bolingbroke's answer of August 11 was a study in stunned hurt. 'I swear I did not imagine, that you could have held out through two pages,

even of small paper, in so grave a style', he began. What followed was a blistering attack on Oxford, charging him with real pride and awkward humility . . . and a heart so void of all tenderness', as well as with 'a temper of engrossing business and power and so perfect an incapacity to manage one'. A final plea was made to Swift to return from Ireland and 'bless me and those few friends who will enjoy you . . . Adieu, love me, and love me the better, because after a greater blow than most have ever felt, I keep up my spirit'. No wonder Swift stayed away. See Williams, H. (1963–65) op. cit., vol. II, p. 117.

13 Ibid., vol. II, p. 206.
14 Davis, H. (1939–68) op. cit., vol. VIII, p. 107.
15 Ibid., vol. VIII, p. xxxiv.
16 Ibid., vol. VIII, p. 107.
17 Idem.
18 Ibid., vol. VIII, p. 108.
19 Williams, H. (1963–65) op. cit., vol. I, p. 262.
20 Davis, H. (1939–68) op. cit., vol. VIII, p. 114.
21 Once again, see Bennett's (1975) *The Tory Crisis in Church and State*, Part I of Chapter 10, 'The Tory Party is Gone', for an analysis of events as high church Tories in England saw them (Oxford: Clarendon, pp. 185–95).
22 Williams, H. (1963–65) op. cit., vol. VII, p. 3. With one exception, the bracketed additions are Harold Williams' and appear in the text from which this is taken. The exception is my reference to the Earl of Oxford. The prosecution reference is to Sacheverell; that to the court appointment is to John Robinson.
23 Ibid., vol. VII, p. 5.
24 Foxcroft, H.C. (1902) *A Supplement to Burnet's* History of My Own Time, Oxford: Clarendon, p. 497.
25 Davis, H. (1939–68) *op cit.*, vol. VII, p. 2.
26 Ehrenpreis, I. (1962–83) op. cit., vol. II, p. 600.
27 Davis, H. (1939–68) op. cit., vol. VII, pp. 96–7.
28 Ibid., vol. VII, p. 107.
29 Ibid., vol. VII, p. 21.
30 Williams, H. (1963–65) op. cit., vol. II, p. 331.
31 Davis, H. (1939–68) op. cit., vol. VIII, p. 88.
32 Ibid., vol. VIII, p. 92.
33 Idem.
34 Ovid (1988) *Epistulae ex Ponto.* (Trans.) A.L. Wheeler. Revised G.P. Gould. Cambridge MA: Harvard University Press, II iii pp. 22–9.
35 Davis, H. (1939–68) op. cit., vol. VIII, p. 131.
36 Ibid., vol. VIII, pp. 132–3.
37 Williams, H. (1963–65) op. cit., vol. II, p. 309.
38 Ibid., vol. II, p. 303.
39 For a reproduction of that title page and Teerink's discovery of it in Marsh's Library, Dublin, see Landa's introduction to Volume IX of Davis, H. (1939–68) op. cit. (xxii).
40 Wilkes, J.H. (1975) 'The Transformation of Dissent: A Review of the Change from the Seventeenth to the Eighteenth Centuries'. *The Dissenting Tradition: Essays for Leland H. Carlson*, (Eds) Cole, C.R. and Moody, M.E. Athens: Ohio University Press, p. 115.
41 Davis, H. (1939–68) op. cit., vol. II, p. 174.
42 Ibid., vol. II, pp. 176–7.
43 Ibid., vol. II, p. 177.
44 Idem.
45 Idem.

46 Although generally included in discussions of Non-juruors, Law's case was significantly different from those deprived of their livings in 1691. Law was born in 1686 and it was the accession of George I, rather than William and Mary, which led to his deprivation. Law's objection to George I was determinedly doctrinal, high church and rooted in his conception of the church–state compact. George's German Lutheranism, with its rejection of episcopacy (in contrast to the Scandinavian Lutherans), made him an unacceptable monarch and head of the Church of England, whose very legitimacy depended, said Law, upon its catholic and apostolic episcopacy.

Ironically, Law's decision to join the Non-jurors came at a time when their influence had almost declined to irrelevance. On the death in 1710 of William Lloyd, Bishop of Norwich, and the last but one of the original Non-juror bishops, Thomas Ken, the popular Non-juror bishop of Bath and Wells, returned to the established church. He was joined, and perhaps encouraged, by Henry Dodwell, the leading lay advocate of the Non-juror position and, incidentally, a graduate of Trinity College, Dublin. Law's deprival, together with a few others, helped breathe life back in to the Non-juror movement. See Cornwall, R.D. (1993) *Visible and Apostolic*. Newark: University of Delaware Press, p. 151.

47 Law, W. (1796) *The Works of the Reverend William Law, M.A., Sometime Fellow of Emmanuel College, Cambridge*, 9 vols. Setley: Hants. vol. II, p. 71.

48 King, W. (1731) *Essay on the Origin of Evil*, London.

49 King, W. (1976) *Sermon on Predestination*, Dublin: Cadenus, pp. 78–9.

50 Ibid., p. 52.

51 King, W. (1731) op. cit., p. 307.

52 Davis, H. (1939–68) op. cit., p. 164.

53 At the Sesquicentennial celebrations at the University of Notre Dame in October 1991, Heinz Vienken told me that marginalia examined by him suggests Swift read the book no more than twice. However, it is unlikely Swift would have bothered commenting on his having read the book four times unless he had done so.

54 Curtis, L.P. (1966) *Anglican Moods of the Eighteenth Century*, Hamden, CT: Archon.

55 Wormwald, B.H.G. (1951) *Clarendon: Politics, History and Religion*, Cambridge: Cambridge University Press.

56 Williams, H. (1963–65) op. cit., vol. III, p. 41.

57 Davis, H. (1939–68) op. cit., vol. IX, p. 158.

58 Ibid., vol. IX, p. 156.

59 Curtis, L.P. (1966) op. cit., p. 47.

60 Tillotson replaced Sancroft as Archbishop of Canterbury when the Non-juror was finally deprived of his post. Tillotson resisted his elevation for some time and allowed Sancroft to remain at Lambeth Palace for several months after his installation as the new primate. Although married to Elizabeth French, a niece of Oliver Cromwell, Tillotson had become chaplain to Charles II soon after that monarch's restoration.

61 Tilloston, J. (1820) *Works*, London, p. 267.

62 Davis, H. (1939–68) op. cit., vol. II, p. 36. John Toland was a native of County Donegal in Ulster and the author of *Christianity Not Mysterious* (1696), a free-thinking tract of significant influence and whose very title was an affront to men such as King and Swift.

63 Ibid., vol. IX, pp. 171–9. For a lengthy consideration of Swift's style in his sermons, see Fanning, C. (1997) 'Sermons on Sermonising: The Pulpit Rhetoric of Swift and Sterne'. *Philological Quarterly* 76:4, pp. 413–37.

64 Ibid., vol. IX, p. 223.

65 Ibid., vol. IX, p. 168.

66   Ibid., vol. IX, P. 63.

67   Ibid., vol. IX, p. 64.

68   Idem. Landa is able to list in a footnote all those present when Swift read his assent to the appointment at Kilroot. It is indicative of the state of the Church of Ireland that the united parishes with Kilroot at their heart had only two parish churches, neither in Kilroot. The church at Ballynure may or may not have had a roof; the one at Templecorran was probably in somewhat better shape. See Landa, L. (1965) *Swift and the Church of Ireland*, Oxford: Clarendon.

69   Rupp, G. (1986) *Religion in England, 1688–1791*, Oxford: Clarendon, pp. 514–15.

70   Ibid., p. 515.

71   Davis, H. (1939–68) op. cit., vol. IX, p. 65.

72   Idem.

73   Ibid., vol. IX, p. 67.

74   Ibid., vol. IX, p. 71.

75   Rupp, G. (1986) op. cit., p. 516.

76   Davis, H. (1939–68) op. cit., vol. IX, p. 68.

77   Ibid., vol. II, p. 57.

78   Ibid., vol. IX, p. 70.

79   Idem.

80   Estabrook, S. (1718) *A Sermon Showing that Peace and Quietness of a People is a main part of the Work of Civil Rulers* . . . New London, CT.

81   Davis, H. (1939–68) op. cit., vol. IX, p. 77.

82   Ibid., vol. IX, pp. 77–8.

83   Ibid., vol. IX, p. 78.

84   Letter to William Wake [5 March 1720] quoted in Ehrenpreis, I. (1962–83) op. cit., vol. III, p. 153.

85   Davis, H. (1939–68) op. cit., vol. IX, p. 81. The Church of England did over time succeed in becoming the church of choice for those who chose not to concern themselves with questions of election and other of the finer issues of doctrine. Then, as now, it was often possible in England to attend services for years without hearing a sermon detailing the specifics of church doctrine. As recently as 1999, a columnist for the *Guardian* reported enthusiastically about a letter he had received from a woman who wrote that:

> I was brought up in the Church of England, and although I don't think I ever believed, I was perfectly prepared to attend irregularly and con-template my spiritual failings . . . But there is now no place for quiet, thinking non-believers who are prepared to conform.

'What is to become of those of us who have the religious temperament but not the faith?' she asked in conclusion (Chancellor, A. (1999), 'Another Country.' 'Pride and Prejudice.' *Guardian Weekend*, 1 May, p. 5).

With the possible exception of that word 'irregularly,' Swift would have thought her an almost perfect member of the Anglican congregation and of society, a shining example of his dictum that freedom of conscience was far from incompatible with the requirement to support the established church.

86   Williams, H. (1963–65) op. cit., vol. II, p. 371.

CHAPTER FOUR

1   Berkeley, G. (1970) *The Querist*. ed. J. Johnston, Dundalk: Dundalgan, No. 80.

2   Davis, H. (ed.) (1939–68) *Prose Works of Jonathan Swift*, 14 vols, Oxford: Basil Blackwell, vol. IX, p. 69.

3 For an analysis of elections throughout Queen Anne's reign, see Richards, J.O. (1972) *Party Propaganda Under Queen Anne: The General Elections of 1702–1713*, Athens: University of Georgia Press.

4 Quoted in Berkeley, G. (1970) op. cit., p. 23.

5 Connolly, S.J. (1998) 'Swift and Protestant Ireland: Images and Reality'. In A. Douglas, P. Kelly and I. Campbell Ross (eds) *Locating Swift*, Dublin: Four Courts Press.

6 In 1711, the Linen Board would be established to try to make the industry national. The Church of Ireland's bishops were reasonably well represented on the board, but along with the other members they had little knowledge of the business and tended to leave the day-to-day operations to the permanent civil service. Although all four provinces were equally represented on the board (18 members from each), the linen trade never became national, and, once the Dublin factors were replaced by their counterparts in Belfast as the principal purchasers of the crop, Ulster's dominance of the industry was assured (adapted from the entry in *The Oxford Companion to Irish History*). For more on the linen trade, see Crawford, W.H. (1988) 'The Evolution of the Linen Trade in Ulster.' *Irish Economic and Social History*, 15, pp. 32–53.

7 Berkeley, G. (1970) op. cit., p. 27.

8 Ibid., p. 28.

9 McDowell, R. (1975) *Irish Public Opinion 1750–1800*, Westport, CT: Greenwood, p. 18. Some of the Anglican Irish analysis of the situation in Ireland was genuinely concerned with theories of freedom and privilege but, as later in the American colonies, many of the secular leaders of Ireland were more concerned with questions of trade and taxation. See Kee, R. (1976) *The Most Distressful Country*, London: Quartet, for a succinct summary of the situation in Ireland at that time (pp. 28–32).

10 Williams, H. (ed.) (1963–65) *The Correspondence of Jonathan Swift*, 5 vols. Oxford: Clarendon, vol. II, p. 369.

11 While Swift was to some extent justified in feeling that promises made to him had not been kept, his treatment by the English ministers was no less fair than that accorded many other Irishmen. See Fischer, J.I. (1986), 'Learning "*David's* Lesson": Some New Information Concerning the Remission of First Fruits and Twentieth Parts in Ireland'. *Swift Studies* 1, pp. 15–23. The variety of uses to which the 'Irish Question' has been put during the past 300 years means that a promise of concession or future favour is best undelivered for as long as possible to preserve temporary alliances. For Swift and Harley, Fischer argues, the longer Harley was promising Swift advancement rather than delivering it, the longer Swift would continue in his retinue. There were other reasons Swift was not promoted to an English deanery, but this was one of the most compelling.

12 Quoted in Mahony, R. (1991) '"Price Posterity" as an Irish Nationalist'. The International Association for the Studies of Anglo-Irish Literature. Rijksuniversiteit te Leiden, Netherlands, 9 July 1991.

13 Like Foot's essay in *Debts of Honour*, Mahony's excellent book is a constant reminder that politicians and polemicists have often better understood Swift than have the literary critics. (Quoted in Mahony, R. (1995) *Jonathan Swift: The Irish Identity*. New Haven: Yale University Press p. 14)

14 Davis, H. (1939–68) op. cit., vol. IX, p. 18. A useful book compiled by Joseph McMinn helps increase awareness of the extraordinary depth and variety of Swift's Irish Pamphlets. McMinn's book offers an excellent selection of the pamphlets, including several lesser known ones and one sermon, which makes clear the essential integrity of the entire Irish corpus.

See McMinn, J. (1991b) *Swift's Irish Pamphlets: An Introductory Selection*, Bucks: Colin Smythe.

15   John Vesey (1638–1716) was another of those courageous clerics whose conduct during the Williamite wars should have been sufficient to put the lie to English stereotypes of Church of Ireland ministers. Unfortunately, he also demonstrated significant interest in his own personal comfort. Vesey may have been ordained during the Commonwealth interregnum, while still too young, by John Lesley, the royalist Bishop of Raphoe. On 18 March 1678, he was translated from Limerick, Ardfert and Arghadoe, to Tuam. In contravention of accepted practice, he insisted on retaining the 'quarta pars episcopalis', or a quarter of most of the tithes collected within the archdiocese, a practice discontinued by Edward Synge on his translation to the see following Vesey's death.

Vesey remained in his archdiocese during the Williamite wars until he felt his life itself was threatened. Along with Richard Tenison, Bishop of Clogher, he was generally reckoned to have provided an example to many of the lower clergy of his province. James II had Vesey's name included on the list of those proscribed by the last Stuart parliament, and upon William of Orange's pacification of Ireland Vesey was rewarded with some honours and in 1712 and 1714 was appointed a lord justice. He died on 28 March 1716 at his palace at Holymount which was then reckoned 'one of the pleasantest places in Ireland' (adapted from the entry in the *DNB.*).

16   Davis, H. (1939–68) op. cit., vol. IX, p. 17. I would like to thank Michael DePorte for repeating to me the story that Eamonn De Valera, Ireland's first president, questioned Swift's suitability as a hero for the newly independent country but was reassured with the phrase 'burn everything English but their coal'. I believe DePorte got the story from the then Dean of St Patrick's. Ehrenpreis provides further evidence of the currency of this saying when he repeats this brief story in a footnote: 'In July 1947 when I was reading in the National Library, Dublin, a stack-boy asked me what I was studying. "Jonathan Swift," I said. "Oh yes", said the page, "Burn everything English but their coal"'. See Ehrenpreis, I. (1962–83) *Swift: The Man, His Works, and the Age*, Cambridge, MA: Harvard University Press, vol. III, p. 126n.

17   Donald Akenson gives information for the religious affiliation of Ireland's population compiled from hearth tax returns in the 1730s:

Province	Protestants	Catholics	Ratio, P:C
Ulster	62,624	38,459	3:2
Leinster	25,241	92,434	1:3.6
Munster	13,337	106,407	1:8
Connaught	4,299	44,101	1:10

These figures are approximate as tax returns included only a portion of the population. If anything, the number of Catholics, who made up a disproportionate percentage of the itinerant population, are underestimated. Note that the number of Protestants includes Presbyterians and other Dissenters, and even in Ulster the Church of Ireland did not constitute a majority. Most of the Protestants in the provinces of Leinster, Munster, and Connaught would have been Church of Ireland adherents. (See Akenson, D.H. [1971] *The Church of Ireland: Ecclesiastical Reform and Revolution, 1800–1885*, New Haven: Yale University Press p. 66.). Alan Harrison (1999) has a brief but interesting discussion of the sociolinguistics of Ireland in his book *The Dean's Friend:*

Anthony Raymond 1675–1726, Jonathan Swift and the Irish Language, Blackrock: de Búrca. The most recent work on the population of Ireland in the eighteenth-century can be found in Dickson, D. Ó Gráda, C. and Daultry, S. (1982) 'Hearth Tax, Household Size and Irish Population Change *c*.1672–1821.' *Proceedings of the Royal Irish Academy* 82(c), pp. 125–81.

18 Ehrenpreis, I. (1962–83) op. cit., vol. III, p. 266.

19 Joining King in opposing the act had been earls Tyrone and Londonderry and Viscount Dungannon. Only James Power, Earl of Tyrone, came from a traditionally Catholic family.

20 Quoted in James, F.G. (1979) 'The Church of Ireland in the Early 18th Century', *Historical Magazine of the Protestant Episcopal Church* 48:4 (Dec.) p. 446.

21 McNally, P. (1995) '"Irish and English Interests": National Conflict within the Church of Ireland Episcopiate in the Reign of George I'. *Irish Historical Studies* XXIX, pp. 295–314.

22 Ibid., pp. 303–4.

23 Lords spiritual were, as their name implies, entitled to sit in the House of Lords by virtue of their clerical rank. In Ireland, all the bishops and archbishops of the Church of Ireland were entitled to a seat in the House of Lords. Lords temporal were the hereditary holders of honours conferred by the monarchy. In Ireland, all lay peers entitled through the Irish list and peers of the joint English and Irish list were entitled to a seat in Dublin. Most peers who were also entitled to a seat in Westminster, by virtue of holding an English as well as an Irish title, preferred to sit there, if they took any part in politics at all.

24 Sources for the composition of the Irish upper house are diverse. See, for example, MacNeill, J.G.S. (1917), *The Constitutional and Parliamentary History of Ireland Till the Union*. Dublin: Talbot (1910–59); copies of the *The Journal of the Irish House of Lords*, the parliamentary record of the upper house; and Cokayne, G.E. (1910–59) *The Complete Peerage of England, Scotland, Ireland, Great Britain and the United Kingdom*, revised by V. Gibbs, G. White and R.S. Lea, London: St Catherine. See also, James, F.G. (1973) *Ireland in the Empire 1688–1770*, Cambridge MA: Harvard University Press, especially Chapter 4, 'The Origins of a Patriot Party.' (pp. 83–109), and (1991) 'The Aristocracy of Ireland's *Ancien regime*.' *Eire–Ireland* XXVI:4, pp. 16–28. Scotland, where the Presbyterian church remained established after the Act of Union, had no lords spiritual as the Presbyterian church has neither bishops nor archbishops.

25 The importance in which Irish peerages were held by all but a handful of native-born Irishmen is most starkly revealed by the steadily declining numbers of temporal peers in the first half of the eighteenth century. By 1751 there were only twenty-eight lords temporal entitled through the Irish list alone, a figure that not coincidentally mirrored the number of Irish peers principally resident in that country. Cokayne provides details of the decline in Irish titles unmerged with English or Scottish titles.

26 Rotten boroughs were those with a constituency so small as to be virtually devoid of eligible voters. Pocket boroughs were those constituencies where the patronage of a local potentate was sufficient to guarantee that the candidate, or candidates, of his choice would be elected. Ireland was, of course, hardly unique. The most famous constituency in England throughout the eighteenth-century was Old Sarum, which in 1728 had an electorate of three people, which grew to five in 1734. The voters would meet under the 'election tree,' an oak which stood until 1905, to cast their votes, invariably for the Whig candidate. Banbury in Oxfordshire had eighteen voters who returned one member to parliament, while Christchurch, Kent, had two members returned

by eighteen voters. In Scotland, Orkney and Shetland's seven voters elected one representative to parliament. On the other hand, Westminster had 8,000 voters returning one member and as a result of its wide franchise tended to elect some of the most radical members of parliament. For further details see Sedgwick, R. (ed.) (1970) *The House of Commons 1715–1754*, Oxford: Oxford University Press. The equivalent Irish term was 'close' borough.

27   See Plowden, F.P. (1803) *An Historical Review of the State of Ireland*, London. Plowden's estimation of affairs, which he wrote at the request of the British government, was independent enough to cost him his patronage. He then lost an 1813 libel case brought against him as a result of the book and was fined the enormous sum of £5,000. He fled to Paris to avoid payment and died there. (Adapted from the *DNB*.)

28   MacNeill, J.G.S. (1917) op. cit., p. 75.

29   One further bizarre consequence of Ireland's uncertain constitutional status was that in addition to its own parliament, and to the Irish peers who sat in the British House of Lords as a result of British peerages held with their Irish titles, there were also members of the British House of Commons elected from Irish constituencies. Most of these MPs were Englishmen who were never resident in Ireland. In 1715, there were 25 such 'Irish' MPs; by 1734 that number had fallen to 13, (see Sedgwick, R. (1970) op. cit., vol. I, pp. 156–8). Many English politicians believed these MPs to be a legitimate representation of Ireland, a situation compounded by the frequent lobbying of 'Irish' members undertaken by both the Dublin Castle administration and their Irish-born opponents.

30   The six were Henry Downes of Killala, John Evans of Meath, Nicholas Forster of Raphoe, Timothy Godwin of Kilmore, Ralph Lambert of Dromore and William Nicholson of Derry. See James, F.G. (1979) op. cit., pp. 433–51.

31   Berkeley, G. (1970) op. cit., p. 12.

32   For this economic summary I am indebted to Johnston's introductory remarks to *The Querist*, especially pp. 10–19 and 36–71.

33   'Rackrent' itself technically refered to the practice of sub-letting and sub-sub-letting and beyond with each tier seeing a profit taken at each level of rent. The final renter, two or three times removed from the landlord and renting a fraction of the land that had usually been originally rented to a single person, was raising a crop on a small plot at a steep rent while the landlord often saw only a part of the total rents being paid on the estate, the remainder of the rents, the 'profit rent,' being kept back by the middlemen. A rackrent was invariably out of balance with the generating capacity of the land.

34   Davis, H. (1939–68) op. cit., vol. IX, p. 68.

35   Ibid., vol. IX, p. 81.

36   Williams, H. (1963–65) op. cit., vol. II, p. 342.

37   When still Bishop of Derry, King had used almost exactly the same terminology when writing to Foy about the 1703 proposal for a convocation: 'I own a Convocation necessary . . . but all assemblies that have been long chained up prove unruly when first let loose and I am afraid this would prove in our present juncture a reason of abrogating them altogether, which I am afraid will happen . . . ' Quoted in Murray, Rev R.H. (1933) 'The Church and the Revolution'. In Phillips, W.A. (ed.) *History of the Church of Ireland from the Earliest Times to the Present Day*, 3 vols, London: Oxford University Press, vol. III, p. 164.

38   Davis, H. (1939–68) op. cit., vol. IX, p. 15.

39   MacNeill, J.G.S. (1917) op. cit., pp. 72–3.

40   Davis H, (1939–68) op. cit., vol. IX, p. 15.

41 Boulter, H. (1770) *Letters written by His Excellency Hugh Boulter D.D. . . .* 2 Vols, Dublin, vol. I. p. 210.

42 Bindon, D. (1738) *A Letter from a Merchant . . .* London, pp. 4–5.

43 Bindon shared with Swift an overarching cynicism about what happened when private and public interests clashed: 'There are,' he writes, 'but few men in any Country who will prefer the public Good to their private Interest, when they happen to be inconsistent with one another.' Ibid., p. 12.

44 Burns, R.E. (1989) *Irish Parliamentary Politics in the Eighteenth Century*, 2 vols, Washington, DC: Catholic University of America Press, vol. I, pp. 92–3.

45 Davis, H. (1939–68) op. cit., vol. XIII, p. 90. Things never changed much, except that what had once annoyed became somehow quaint, and the man who was perhaps Anglo-Ireland's last poet, Louis MacNeice (son of the Anglican bishop of Down, Connor, and Dromore) remarked more than two hundred years after Swift on 'His glint of joy in cunning as the farmer asks / Twenty per cent too much'. From 'Train to Dublin' in MacNeice, L. (1966) *Collected Poems*. (Ed.) E.R. Dodds, London: Faber, p. 28.

46 Davis, H. (1939–68) op. cit., vol. IX, p. 15.

47 Idem.

48 McMinn, J. (1991a) *Jonathan Swift: A Literary Life*, Basingstoke, Hants: Macmillan, p. 80.

49 Williams, H. (1963–65) op. cit., vol. II, p. 312.

50 Ibid., vol. II, pp. 329–30.

51 Ibid., vol. II, p. 342.

52 Idem.

53 Poynings' Law, named for Henry VII's Lord Lieutenant in Ireland, also functioned as a classic housekeeping bill which simply announced that all English statutes then in force also applied to Ireland. Since those statutes included the measures which gave the English parliament its very authority to legislate, most English jurists interpreted Poynings' Law effectively to give the English parliament authority over the Irish by virtue of English enabling acts, some dating back as far as the Magna Carta of 1215. The first sustained Irish critique of Poynings' Law was perhaps *An Argument delivered by Patricke Darcy, Esquire; by the Expresse Order of the House of Commons in the Parliament of Ireland*. This seminal work helped shape a brief 1641 alliance between Catholics and Ulster Protestants and was important in shaping the ideas of several framers of the United States' declaration of independence. It deserves to be better known. See Rowan P.B. (nd) *Catalogue 51 Books and perodicals of Irish Interest*. Belfast.

54 Burns, R.E. (1989) op. cit., vol. I, p. 105.

55 As with so much of Westminster's legislation directed at Ireland, the Declaratory Act left plenty of loose ends for all sides to continue to worry at until they could find some aspect of the legislation to benefit their particular case. While it sought to explain the connection between the Irish and British parliaments, the Declaratory Act failed to address the matter of relations between the two government-sanctioned Anglican churches – the Church of Ireland and the Church of England. These relations had long been confusing and had never really been clear, however much either side of the debate in the early 1700s liked to imagine the state of affairs had once been different. Alan Ford offers a useful thumbnail sketch of relations between the two churches from the twelfth century onwards. In 1140, for example, 'Bishop Patrick of Limerick was consecrated . . . at Canterbury and acknowledged the Archbishop of Canterbury as "totius Britanniae primas"' (Ford, A. (1995) 'Dependent or

Independent? The Church of Ireland and its Colonial Context, 1536–1649'. *The Seventeenth Century*. X:2, p. 165). Naturally, it was the Reformation which exposed the uncertain nature of the relationship between the two churches. Equally unsurprising was that Henry VIII's solution actually just complicated the matter. In 1536, the Irish Act of Supremacy was passed, mirroring the English act of two years earlier. It acknowledged Henry as '"the only supreme head in earth of the whole church of Ireland, called Hibernica Ecclesia". Just as in the secular sphere, so to in the ecclesiastical: the King joined the two polities together in his person' (Ford, pp. 165–6). As Ford goes on to demonstrate, this joining of the two polities in one person failed to clarify whether the polities themselves were commingled or whether they relied upon the same royal personage for their authority but continued to function, to some degree, as independent entities.

Another distinction between the two churches was their confessions of faith. It took the Church of England some time to arrive at the Thirty-Nine Articles, but the Church of Ireland began with Archbishop Parker's Eleven Articles (1561) which became the Twelve Articles in 1567. From then until 1615 these remained the Church of Ireland's confession of faith. In 1615, convocation produced the One-Hundred-and-Four Articles. These included the Church of England's Thirty-Nine Articles and a good number of the Homilies which the English Articles had described as 'godly and wholesome doctrine' even as they were not included in the Articles themselves; but there are distinctions, too, most noticeably in the Church of Ireland's much clearer, and far more Calvinist, definition of the church's position on predestination. While obviously related to the Church of England's confession of faith, the Church of Ireland's confession was not the same as its English counterpart's (Ford, 168–70). The history of the Church of England at this time is also important for understanding certain Church of Ireland fears and assumptions. A good place to start is Walsh J., Haydon, C. and Taylor, S. (eds) (1993) *The Church of England c.1689–c.1833: From Toleration to Tractarianism*, Cambridge: Cambridge University Press. See also Young, B.W. (1998) *Religion and Englightenment in Eighteenth-Century England; Theological Debate from Locke to Burke*, Oxford: Clarendon.

56   Ehrenpreis, I. (1962–83) op. cit., vol. III, p. 125.
57   Ibid., vol. IX, p. 16.
58   McMinn, J. (1991b) op. cit., p. 15.
59   Davis, H. (1939–68) op. cit., vol. IX, p. 16.
60   Idem.
61   Davis, H. (1939–68) op. cit., vol. IX, p. 16.
62   Idem.
63   MacNeill, J.G.S. (1917) op. cit., p. 72.
64   Davis, H. (1939–68) op. cit., vol. IX, p. 16.
65   Ibid., vol. IX, p. 16.
66   McMinn, J. (1991a) op. cit., p. 96.
67   Davis, H. (1939–68) op. cit., vol. IX, pp. 16–17.
68   This letter is useful in demonstrating the tricky ground upon which both sides walked when discussing 'Irish' rights. Here, King is relying upon the Magna Carta and the rights granted the Church of England to make his case for the Church of Ireland, a church he would not have considered subservient to the Church of England, although presumably as it drew its rights from those granted that church it could just as easily lose them if the Church of England were to lose its privileges. This would become another tricky point

as the Church of England did start losing its protections as a landholder and as toleration increasingly became the policy in England, both trends the Church of Ireland clerics sought to oppose (in these two cases largely without regard to their country of birth). It is not surprising that King, Stearne, Synge and others were careful with their language so that, as McNally notes:

> there is little evidence of a conscious sense of national identity on the part of the Irish clergy. References to the 'Irish interest' are normally found only in the letters of English politicians and bishops, who also referred to the Irish-born Anglican clergy as 'the natives'. King, Stearne, Synge, and Swift might have increasingly made their claims for political rights in light of events in Ireland, but that did not mean they saw themselves as arguing for uniquely 'Irish' rights.

See McNally, P. (1995) op. cit., pp. 313–14.

69   Davis, H. (1939–68) op. cit., vol. IX, p. 17.

70   Ibid., vol. IX, p. 18.

71   Ibid., vol. IX, p. 17.

72   James observes that the quintessential historian of the period, J.C. Beckett, 'notes that the episcopal bench was evenly divided between Irish and English prelates at Boulter's death in 1742, but he fails to point out that the ratio was the same when Boulter became primate in 1724' (see James, F.G. (1979) op. cit., p. 442). What James in turn fails to point out is that the disposition of various livings was increasingly advantageous to non-Irish born clergy. After King's death, the archdiocese of Dublin was granted to an Irish-born cleric on only one of five occasions when the see became vacant prior to 1801. Similarly, Derry, which was wealthier even than Dublin, was held without interruption by English-born clerics from Nicolson's appointment until well into the nineteenth century. Kildare, too, was consistently held by Englishmen; it was prized because it came with the Deanship of Christ Church Cathedral, Dublin and allowed permanent residence in that city. Akenson has detailed these and other trends, among them that 'appointments to the Provinces of Cashel and Tuam, generally the poorest parts of the country . . . were dominated by the Irish-born prelates' (Akenson, D.H. (1971) op. cit., p. 25). Indeed, by 1725 King was complaining to Southwell [29 December 1725], the one ally he had left in the British government, that 'there have been above £20,000 [given to "strangers"], & I understand several have not yet come to my knowledge. There are several vacancies now in prospect to the value of some thousands, & I hear strangers are already named for them'. (King, C.S. (ed.) (1906) *A Great Archbishop of Dublin*, London: Longmans, Green, p. 252). On Synge's death, the living of Tuam was awarded to Josiah Hort, a former chaplain to Lord Wharton, and, more tellingly, the product of a Nonconformist education. King, Synge, Swift and Beckett might have been wrong on the numbers, but James is perhaps more seriously mistaken when he confuses numbers with influence.

73   Davis, H. (1939–68) op. cit., vol. IX, p. 18.

74   Idem.

75   Ibid., vol. IX, p. 20.

76   Idem.

77   Ibid., vol. IX, p. 21.

78   Williams, H. (1963–65) op. cit., vol. IV, p. 70.

79   Boulter, H. (1770) op. cit., vol. I, p. 12.

80   Davis, H. (1939–68) op. cit., vol. IX, p. 21.

81   Ibid., vol. IX, p. 20.

82   Idem.
83   Ibid., vol. IX, p. 18.
84   Ibid., vol. IX, p. 21.
85   Quoted in Mahony, R. (1995) *Swift's Irish Identity*, New Haven: Yale University Press, pp. 74–5.
86   Idem.

CHAPTER FIVE

1   Pocock, J.G.A. (1987) (ed.) 'Introduction' from *Reflections on the Revolution in France* by Edmund Burke. Indianapolis: Hackett, p. xi.
2   The first professor of economics at a British university was not appointed until the beginning of the nineteenth century, an appointment that went to the Rev. Thomas Robert Malthus. Even then, the new college at Haileybury combined the history professorship with that of political economy. Adam Smith and others whom we today think of as the founders of modern economics held professorships in mathematics or philosophy, if they held any academic position at all. Charles Mann's essay on the legacy of Malthus reminds us that it was Malthus's *Essay on Population* (first published, anonymously, in 1798) that earned the field the sobriquet 'dismal science', a term coined by Thomas Carlyle. See Mann, C. (1993) 'How many is too many' *Atlantic Monthly* (Feb.) pp. 47–67.
3   In his *Short View of the State of Ireland*, Swift encapsulates his opinion of Whitshed, who had *'Libertas & natale Solum* [Liberty and my native country] written as a Motto on his Coach, as it stood at the Door of the Court, while he was perjuring himself to betray both'. See Davis, H. (ed.) (1939–68) *Prose Works of Jonathan Swift*, 14 vols, Oxford: Basil Blackwell, vol. XII, p. 8. This mutual animosity should serve to remind us that personality often prevents what might otherwise be alliances. Whitshed was a committed Anglican and the leading opponent of toleration within Dublin Castle. He was also a close friend of William King, who sought to intervene on his behalf during the pamphlet assault by Swift.
4   Ehrenpreis, I. (1962–83) *Swift: The Man, His Works and the Age*, 3 vols, Cambridge, MA: Harvard University Press, vol. III, pp. 129–30.
5   Williams, H. (ed.) (1963–65) *The Correspondence of Jonathan Swift*, 5 vols., Oxford: Clarendon, vol. II, p. 358.
6   Swift's efforts on behalf of Waters were extensive and exhaustive, but Burns and others argue with good reason that Grafton had already decided to drop the case against Waters before Swift made his final approach through Sir Thomas Hanmer. See Burns, R.E. (1989) *Irish Parliamentary Politics in the Eighteenth Century*, 2 vols, Washington, DC: Catholic University of America Press, vol. I, p. 113.
7   Rogers, P. (ed.) (1983) *Jonathan Swift: The Complete Poems*, New Haven: Yale University Press.
8   Idem.
9   McMinn, J. (1991a) *Jonathan Swift: A Literary Life*. Hants: Macmillan, p. 98.
10 Mahony provides an excellent account of Swift's reputation among both the Protestant and Catholic Irish from his death in 1745 until the modern era in *Swift's Irish Identity* (1995) New Haven: Yale University Press. In short, he argues that one reason Swift was not extolled by certain late eighteenth- and early nineteenth-century Catholic advocates was that:

Swift's patriotic efforts were frequently regarded in England as spurious, motivated by disappointment at the thwarting of his ambitions for preferment or influence there . . . He had, moreover, a popular reputation in England as an eccentric, ribald parson, unduly given to scatology; Irish Catholic leaders, anxious to demonstrate their respectability, had all the greater reason therefore to make little mention of him. ('"Prince Posterity" as an Irish Nationalist: The Posthumous Course of Swift's Patriotic Reputation' Rijksuniversiteit te Leiden, Netherlands)

11   Williams, H. (1963–65) op. cit., vol. II, p. 353.
12   Ibid., vol. II, p. 378.
13   Ibid., vol. II, p. 392.
14   Ibid., vol. II, p. 342.
15   Quoted in Ehrenpreis, I. (1962–83) op. cit., vol. III, p. 136.
16   References to this particular letter are to Angus Ross and David Woolley's edition of *Jonathan Swift* in the Oxford Authors series. The letter is more an essay than an epistle, a point reinforced by taking it out of the context of the *Correspondence*. See Ross, A. and Woolley, D. (eds.) (1984) *Jonathan Swift*, Oxford University Press, p. 411.
17   McMinn, J. (1991a) op. cit., p. 98.
18   Ross and Woolley (1984) op. cit., p. 411.
19   Idem.
20   Ibid., p. 412.
21   Idem.
22   Ibid., p. 416.
23   Ibid., pp. 412–13.
24   Ibid., p. 413.
25   Idem.
26   Ibid., p. 416.
27   Ibid., p. 417.
28   Ferguson, O.W. (1962) *Jonathan Swift and Ireland*, Urbana: University of Illinois Press, pp. 187–8.
29   Ibid., p. 188.
30   Montag, W. (1994) *The Unthinkable Swift*, London: Verso, p. 128.
31   Ibid., p. 144.
32   The modern-day relationship between the Iranian *Majlis* and the *velayat-e-faqih* is perhaps the closest model to Swift's view of the ideal church-state compact that has ever existed, not in the sense of the policies but certainly in the manner of the apparatus of polity. That that apparatus has proved increasingly strained since the death of Ayatollah Khomeini only serves to highlight the idealistic nature of such a system (see Rouleau, É. (June 1999) 'Islam Confronts Islam in Iran', *Le Monde Diplomatique*, pp. 1–3, for an explanation of the *Majlis/velayat-e-faqih* relationship and the stresses that are appearing). Swift, of course, was not theocratic and he would not have recognised the idea of a theocratic state in its modern incarnation. He did, however, support the idea of a civil government faithful to the demands of an established church and requiring all civil officers to be adherents of that church and, in some manner, loyal to its principles. Whether he would have required belief in addition to action is a different matter.
33   Davis, H. (1939–68) op. cit., vol. XI, pp. 197–202.
34   Ibid., p. 196.
35   Ibid., p. 198.
36   DePorte, M. (1993b) 'Swift's Horses of Instruction'. In Rodino, R.H. and Real, H.J. (eds) *Reading Swift*, Munich: Wilhelm Fink, pp. 207, 211.

37   This admission by Caesar would seem not only to demonstrate Swift's orthodox belief in the afterlife (as does the whole process of summoning the dead), it also suggests he believed that upon death the sins of our lives are revealed to us, and we, presumably, repent of them. Whether there is a hell or not Swift does not address, but here he may have been in advance of Anglican thought. The Church of England ruled in 1999 that there is no hell, merely a moment of recognition of our failings when we confront God at our death. Davis, H. (1939–68) op. cit., vol. XI, p. 196.

38   Davis, H. (1939–68) op. cit., vol. XI, p. 131. See also pp. 50, 60.

39   In an interesting but often overlooked tract, Swift advocates the active elimination of the Irish language, among the benefits of which would be that it would 'reduce great numbers [of the Irish] to the national religion, *whatever kind may then happen to be established* (emphasis added) (*An Answer to Several Letters Sent Me From Unknown Hands*. In Davis, H. (1939–68) op. cit., vol xii, p. 89). This is the clearest statement Swift makes anywhere that what matters is the fact of establishment, not the doctrine of the established church.

40   This analysis of the church-state compact helps explain Swift's principal objections to the Catholic church, objections which are more often expressed as social than as doctrinal points of contention. For Swift, the church in Spain, France, and the Papal states was the state, an abettor and beneficiary of absolutist powers. In Ireland, and in England, the Churches of Ireland and England, established though they were, were, or could be, guarantors of protection from absolutism.

41   Davis, H. (1939–68) op. cit., vol. XI, p. 225.

42   Pope, A. (1940–69) *The Poems*, (ed.) J. Butt, 11 vols, London: Methuen. Lines 69–74 of 'Epistle to Bathurst'.

43   In fact, Poynings' Law had been designed to curb the powers of the lord lieutenancy not of Parliament. See, Darcy, P. (1641) *An Argument delivered by Patricke Darcy, Esquire . . .* Dublin.

44   Davis, H. (1939–68) op. cit., vol. IX, p. 21.

45   Burns, R.E. (1989) op. cit., vol. I, p. 114.

46   While the English parliament and court made liberal use of Poynings' Law, there was no corollary that meant English laws passed after 1495 (the date of Poynings' Law) necessarily applied to Ireland. So just as today parliament in Westminster must specifically include Scotland in legislation that would otherwise affect only England and Wales, eighteenth-century laws that did not specifically mention Ireland could be held not to apply to that country. Failure, deliberate or otherwise, to mention Ireland in various electoral reform bills passed in Westminster after 1688 meant the Irish parliament was not required to meet on any stipulated schedule. When parliament did meet, it traditionally tried to follow a biennial pattern, sitting only every other year. The increasing frequency with which the Irish parliament met after 1709 indicates the steadily worsening Irish fiscal situation.

47   Burns, R.E. (1989) op. cit., pp. 114–20.

48   At the first session of the Irish parliament after his return, Grafton was asked to produce the royal warrant concerning the bank charter by that Friday. On Friday he was forced to tell the House of Lords that the warrant had been misplaced – a story they were loath to believe despite its truthfulness. Soon thereafter, the warrant was found among a stack of timber shipped from England with Grafton. Grafton returned to the House with the news immediately, but the idea that a royal warrant had been lost in a woodpile resulted only in ridicule and a suspicion that the House was being

deliberately mocked. In many ways this event was typical of Grafton, a man who was unsuccessful more for being unfortunate than incompetent.

49 See Burns, R.E. (1989) op. cit., vol. I, p. 122. Specie is the term for the actual coinage in circulation. It does not measure available money, that is credit, promissory notes, etc.

50 Burns, R.E. (1989) op. cit., vol. I, p. 129.

51 Idem.

52 Ibid., vol. I, p. 130.

53 Kelly, P.H. (1991) *Locke on Money*, 2 vols, Oxford: Clarendon.

54 Ibid., vol. I, p. 67.

55 Kelly, J. (1990) 'Jonathan Swift and the Irish Economy in the 1720s'. *Eighteenth-Century Ireland*, 6, pp. 13–14.

56 Davis, H. (1939–68) op. cit., vol. IX, pp. 58–9.

57 Kelly, P.H. (1991) op. cit., vol. I, p. 67. Joseph Harris, Joseph Massie and Sir James Steuart were among the founders on modern economic theory. The tracts to which Kelly refers are Harris's *An Essay upon Money and Coins*, part ii (1757); Massie's *Observations Relating to the Coinage of Great Britain; consisting partly of Extracts from Mr Locke's Treatise concerning Money, but chiefly of such Additions thereunto, as are thought to be very Necessary at this Juncture . . .* (1760); and Steuart's *An Inquiry into the Principles of Political Œconomy. Being an Essay on the Science of Domestic Policy in Free Nations* (1767).

58 Ibid., vol. I, pp. 68–9.

59 Ibid., p. 311. As with Royalist forces in besieged garrisons during the English Civil War, who minted so-called 'siege currency' in base metals secured against later access to precious metals, so James in Ireland, appealing to precedent in addition to his royal prerogative to mint money outside England, issued copper currency in Ireland in 1688 and 1689. After the Williamite Wars, Irish copper money was bought in bulk by English and Scottish speculators at vast discounts, further undermining Irish specie.

60 King, W. (1768) *The State of the Protestants of Ireland under the Late King James's Government*, London, p. 43.

61 Davis, H. (1939–68) op. cit., vol. X, p. 8.

62 Kelly, P.H. (1991) op. cit., p. 88.

63 Maxwell, H. (1721) *Reasons offered for erecting a Bank in Ireland*, Dublin, p. 11.

64 Ibid., p. 14.

65 Ibid., p. 11.

66 Ibid., pp. 50–1, emphasis added.

67 Rowley, H. (1721) *An Answer to a Book Entitled 'Reasons Offered for Erecting a Bank in Ireland'*, Dublin, p. 5.

68 Ibid., p. 39.

69 Ibid., p. 26.

70 Davis, H. (1939–68) op. cit., vol. XII, p. 5.

71 McMinn, J. (1991a) op. cit., pp. 100–1.

72 Williams, H. (1963–65) op. cit., vol. II, p. 405.

73 Ehrenpreis, I. (1962–83) op. cit., vol. III, p. 162.

74 Williams, H. (1963–65) op. cit., vol. II, p. 387.

75 Ibid., vol. II, p. 412.

76 Ibid., vol. II, p. 411.

77 In his introduction to Volume IX of the *Prose Works*, Landa assesses the relative merits of these attributions (pp. xvii–xxvi).

78 Davis, H. (1939–68) op. cit., vol. IX, p. 288. The two bishops were John Smyth, Bishop of Down and Connor, and Ralph Lambert, Bishop of Dromore. Both

were English transplants. Swift's relationship with Lambert dated back to 1708 when Lambert had been offered the position of Chaplain to the Earl of Wharton, a post Swift himself had anticipated.

79 This number of 2,000,000 included Catholics. Swift considered their labour an integral part of Ireland's wealth, even if he saw no reason for them to participate in any of Ireland's political institutions. The estimate of 2,000,000 is somewhat lower than most contemporary observers', but is typical of Swift's consistently low estimates and is perhaps the best argument for his authorship of the *Subscribers* pamphlet. See Lein, C. (1975) 'Jonathan Swift and the Population of Ireland'. *Eighteenth-Century Studies*, 8:4, pp. 451–3. See also the note to Chapter 4 of this study discussing hearth tax returns for this period.

CHAPTER SIX

1 King, W. (1731) *Essay on the Origin of Evil*, London. Appendix III, p. 318.
2 This relationship was well recognised. Ford's verses, 'To Swift, on His Birthday 30 November 1727', refer to the affair of Wood's half-penny by remarking on:

> . . . fraudulentus Præses Hiberniæ,
> Et turpe scortum, et latro paraverant
> mpune partiri labores
> Artificis miseri at coloni.

[the deceitful Governor of Ireland, and a filthy whore, and a bandit had prepared to divide among themselves with impunity (the profits of) the toils of the wretched of the colony.] (Quoted in Carpenter, A. (ed.) (1978) *Adventure At Sienna*, Dublin: Cadenus, pp. 80, 82. [prose translation by Ray Astbury with minor modifications].)
3 This summary of the early days of the patent is adapted from Coxe, W. (1816) *Memoirs of . . . Sir Robert Walpole* (vol. I: pp. 217–20), of which Ehrenpreis gives an excellent summary ((1962–83) *Swift: The Man, His Works and the Age*, Cambridge, MA: Cambridge University Press, vol. III, pp. 187–9).
4 Berkeley, G. (1970) *The Querist*. (Ed.) Johnston, J. Dundalk: Dundalgan, pp. 52–71.
5 Davis, H. (1939–68) *Prose Works of Jonathan Swift*, 14 vols. Oxford: Basil Blackwell, vol. X. p. 189.
6 Rents were usually set in Irish currency and the acreage measured in Irish acres which were some 1.6 times larger than English acres (the ratio of Irish to English acres was 49:30.25).
7 Quoted in Berkeley, G. (1970) op. cit., p. 63.
8 Davis, H. (1939–68) op. cit., vol. XII, p. 11.
9 Williams, H. (ed.) (1963–65) *The Correspondence of Jonathan Swift*. Oxford: Claredon, vol. II, pp. 419–20. The guinea, first minted in 1663 and designed for trade with the west coast of Africa, hence its name, was fixed at a value of 21*s* in England in 1717 (£1.1*s*.0*d*). Prior to that it had fluctuated in value, ranging anywhere from its nominal face value of 20*s* (£1.0*s*.0*d*) to 30*s* (£1.10*s*.0*d*) in 1695. It is indicative of English negligence of Irish affairs when passing domestic reforms that the 1717 fixing of the guinea's value in Britain did not fix its value in Ireland. (Prior to decimalisation in Britain on 15 February 1971, there were 12 pence to a shilling and 20 shillings to a pound.)
10 Ibid., p. 419.

11 Among his English contacts, only Bolingbroke claimed to understand Ireland's plight (doubtless for his own reasons) and actually admonished Swift, in a letter of 28 July 1721, that 'the condition of your wretched country is worse than you represent . . . I mourn over Ireland with all my heart, but I pity you more . . . [Y]ou are really in a very bad way'. See Williams, H. (1963–65) op. cit., vol. II, p. 397.

12 Jones, D.W. (1991) 'Sequel to Revolution: The Economics of England's Emergence as a Great Power, 1688–1712'. In Israel, J.I. (ed.) *The Anglo–Dutch Moment*, Cambridge: Cambridge University Press, pp. 389–406.

13 See Dickson, P.G.M. (1967) *The Financial Revolution in England*, New York: St Martin's.

14 Daston, L. (1988) *Classical Probability in the Enlightenment*, Princeton: Princeton University Press.

15 Ibid., p. 164.

16 From 'An Essay on Projects' (1697) quoted in Daston (1988) op. cit., pp. 164–5.

17 Horne, T. (1978) *The Social Thought of Bernard Mandeville: Virtue and Commerce in Early Eighteenth Century England*, New York: Columbia University Press, p. 54.

18 Ekelund, R. and Tollison, R. (1981) *Mercantilism as a Rent–Seeking Society: Economic Regulation in Historical Perspective*, College Station, TX: Texas A&M University Press.

19 Ehrenpreis, I. (1962–83) op. cit., vol. III, pp. 188–9.

20 Ibid., p. 190n.

21 Berkeley, G. (1957) *Letters. The Works of George Berkeley, Bishop of Cloyne.* Luce, A.A. and Jessop, T.G. (eds) 9 vols., London: Nelson.

22 The legal word used to define such fees was 'fine'.

23 Landa, L. (1965) *Swift and the Church of Ireland*, Oxford: Clarendon, pp. 100–1.

24 Idem.

25 Davis, H. (1939–68) op. cit., vol. IX, p. 21.

26 For a thorough investigation of patterns of Irish rents, see 'A Sample of agricultural rents, 1700–1850', Chapter X of Johnston's (1970) edition of *Bishop Berkeley's Querist in Historical Perspective* (pp. 100–11).

27 Landa, L. (1965) op. cit., p. 101.

28 Quoted in Ehrenpreis, I. (1962–83) op. cit., vol. III, p. 169.

29 Rogers, P. (1983) (ed.) *Jonathan Swift: The Complete Poems.* New Haven: Yale University Press. 'Excellent New Song upon His Grace Our Good Lord Archbishop of Dublin', lines 9–10.

30 Quoted in Berkeley, G. (1970) op. cit., pp 30–1.

31 Ehrenpreis, I. (1962–83) op. cit., vol. III, p. 177.

32 Ibid., p. 33.

33 'An Excellent New Song,' line 26 from Rogers, P. (1983) op. cit.

34 Ehrenpreis, I. (1962–83) op. cit., vol. III, p. 178.

35 Landa, L. (1965) op. cit., p. 99.

36 Williams, H. (1963–65) op. cit., vol. I, p. 339 (28 March 1713).

37 Davis H. (1939–68) op. cit., vol. IX, p. 45.

38 Idem.

39 Williams, H. (1963–65) op. cit., vol. II, p. 11.

40 Davis, H. (1939–68) op. cit., vol. IX, p. 45.

41 Ibid., vol. IX, p. 220.

42 Ibid., vol. IX, pp. 45–6.

43 Ibid., vol. IX, pp. 47, 48.

44 Ibid., vol. IX, pp. 46–7.

45   Ibid., vol. IX, p. 48.
46   Ibid., vol. IX, p. 51.
47   Ibid., vol. IX, p. 53.
48   Idem.
49   Ibid., vol. IX, p. 54.
50   Idem.
51   Idem.
52   Ibid., vol. IX, p. 57.
53   Ibid., vol. IX, p. 57.
54   Ibid., vol. X, p. 20.
55   Ibid., vol. IX, p. 57.

EPILOGUE

1   Halifax, Marquis of (1989) *Miscellaneous Thoughts and Reflections,* Brown, M.N. (ed.) Oxford: Clarendon, vol. 3, p. 474.
2   Ireland became part of the United Kingdom on 1 January 1801. The scale of the inducements necessary to secure Irish votes in favour of the Union can perhaps best be grasped when one considers that Lord Cornwallis, the Viceroy given the task of deploying sufficient patronage and bribery to win the day, admitted that 'I despise and hate myself every hour for engaging in such dirty work'. Quoted in Kee, R. (1976) *The Most Distressful Country,* London: Quartet, p. 159.
3   'Verses on the Death of Dr. Swift'. Lines 447, 449–52, from Rogers, P. (ed.) (1983) *Jonathan Swift; The Complete Poems,* New Haven: Yale University Press.
4   'A Paper Book is Sent by Boyle', lines 8–12, from Rogers, P. (1983) op. cit.

Bibliography

Acheson, Alan (1997) *A History of the Church of Ireland, 1691–1996*, Dublin: Columba, APCK.

Akenson, Donald Harman (1971) *The Church of Ireland: Ecclesiastical Reform and Revolution, 1800–1885*, New Haven: Yale University Press.

Andrewes, Lancelot (1978) *Collected Works*, J.P. Wilson and J. Bliss (eds) New York: AMS Press.

Beckett, J.C. (1971) 'Jonathan Swift as an Ecclesiastic Statesman'. In Denis Donoghue (ed.) *Jonathan Swift: A Critical Anthology*, Harmondsworth: Penguin, pp. 153–68.

Bennett, G.V. (1975) *The Tory Crisis in Church and State 1688–1730: The Career of Francis Atterbury Bishop of Rochester*, Oxford: Clarendon.

Berggrav, Eivind (1943) *With God in the Darkness. And Other Papers Illustrating the Norwegian Church Conflict*, G.K.A. Bell and H.M. Waddams (eds) London: Hodder and Stoughton.

Berkeley, George (1957) *Letters. The Works of George Berkeley, Bishop of Cloyne*, vol. 8. A.A. Luce and T.G. Jessop (eds) 9 vols. London: Nelson.

—— (1970) *The Irish Patriot or Queries upon Queries: Whereby it is made manifest that a National Bank is utterly inconsistent with the rights, privileges and interests of Ireland*. In Joseph Johnston (ed.) *Bishop Berkeley's Querist in Historical Perspective*, Dundalk, Ireland: Dundalgan, pp. 210–13.

—— (1970) *The Querist, containing several Queries proposed to the consideration of the Public*, Joseph Johnston (ed.) pp. 124–75.

Bindon, David (1738) *A Letter from a Merchant Who Has Left Off Trade, to a Member of Parliament, in which The Case of the* British *and* Irish *manufacture of Linen, Threads, and Tapes, is fairly stated; and all the Objections against the Encouragement proposed to be given to that Manufacture, fully answered*, London.

Boulter, Hugh (1770) *Letters Written by His Excellency Hugh Boulter, D.D., Lord Primate of All Ireland, &c. To Several Ministers of State in England, and some Others. Containing an Account of the Most Interesting Transactions which Passed in Ireland from 1724 to 1738*, 2 vols, Dublin.

Boyer, Abel (1719) *Political State*, London.

Burns, Robert E. (1989) *Irish Parliamentary Politics in the Eighteenth Century*, 2 vols, Washington, D.C.: Catholic University of America Press.

Carpenter, Andrew (1972) 'William King and the Threats to the Church of Ireland During the Reign of James II'. *Irish Historical Studies* XVII , pp. 22–8.

—— (ed.) (1974) *Letters to and from Persons of Quality*, Monkstown, Co. Dublin: Cadenus.

—— (1978) 'To Swift on his Birthday 30 November 1727'. In Charles Ford, *Adventure at Sienna*, trans R. Astbury, Dublin: Cadenus, pp. 80–5.

Chancellor, Alexander (1999) 'Another Country'. 'Pride and Prejudice'. *The Guardian Weekend*, 1 May.

Chandler, Thomas Bradbury (1767) *An Appeal to the Public, in Behalf of the Church of England in America*, New York.

Cokayne, G.E. (1910–59) *The Complete Peerage of England, Scotland, Ireland, Great Britain and the United Kingdom*. Revised by Vicary Gibbs, Geoffrey White and R.S. Lea. 12 vols, London: St Catherine.

Connolly, S.J. (ed.) (1998a) *The Oxford Companion to Irish History*, Oxford: Oxford University Press.

—— (1998b) 'Swift and Protestant Ireland: Images and Reality'. In Aileen Douglas, Patrick Kelly and Ian Campbell Ross (eds) *Locating Swift: Essays from Dublin on the 250th Anniversary of the Death of Jonathan Swift 1667–1745*, Dublin: Four Courts Press, pp. 284–6.

Cook, Richard I. (1967) *Jonathan Swift as a Tory Pamphleteer*, Seattle: University of Washington Press.

Cornwall, Robert D. (1993) *Visible and Apostolic: The Constitution of the Church in High Church Anglican and Non-Juror Thought*, Newark: University of Delaware Press.

Coxe, William (1816) *Memoirs of the Life and Administration of Sir Robert Walpole*, 4 vols, London.

Crawford, William Henry (1988) 'The Evolution of the Linen Trade in Ulster'. *Irish Economic and Social History* 15, pp. 32–53.

Cross, F.L. and E.A. Livingstone (eds) (1997) *The Oxford Dictionary of the Christian Church*, 3rd edn, Oxford: Oxford University Press.

Curtis, L.P. (1966) *Anglican Moods of the Eighteenth Century*, Hamden, CT: Archon.

Darcy, P. (1641). *An Argument delivered by Patricke Darcy, Esquire: by the Expresse Order of the House of Commons in the Parliament of Ireland*, Dublin.

Daston, Lorraine (1988) *Classical Probability in the Enlightenment*, Princeton: Princeton University Press.

Davie, Donald (1978) *A Gathered Church: The Literature of the English Dissenting Interest, 1700–1930*, New York: Oxford University Press.

Davis, H. (ed.) (1939–68) *Prose Works of Jonathan Swift*, 14 vols, Oxford: Basil Blackwell.

Daw, Carl P. (1970) 'An Annotated Edition of Five Sermons by Jonathan Swift'. Dissertation, University of Virginia.

Dawe, G. and E. Longley (eds) (1985) *Across a Roaring Hill: The Protestent Imagination in Modern Ireland. Essays in Honour of John Hewitt*, Belfast: Blackstaff, p. 120.

Defoe, Daniel (1697) *An Essay on Projects*, London.

—— (1713) *The Honour and Prerogative of the Queen's Majesty Vindicated*, London.

DePorte, Michael (1993a) 'The Road to St Patrick's: Swift and the Problem of Belief'. *Swift Studies* 8, pp. 5–17.

—— (1993b) 'Swift's Horses of Instruction'. In Richard H. Rodino and Herman J. Real (eds) *Reading Swift: Papers from the Second Münster Symposium on Jonathan Swift*, Munich: Wilhelm Fink, pp. 199–211.

Dickson, David, Cormac Ó Gráda and Stu Daultry (1982) 'Hearth Tax, Household Size and Irish Population Change c.1672–1821'. *Proceedings of the Royal Irish Academy* 82(C) , pp. 125–81.

Dickson, Peter George Muir (1967) *The Financial Revolution in England: A Study in the Development of Public Credit, 1688–1786*, New York: St Martin's.

Doherty, Richard (1998) *The Williamite War in Ireland, 1688–1691*, Dublin: Four Courts Press.

Douglas, Aileen, Patrick Kelly and Ian Campbell Ross, (eds)(1998) 'Introduction: Locating Swift'. *Locating Swift: Essays from Dublin on the 250th Anniversary of the Death of Jonathan Swift 1667–1745*, Dublin: Four Courts Press, pp. 9–27.

Douglas, D.C. (1951) *English Scholars, 1600–1730*, London: Eyre and Spottiswoode.

Downie, J.A. (1984) *Jonathan Swift: Political Writer*, London: Routledge & Kegan Paul.

Edgeworth, Maria (1964) *Castle Rackrent*, Bruce Teets (ed.) Coral Gables, FL: University of Miami Press.

Ehrenpreis, Irvin (1962–83) *Swift: The Man, His Works, and the Age*. 3 vols, Cambridge, MA: Harvard University Press.

Ekelund, Robert and Robert Tollison (1981) *Mercantilism as a Rent-Seeking Society: Economic Regulation in Historical Perspective*, College Station, TX: Texas A&M University Press.

Elias, A.C. Jr. (1982) *Swift at Moor Park: Problems in Biography and Criticism*, Philadelphia: University of Pennsylvania Press.

Enright, D.J. (1986) *The Alluring Problem: An Essay on Irony*, Oxford: Oxford University Press.

Estabrook, Samuel (1718) *A Sermon Showing that Peace and Quietness of a People is a Main Part of the Work of Civil Rulers, and that it is the Duty of all to Pray for them: Deliver'd at Hartford May the 8th, 1718, being the day for the Election of the Honourable the Governour, Lieutenant Governour, and the Worshipful Assistants, for the Government of Connecticut*, New London, CT.

Fabricant, Carole (1982) *Swift's Landscape*, Baltimore: Johns Hopkins University Press.

—— (1995) 'Swift as Irish Historian'. In Christopher Fox and Brenda Tooley (eds) *Walking Naboth's Vineyard: New Studies of Swift*, Notre Dame, IN: University of Notre Dame Press, pp. 40–72.

Fanning, Christopher (1997) 'Sermons on Sermonizing: The Pulpit Rhetoric of Swift and Sterne'. *Philological Quarterly* 76:4 (Fall) pp. 413–37.

Ferguson, Oliver W. (1962) *Jonathan Swift and Ireland*, Urbana: University of Illinois Press.

Fischer, John Irwin (1986) 'Learning "*David's* Lesson": Some New Information Concerning the Remission of First Fruits and Twentieth Parts in Ireland'. *Swift Studies* 1, pp. 15–23.

Foot, Michael (1981) 'Round the Next Corner'. *Debts of Honour*, London: Picador.

Ford, Alan, James McGuire and Kenneth Milne (eds) (1995) *As by Law Established: The Church of Ireland since the Reformation*, Dublin: Lilliput Press.

Ford, Alan (1995) 'Dependent or Independent? The Church of Ireland and its Colonial Context, 1536–1649'. *The Seventeenth Century* X:2, pp. 163–87.

—— (1998) 'James Ussher and the Creation of an Irish Protestant Identity'. In Brenda Bradshaw and Peter Roberts (eds) *British Consciousness and Identity: The Making of Britain, 1533–1707*, Cambridge: Cambridge University Press, pp. 185–212.

Ford, Charles (1978) 'To Swift, On his Birthday Nov. 30, 1727'. In Andrew Carpenter *Adventure at Sienna*, trans. Ray Astbury, (ed.) Dublin: Cadenus, pp. 80–5.

Foxcroft, H.C. (1902) *A Supplement to Burnet's* History of My Own Time. *Derived from his Original Memoirs, his Autobiography, his Letters to Admiral Herbert, and his Private Meditations, all hitherto unpublished*, Oxford: Clarendon.

Glendenning, Victoria (1998) *Jonathan Swift: A Portrait*, London: Hutchinson.

Green, David (1970) *Queen Anne*, New York: Charles Scribner's.

Halifax, Marquis of (1989) *The Character of a Trimmer. The Works of George Savile, Marquis of Halifax*, ed. Mark N. Brown, Vol. 1, Oxford: Clarendon, pp. 178–243.

—— (1989) *Miscellaneous Thoughts and Reflections*, ed. Mark N. Brown, Vol. 3, pp. 469–83.

Harris, Joseph (1757) *An Essay upon Money and Coins*, London.

Harrison, Alan (1999) *The Dean's Friend: Anthony Raymond 1675–1726, Jonathan Swift and the Irish Language*, Caisleán an Bhúrcaigh (Blackrock), Co. Dublin: Éamonn de Búrca for Edmund Burke.

Hatton, R.M. (1955) 'John Robinson and the *Account of Sweden*'. *Bulletin of the Institute of Historical Research* XXVIII, pp. 128–59.

Hayton, David (1981) 'The Crisis in Ireland and the Disintegration of Queen Anne's Last Ministry'. *Irish Historical Studies* XXII, (March) pp. 193–215.

Healey, Denis (1990) *The Time of My Life*, London: Penguin.

Hewitt, John (1991) 'The Colony'. In Frank Ormsby (ed.), *The Collected Poems of John Hewitt*, Belfast: Blackstaff, pp. 76–9.

Higgins, Ian (1994) *Swift's Politics: A Study in Disaffection*, Cambridge: Cambridge University Press.

Hill, Christopher (1985) 'Censorship and English Literature'. *The Collected Essays of Christopher Hill. Volume One: Writing and Revolution in 17th Century England*, Amherst, MA: The University of Massachusetts Press, pp. 32–71.

Holmes, G.S. (1973) *The Trial of Doctor Sacheverell*, London: Methuen.

Hook, Walter F. (1871) *A Church Dictionary*, 7th edn, London.

Hooker, Richard (1977) *The Laws of Ecclesiastical Polity: Books I–V*, (eds) W. Speed Hill and Georges Edelen. Folger Library Edition of the Works of Richard Hooker, Cambridge, MA: Belknap Press.

Horne, Thomas (1978) *The Social Thought of Bernard Mandeville: Virtue and Commerce in Early Eighteenth Century England*, New York: Columbia University Press.

Hunter, J. Paul (1990) *Before Novels: The Cultural Contexts of Eighteenth-Century English Fiction*, New York: Norton.

Hutchinson, Francis (1723) *A Letter to a Member of Parliament Concerning the imploying and Providing for the Poor*, Dublin.

James, Francis Godwin (1973) *Ireland in the Empire 1688–1770: A History of Ireland from the Williamite Wars to the Eve of the American Revolution*, Cambridge, MA: Harvard University Press.

—— (1979) 'The Church of Ireland in the Early 18th Century'. *Historical Magazine of the Protestant Episcopal Church* 48:4, (Dec.) pp. 433–51.

—— (1991) 'The Aristocracy of Ireland's *Ancien Regime*'. *Éire-Ireland* XXVI:4, pp. 16–28.

Johnson, J.W. (1967) *The Formation of English Neo-Classical Thought*, Princeton: Princeton University Press.

Johnson, Samuel (1755) *A Dictionary of the English Language*, 2 vols, London.

—— (1905) *Lives of the English Poets* (ed.) George Birkbeck Hill, 3 vols, Oxford: Clarendon.

Jones, D.W. (1991) 'Sequel to Revolution: The Economics of England's Emergence as a Great Power, 1688–1712. In Jonathan I. Israel (ed.) *The Anglo-Dutch Moment: Essays on the Glorious Revolution and Its World Impact*, Cambridge: Cambridge University Press, pp. 389–406.

Kanfer, Stefan (1985) *The International Garage Sale*, New York: Norton.

Kee, Robert (1976) *The Most Distressful Country*, London: Quartet.

Kelly, James (1990) 'Jonathan Swift and the Irish Economy in the 1720s'. *Eighteenth-Century Ireland* 6, pp. 7–36.

Kelly Patrick (ed.) (1991) *Locke on Money*, 2 vols, Oxford: Clarendon.

—— (1998) '"Conclusions by no Means Calculated for the Circumstances and Condition of Ireland": Swift, Berkeley and the Solution to Ireland's Economic Problems'. In Aileen Douglas, Patrick Kelly and Ian Campbell Ross (eds) *Locating Swift: Essays from Dublin on the 250th Anniversary of the Death of Jonathan Swift 1667–1745*, Dublin: Four Courts Press, pp. 47–59.

Kierkegaard, Søren (1989) *The Concept of Irony, with Continual Reference to Socrates*, (eds and trans.) Howard V. and Edna H. Hong, Princeton: Princeton University Press.

King, Sir Charles Simeon (ed.) (1906) *A Great Archbishop of Dublin, William King. D.D., 1650–1729: His Autobiography, Family, and a Selection from His Correspondence*, London: Longmans, Green.

King, William (1731) *Essay on the Origin of Evil. [De Origine mali.] By Dr. William King, late Lord Archbishop of Dublin. Translated from the Latin, with large Notes; tending to explain and vindicate some of the Author's Principles Against the Objections of* Bayle, Leibnitz, *the Author of a* Philosophical Enquiry concerning Human Liberty; *and others*. London.

—— (1768) *The State of the Protestants of Ireland under the Late King James's Government*. 1691, London.

—— (1976) *Sermon on Predestination*, (ed.) Andrew Carpenter. Intro. David Berman, Dublin: Cadenus.

Klein, Lawrence E. (1994) *Shaftesbury and the Culture of Politeness: Moral Discourse and Cultural Politics in Early Eighteenth-century England*, Cambridge: Cambridge University Press.

Kramnick, Isaac (1968) *Bolingbroke and His Circle: The Politics of Nostalgia in the Age of Walpole*, Cambridge, MA: Harvard University Press.

Landa, Louis (1965) *Swift and the Church of Ireland*, Oxford: Clarendon.
—— (1980) 'Jonathan Swift and Charity' pp. 49–62 and 'Not the Gravest of Divines' pp. 63–88. *Essays in Eighteenth Century Literature*, Princeton: Princeton University Press.

Law, William (1893) *The Works of the Reverend William Law, M.A., Sometime Fellow of Emmanuel College, Cambridge*, 9 vols, 1796, Setley, Hants.

Leavis, F.R. (1953) 'The Irony of Swift'. *The Common Pursuit*, London: Chatto & Windus, pp. 73–87.

Lein, Clayton D. (1975) 'Jonathan Swift and the Population of Ireland'. *Eighteenth-Century Studies* 8:4, pp. 431–53.

Lock, F.P. (1980) *The Politics of* Gulliver's Travels, Oxford: Clarendon.
—— (1983) *Swift's Tory Politics*, Newark: University of Delaware Press.

Locke, John (1991) *Some Considerations of the Consequences of the Lowering of Interest, and Raising the Value of* MONEY. *In a Letter sent to a Member of Parliament, 1691*. In Patrick Hyde Kelly (ed.) *Locke on Money*, 2 vols, Oxford: Clarendon, pp. 203–342.

Longley, Edna (1985) 'Louis MacNeice: "The Walls are Flowing"'. In G. Dave and E. Longley (eds) *Across a Roaring Hill: The Protestant Imagination in Modern Ireland. Essays in Honour of John Hewitt*, Belfast: Blackstaff, pp. 99–123.

McDowell, R[obert] B. (1975) *Irish Public Opinion 1750–1800*, Westport, CT: Greenwood.

McMinn, Joseph (1991a) *Jonathan Swift: A Literary Life*, Basingstoke, Hants: Macmillan.
—— (ed.) (1991b) *Swift's Irish Pamphlets: An Introductory Selection*, Gerrards Cross, Bucks: Colin Smythe.

McNally, Paddy (1995) '"Irish and English Interests": National Conflict Within the Church of Ireland Episcopate in the Reign of George I'. *Irish Historical Studies* XXIX, (May) pp. 295–314.

MacNeice, Louis (1966) *Collected Poems*, (ed.) E.R. Dodds, London: Faber.

MacNeill, John Gordon Swift (1917) *The Constitutional and Parliamentary History of Ireland till the Union*, Dublin: Talbot.

Mahony, Robert (1991) '"Prince Posterity" as an Irish Nationalist: The Posthumous Course of Swift's Patriotic Reputation'. International Association for the Studies of Anglo-Irish Literature, Rijksuniversiteit te Leiden, Netherlands, 9 July 1991.
—— (1995) *Swift's Irish Identity*. New Haven: Yale University Press.

Mann, Charles C. (1993) 'How Many Is Too Many?' *Atlantic Monthly* (Feb.) pp. 47–67.

Mant, Richard (1840) *History of the Church of Ireland, from the Reformation to the Revolution; with a Preliminary Survey, from the*

Papal Usurpation, in the Twelfth Century, to its Legal Abolition in the Sixteenth, 2 vols, London.

Massie, Joseph (1912) *Observations Relating to the Coinage of Great Britain; consisting partly of Extracts from Mr Locke's Treatise concerning Money, but chiefly of such Additions thereunto, as are thought to be very Necessary at this Juncture*, London, 1760. Baltimore: Lord Baltimore Press.

Maxwell, Henry (1721) *Reasons Offered for Erecting a Bank in Ireland*, Dublin.

Molesworth, Viscount, Robert (1723) *Some Considerations for Promoting the Agriculture of Ireland and Employing the Poor*, Dublin.

Molyneux, William (1698) *The Case of Ireland's Being Bound by Acts of Parliament in England Stated*, Dublin.

Montag, Warren (1994) *The Unthinkable Swift: The Spontaneous Philosophy of a Church of England Man*, London: Verso.

Moore, John Robert (1950) 'Defoe, Steele, and the Demolition of Dunkirk'. *Huntington Library Quarterly* 13, pp. 279–302.

Murray, Rev R.H. (1933) 'The Church and the Revolution'. In Walter Alison Phillips (ed.) *History of the Church of Ireland from the Earliest Times to the Present Day*, 3 vols, London: Oxford University Press, III: pp. 148–74.

Nenner, Howard (1996) 'Sovereignty and the Succession in 1688–89'. In Dale Hoak and Mordechai Feingold (eds) *The World of William and Mary: Anglo-Dutch Perspectives on the Revolution of 1688–89*, Stanford, CA: Stanford University Press, pp. 104–17.

Newcomb, Robert (1955) 'Poor Richard's Debt to Lord Halifax'. *PMLA* 70, pp. 535–9.

Nokes, David (1985) *Jonathan Swift, a Hypocrite Reversed: A Critical Biography*, Oxford: Oxford University Press.

O'Regan, Philip (2000) *Archbishop William King (1650–1729) and the Constitution in Church and State*, Dublin: Four Courts Press.

Ovid (1988) *Epistulae ex Ponto. Tristia. Ex Ponto.* Trans. Arthur Leslie Wheeler. Rev. G.P. Gould. Loeb Classical Library 151. 2d. (ed.) Cambridge, MA: Harvard University Press, pp. 263–489.

Pascal, Blaise (1941) *Pensées.* Trans. W.F. Trotter, New York: Modern Library.

Pears, Iain (1999) *An Instance of the Fingerpost*, New York: Berkeley.

Phillips, Walter Alison (1933) (ed.) *History of the Church of Ireland from the Earliest Times to the Present Day*, 3 vols, London: Oxford University Press.

Plowden, Francis Peter (1803) *An Historical Review of the State of Ireland from the Invasion of that Country under Henry II to its Union with Great Britain, 1 Jan. 1801*, London.

Pocock, J.G.A. (ed.) (1987) *Reflections on the Revolution in France by Edmund Burke*, Indianapolis: Hackett.

Pope, Alexander (1940–69) *The Poems*, (ed.) John Butt, 11 vols, London: Methuen.

Prior, Thomas (1729) *Observations on Coin*, Dublin.

Probyn, Clive T. (ed.) (1979) *Jonathan Swift: The Contemporary Background*, New York: Barnes and Noble.

Richards, James O. (1972) *Party Propaganda Under Queen Anne: The General Elections of 1702–1713*, Athens: University of Georgia Press.

Richardson, Joseph (1999) 'Archbishop William King (1650–1729), Man of Faith and Reason'. Dissertation, National University of Ireland, Maynooth.

Rogers, Pat (ed.) (1983) *Jonathan Swift: The Complete Poems*, New Haven: Yale University Press.

Rosenheim, Edward W. Jr. (1963) *Swift and the Satirist's Art*, Chicago: University of Chicago Press.

Ross, Angus and David Woolley (eds) (1984) *Jonathan Swift*, The Oxford Authors, Oxford: Oxford University Press.

Rouleau, Éric (1999) 'Islam Confronts Islam in Iran'. Trans. Derry Cook-Radmore. *Le Monde Diplomatique* (June) pp. 1–3.

Rowan, P.B. (n.d.) *Catalogue 51 Books and Periodicals of Irish Interest*, Belfast.

Rowley, Hercules (1721) *An Answer to a Book Entitled 'Reasons Offered for Erecting a Bank in Ireland.' by Hercules Rowley, Esq.* Dublin.

Rupp, Gordon (1986) *Religion in England, 1688–1791*. Oxford: Clarendon.

Said, Edward (1969) 'Swift's Tory Anarchy'. *Eighteenth-Century Studies*. 3, (Fall) pp. 48–66.

Schochet, Gordon J. (1996) 'The Act of Toleration and the Failure of Comprehension: Persecution, Nonconformity, and Religious Indifference'. In Dale Hoak and Mordechai Feingold (eds) *The World of William and Mary: Anglo-Dutch Perspectives on the Revolution of 1688–89*. Stanford, CA: Stanford University Press, pp. 165–87.

Sedgwick, Romney (ed.) (1970) *The House of Commons 1715–1754*, 2 vols, Oxford: Oxford University Press.

Simms, J.G. (1969) *Jacobite Ireland 1685–91*, London: Routledge & Kegan Paul.

Smedley, Jonathan (1728) *Gulliveriana: or, A Fourth Volume of Miscellanies*, London.

Smith, Edward (1999) 'Mad Poet's Society'. Review of Alan Wall, *The Lightning Cage* (London: Chatto & Windus, 1999). *The Sunday Telegraph Review* (1 Aug.) p. 14.

Speck, W.A. (1977) *Stability and Strife: England, 1714–1760* Cambridge, MA: Harvard University Press.

—— (1985) 'Swift and the Historian'. In Hermann J. Real and Heinz J. Vienken (eds) *First Munster Symposium on Jonathan Swift*, Munich: Wilhelm Fink, pp. 257–68.

Steele, Richard (1982) *The Guardian*, (ed.) John Calhoun Stephens, Lexington, KY: The University Press of Kentucky.

Steuart, Sir James (1767) *An Inquiry into the Principles of Political Œconomy. Being an Essay on the Science of Domestic Policy in Free Nations*, 2 vols London.

Swift, Jonathan and Thomas Sheridan (1992) *The Intelligencer*. (ed.) James Woolley, Oxford: Clarendon.

—— (1999) *The Correspondence of Jonathan Swift, D.D.*, (ed.) David Woolley, 4 vols, Frankfurt: Peter Lang.

Tillotson, John (1820) *Works*, 9 vols, London.

Toland, John (1998) *Christianity Not Mysterious*, (eds) Philip McGuiness and Alan Harrison, Dublin: Lilliput Press.

Torism and Trade can Never Agree, to which is added an Account of the Mercator and his Writings, particularly his former discourses against the Land-interest and a trade with France: in a Letter to Sir G— H——. London, 1713.

Walsh, John, Colin Haydon and Stephen Taylor (eds) (1993) *The Church of England c.1689–c.1833: From Toleration to Tractarianism*, Cambridge: Cambridge University Press.

Wand, J.W.C. (1951) *The High Church Schism: Four Lectures on the Nonjurors*, New York: Morehouse-Gorham.

Wilkes, John H. (1975) 'The Transformation of Dissent: A Review of the Change from the Seventeenth to the Eighteenth Centuries'. In C. Robert Cole and Michael E. Moody (eds) *The Dissenting Tradition: Essays for Leland H. Carlson*, Athens: Ohio University Press, pp. 108–22.

Williams, Sir Harold (ed.) (1948) *Journal to Stella by Jonathan Swift*, 2 vols, Oxford: Clarendon.

—— (ed.) (1963–65) *The Correspondence of Jonathan Swift*, 5 vols, Oxford: Clarendon.

Wilson, A.N. (1993) *Daughters of Albion*, New York: Norton.

Wormwald, B.H.G. (1951) *Clarendon: Politics, History, and Religion*, Cambridge: Cambridge University Press.

Young, B.W. (1998) *Religion and Enlightenment in Eighteenth-Century England: Theological Debate from Locke to Burke*, Oxford: Clarendon.

Index

Where a person was known by more than one name (e.g. Henry St John, who became Viscount Bolingbroke), the name provided below is that used most often in the text. Clerical titles are of the appointment for which the person concerned is best known. References to the notes (pp. 149–75) are provided only when there is something substantive to be found there.